Erratum

Add to Acknowledgments, page 11:

Carl Winter Universitätsverlag (Heidelberg, Germany), Yoshinobu Hakutani and Lewis Fried, eds., *American Literary Naturalism: A Reassessment*, 1975, for permission to reprint in modified form the "Introduction" by Lewis Fried and Yoshinobu Hakutani, pp. 1-10.

Young Dreiser

Theodore Dreiser, aged twenty-two in the spring of 1894, a Pittsburgh newspaperman. *Courtesy of the University of Pennsylvania Library.*

Young Dreiser

A Critical Study

Yoshinobu Hakutani

Rutherford • Madison • Teaneck
Fairleigh Dickinson University Press
London: Associated University Presses

Also by YOSHINOBU HAKUTANI:

The World of Japanese Fiction
American Literary Naturalism: A Reassessment

Associated University Presses, Inc.
Cranbury, New Jersey 08512

Associated University Presses
Magdalen House
136-148 Tooley Street
London SE1 2TT, England

Library of Congress Cataloging in Publication Data

Hakutani, Yoshinobu, 1935-
    Young Dreiser.

    Bibliography: p.
    Includes index.
    1. Dreiser, Theodore, 1871-1945—Criticism and interpretation. I. Title.
PS3507.R55Z638   813'.5'2   78-66797
ISBN 0-8386-2268-2

Printed in the United States of America

To Yoshiki and Naoki

Contents

Preface

It would appear from the intensive commentary of the past sixty-five years that the greatness of Theodore Dreiser's writings comes not so much from his technique but from his particular knowledge of American life. Dreiser took his experience seriously. Helen Dreiser, his second wife, discussing her husband's works, wrote, "With all his novels, the ideas were carried in his mind for years before ever he sat down to work them out." How Dreiser found and shaped these "ideas" before he wrote his earliest fiction is a crucial question in Dreiser criticism. To Dreiser, life was a struggle, and that struggle led him to a decided view of the nature of existence. His fictional efforts and the history of his early life were inseparably intertwined.

Many of his early critics, however, regarded Dreiser's work primarily as the product of a literary influence—that of naturalism, particularly the works of Balzac and Zola. It is necessary to keep in mind Dreiser's relationship to the French sources, and this study is concerned initially with the nature of the influence of literary naturalism on him. Nonetheless, I hope to establish the fact that, unlike Frank Norris, Dreiser was not, at least in his early works, influenced in any conscious way by the naturalistic movement. Dreiser's presumed indebtedness to French and American naturalists is the result of a superficial reading of his early works. Such indebtedness, if it exists, is superficial—the kind produced by the process of assimilation of the literary fashion of the day.

But if we are to dispute an influence that has been so frequently claimed, it is essential to investigate thoroughly the whole of Dreiser's education in America. The major part of the study, then, is intended to elucidate the personal experiences of Dreiser's youth, his newspaper work, and his career as an editor and as a free-lance magazine writer before he wrote the first works of fiction. The ultimate purpose of this study is to demonstrate the significance of these experiences and concepts in molding Dreiser's earliest short stories and his first novel, *Sister Carrie*.

Because of the scarcity of the material relating to Dreiser's editorial and periodical writings before 1900, and because of the difficulty of gaining access to the material that is available, previous studies of

Dreiser have treated this period inadequately. In the area of his nonfiction, new studies of Dreiser are needed. The three-volume edition of Dreiser's letters by Robert H. Elias, published in 1959, does, to a limited extent, add to our knowledge of Dreiser's life before the turn of the century. The value of these letters for the present study is relatively slight, however, since few letters written by Dreiser before 1900 are included. Dreiser's *Notes on Life*, edited by Marguerite Tjader and John J. McAleer in 1974, helps us to reevaluate Dreiser's entire philosophy, but none of the statements collected in the book, however revealing and important it is, comes from his early career.

Dreiserian criticism has long been in the nature of attacks and defenses, of counterattacks and apologies. As Dreiser comes to occupy a permanently accepted position in American literary history, more scholarly and critical, and less polemical, attention must be paid to his works. In studying Dreiser, we discover a writer of stature who emerged, as it were, out of nowhere, with a voice so strikingly new as to raise not only contemporary literary eyebrows but many still unresolved critical questions. It is because he puzzles and troubles us that we find it difficult or impossible—and yet necessary—to trace his achievement to its origins. Thus, a French critic once complained in reviewing one of Dreiser's books by saying, "One doesn't see how it's made."

This is the inherent difficulty in the evaluation of Dreiser's work, and yet this is also a sign of its greatness. We must continue to appreciate each of the various stages of his achievement as a writer. This achievement has justified Dreiser's present stature as one of America's great novelists, a rare and original man who created art out of his own vision of life. The present study is, in a way, an attempt to judge and appreciate the beginning and the most important stage in his development. It is not true, as Fred Lewis Pattee once said, that "to weigh the man as a force in the period one must begin with his six novels, the rest of his output is but chips and explanations and excursions." It is precisely to such chips and explanations and excursions that we must go if we are to understand the essential nature of Dreiser's accomplishment.

Yoshinobu Hakutani

Kent, Ohio
April 1979

Acknowledgments

This book owes much to a number of people, including previous writers on Dreiser, who have been of direct or indirect help. Among them my gratitude is due to Robert H. Elias and W. A. Swanberg, who furnished me with information concerning the early issues of *Ev'ry Month*. I am particularly indebted to David Ewbank, Arthur O. Lewis, and Chester Rebok who read all or part of the manuscript at some stage of its development and made many useful suggestions. I am also grateful to Drs. Neda Westlake and William E. Miller, both of the Charles Patterson Van Pelt Library of the University of Pennsylvania, for the graceful assistance I have received over the years. Finally, I want to thank my wife, Michiko, for typing and proofreading with patience.

In the course of my work I have benefited from grants-in-aid by the Research Council of the Kent State University Graduate School.

Mr. Harold J. Dies, executor of the Dreiser estate, has readily allowed me to quote from *Dawn*. The University of Pennsylvania has generously granted me permission to consult and quote from unpublished material in the Theodore Dreiser Collection.

And I wish to thank the following publishers for having given me permission to quote from published works:

The *Library Chronicle*, for permission to reprint in modified form my essay "Theodore Dreiser's Editorial and Free-Lance Writing," 37 (Winter 1971): 70–85; and my "Dreiser and American Magazines of the 1890s," 43 (Spring 1978): 55–80.

Studies in American Fiction, for permission to reprint in modified form my essay "The Making of Dreiser's Early Short Stories: The Philosopher and the Artist," 6 (Spring 1978): 48–63.

Twentieth Century Literature, for permission to reprint in modified form my essay "*Sister Carrie* and the Problem of Literary Naturalism," 13 (April 1967): 3–17.

University of Texas Press, *Texas Studies in Literature and Language*, for permission to reprint in modified form my essay "Dreiser and French Realism," 6 (Summer 1964): 200–212.

Y. H.

Young Dreiser

1 American Literary Naturalism

The career of Theodore Dreiser has always been associated with American naturalism, that vaguely defined literary movement that reached its apogee in the 1890s. This association is easy to understand because Dreiser's most formative years coincided with the rise of naturalism in America. *Sister Carrie*, his first novel, appeared at the end of that decade, and critics then immediately labeled it as a typical product of the movement. The critics even went so far as to call Dreiser an American Zola. Even today Dreiser is often classified as a famous, if not the most famous, American literary naturalist.

Such views raise the question of the relation of life and art. Dreiser is known as a faithful recorder of American life as he experienced it. Does this mean that he simply transcribed actuality and happened to conform to naturalistic doctrine? Dreiser's fiction as well as that voluminous autobiographical writing prove that he was peculiarly an American and a highly original thinker. French naturalism when it came to America contradicted in many ways the idealism that was rooted in her soil. It is unlikely that Dreiser, as he was in his early career, a believer of the American values and himself an exemplar of national character, would have so easily absorbed such tenets that naturalism stood for.

As Philip Rahv argued almost four decades ago, experimentation with symbolism, surrealism, and myth not only has stylistically liberated the modern artist but also has demolished the naturalistic assumption that "reality" was reducible to biological and social determinism. The naturalistic formula proved inadequate; it was not a comprehensive view of human nature and experience. The imaginative prose writer must look elsewhere.[1] Rahv probably had in mind such experimenters as Proust, Joyce, and Faulkner, and indirectly criticized a novelist such as Dreiser as *démodé*. The problem with this point of view is that Rahv assumes that Dreiser is a pure literary naturalist and, therefore, he minimizes Dreiser's contribution as a unique American artist. Rahv's thesis, then, as it is now, is attractive if it does not apply to Dreiser; whether or not such a viewpoint is entirely accurate depends upon our assumptions and theories about naturalism.

15

The controversy about whether or not Dreiser is a naturalist still remains unsettled. Many critics, focusing upon *Sister Carrie*, have discussed his relationship to the works of other writers and movements. Malcolm Cowley, for example, regards the failure of Dreiser's first novel in 1900 as "part of a general disaster that involved the whole literary movement of the 1890's," many of whose representative writers Cowley identifies. Lars Åhnebrink, in "Dreiser's *Sister Carrie* and Balzac," demonstrates the French novelist's influence on the novel not only in theme, spirit, and character but also in the description of city contrasts and liaisons and in the use of reflective passages. But it can also be argued that the setting, the tone, and the handling of such incidents as Hurstwood's theft in the novel clearly indicate Dreiser's romantic sensibility.[2]

It is, therefore, time to reexamine what naturalism is. Is it a single, identifiable movement? Is it equivalent to positivism? We must ask ourselves what is the relationship between a bold philosophical innovation that claimed to have transcended barren philosophical meditation and a daring literary experiment that sought to deal with the pathology of everyday life. Was the naturalistic novelist genuinely insensitive to the demands of novelty, of an evolving, pluralistic society? Or was the very nature of the naturalist writer's vision wide, accommodating, and often misunderstood? And finally, have we paid too slight attention to the spirit and durability of the naturalistic enterprise?

We must state at once that literary naturalism differs from its philosophical counterpart, positivism. The positivist imagination demanded that speculation and interest not only in "the thing-in-itself" but also in the manifestation of the Absolute cease as unfruitful and unverifiable. For, the positivists argued, only the claims of the phenomenal world constitute our experience; only that which is empirically verifiable composes our genuine reality. That post-Kantians and Hegelians alike scorned such a concept is understandable. Yet it is clear that such a scheme, taking as its approach the scientific method and grandly striving for the reduction of all phenomenal experience into one or even several overarching laws, would fascinate a certain kind of imagination. Could not the same method be applied to man and his social life? Could we not have an authentic sociology and, as Zola argued, a genuine picture of man?

Yet there is a tenuous line between the influence of an idea and its power of inspiration. Above all, literary naturalism refers to the writers' products. Although based on the positivist approach, literary naturalism involves the very craft of fiction. However rigorously Zola's experimental formula might be applied, it is nevertheless a personal and necessarily subjective activity. Moreover, as Zola argued, the writer should rely on his imaginative powers when the very conclusions of science were simply lacking. When we talk about nineteenth-century naturalistic novelists, we must see them within the context of artificers struggling to dramatize in their works the conclusions of a historically relevant biology and physics, of the diverse and often opposing speculations of Prosper Lucas, Despine, Darwin, Spencer, and Taine. We must also see naturalistic authors adjusting themselves to the gradual refinement of scientific law. As such, the naturalists, both early and late, are artists who cling to the theory of phenomenalism while subjectively interpreting and choosing a subject, an issue, a milieu. Whether naturalism is pessimistic or optimistic, therefore, depends upon the individual novelist's handling of his given material; there is a vast difference between Zola's *Nana* and Phillips' *Susan Lenox: Her Fall and Rise*.

If the scope of naturalism is seen in this light, we must conclude that the movement, from its inception, was not monolithic but rather fluid and variable; in fact, it was open to novelty. The various modes of expression were incorporated stylistically, and its philosophical durability resides in a decided view of human nature that is much with us even today. Whereas naturalism in America may not be directly traceable to any one particular national philosophy, character, or attitude, all observers agree that naturalism attained its eminence in France; Balzac, Taine, the Goncourt brothers, and Zola are its masters. In tune with the positivist spirit, the French naturalists developed a keen eye for empirical detail, and often paid homage to their concept of the scientist by conceiving of themselves as novelists in the clothes of biologists and chemists, anatomists and surgeons.[3]

Balzac's preface to the *Comédie humaine* is considered one of the earliest statements of the naturalistic thought. Balzac argued that man was the product of his surroundings and developed his individual characteristics accordingly. In his fiction, Balzac was enormously interested in describing the architecture and conditions of the houses, the furniture, the food people ate, and the clothes they wore—not because he wanted to create an illusion of reality, but because he thought the surroundings as both an extension of personality and a controlling force. Flaubert, too, believed in the environmental influence on character, illustrating the tragedy of Emma Bovary by the bourgeois society of which she was a necessary part. Like Balzac, who cited contemporary biological classification, Flaubert too adhered to scientific principles in describing characters and events; witness Flaubert's words to George Sand: "Great Art is scientific and impersonal. By an effort of the mind you must put yourself into your characters, not draw them to you. That, at least, is the method."[4] The Goncourt brothers, in their preface to *Germinie Lacerteux*, called their public to notice how Germinie would be depicted, dissected like a corpse upon a slab. Equally important, they forcefully urged novelists to describe the inhabitants of the lower world, a challenge to the bourgeois and genteel reading public. As the Goncourt brothers argued, the public is fond of sensation:

> It loves smutty little works, prostitutes' memoirs, alcove confessions, erotic dirt, scandal adjusting its dress in a picture in a bookstore window: what it is about to read is severe and pure. It must not expect the decolleté photograph of Pleasure; what follows is a clinical study of love.
> The public also loves vapid and consoling reading, adventures that end happily, imaginings which upset neither its digestion nor its serenity: this book with its sad and violent distraction is bound to challenge its habits and upset its hygiene.[5]

By far the most influential exponent of French naturalism was Zola. Throughout his Rougon-Macquart series, Zola portrayed French life in its entirety through a detailed yet passionate study of a family seen in the light of its environment and heredity. Although Zola often professed to be scientifically impersonal and dispassionate in his treatment of his fictional material—his preface to *Thérèse Raquin* is one such public statement among many—he may well have been the least objective among the French naturalists. What distinguishes Zola from a scrupulously objective narrator like Flaubert is his eagerness to be a moralist, a social reformer. In fact, the sensational details woven into *L'Assommoir*, the fascination with brutality in *La Bête humaine*, and the sweeping romantic vision that looms large at the end of *Germinal*, the very allusion to the cycle of life, death, and rebirth that redeems his almost journalistic prose, seem to be pursued for their own sake. These elements have allowed critics to cast Zola as an extreme example of romanticism; in fact, Norris claimed that Zola was the chief exponent of such romantic sensationalism.

We may well ask if this is not another case of discrepancy so often found between theory and practice. But first, we must consider whether or not physio-chemical determinism and such grandiose sensationalism are incompatible. We are not necessarily refuting the idea that both can—and often do—coexist within both personality and work. In Zola's case, such explanations reside in his manifesto, *The Experimental Novel*. Zola insisted that his method of observation was that of the empirical sciences; he admitted that he lifted much of his polemic from Claude Bernard's *Introduction to the Study of the Experimental Medicine* and simply replaced the word *novelist* with the word *doctor*. However, the reason that this scientific method did not turn out to be a wholly objective approach for Zola lies both in the social legacy of positivism and in Zola's ulterior desire to portray realistically the conditions of man and his environment for their own sake. Zola passionately argued that his ultimate intention as a novelist was to correct the conditions under which man suffered; he wished to further a liberal, progressive spirit that was so often smothered by the legacy of the Second Empire. Yet not only were the injustices that Zola disclosed so objectively the predictable outgrowth of a moralistic temper but also his attitude toward the injustices was at variance with the clinically ontological status of man under positivism. Although this conflict pervades his work, Zola remarkably avoided a genuine confrontation with its implication. If Zola focused on the lower classes in which women like Nana and Gervaise became victims of, and mirrored, the gutter-life, or on the revolutionary Etienne, it was not because he wanted to create in his reader an attitude of pessimism and despair but rather because he believed in the possibility of reform and the validity of hope. Thus, Zola himself was no mechanical naturalist, but employed the naturalistic formula imaginatively and powerfully, portraying realms of human experience that were neither conventionally nor dogmatically defined.

There have been conflicting speculations about the origins and manifestations of American literary naturalism. Writers as diverse as Howells, Garland, Crane, Norris, London, and Dreiser, as well as such modern novelists as Hemingway, Faulkner, Wright, Farrell, Steinbeck, Mailer, and Bellow have sometimes been placed in the naturalistic camp. The more we examine this pervasive stream of naturalism the more apparent are the differences between its American and European aspects. Moreover, since its tumultuous beginnings in the late nineteenth century, American naturalism has undergone a drastic transformation. There have been no two American writers who were alike in their use and interpretation of the doctrine. Norris used to be labeled a Zolaesque naturalist, but contemporary criticism often places him apart from his avowed master.[6] Dreiser might not be the thoroughgoing determinist he was once described as being despite his often sententious pronouncements about "chemisms" and the vast forces that control human behavior. We can conclude from these observations that naturalism is not a "pure" or "undifferentiated" movement, especially in the American context. This is perhaps why Edwin Cady, in *The Light of Common Day*, went so far as to declare that "there are not finally any naturalists" in American literature.[7]

Although the American character has so many facets and modes of expression, literary historians often maintain the commonplace that American naturalists were pessimistic determinists. Charles C. Walcutt traces American naturalism to the kernel of American transcendentalism. Spirit and Nature, initially united, separated. Idealistic social radicalism owes much to its interpretation of Spirit; pessimistic determinists, emphasizing the exploration of Nature by science, become the dark children of their Concord parents. However interesting this view may be for an adequate account of the subject, modern criticism has continued to employ such terms as *dualism, tensions*, and *contradictions* in defining the essential character of American literary naturalism. For many of our thinkers and writers, the concept of determinism naturally suggested the limits of man's freedom. No doubt Dreiser instinctively employed this intimation when he referred to Mark Twain as the "double" Twain. We are also reminded of Henry Adams' words that "[from] earliest childhood the boy was accustomed to feel that, for him, life was double." If American naturalists admitted the stifling conditions of man's life—Crane's *The Red Badge of Courage* serves as a striking example—they could also affirm the significance of men as individuals. This problem, so often the tension within the naturalistic canon, is dramatized in another way: the choice between the lower-class characters coming to bad ends and the heroic, adventurous image of man, e.g., *George's Mother* and *Moran of the Lady Letty*.[8]

Some critics find the sources of American pessimistic determinism in the ineradicable Calvinism that was rooted strongly in the early years of American national development and in the moral sterility produced by the growth of materialism. The argument of these critics further states that the theory of predestination was seriously breached by the impact of the Enlightenment, though the latter was never successful in demolishing the traditional sense of Original Sin that was later superseded—in fact easily accommodated by the American mind—by pessimistic determinism in the guise of evolution. In effect, then, the development of science in the nineteenth century liberated America from its earlier religious pessimism, but ironically the latter was now replaced by scientific pessimism.[9]

Still another argument states that the American mood was different following the Civil War and that new ways of living and thinking challenged the established codes of life. The growth of industrialism, the frontier movements, and the development of science all had a penetrating effect on American life. On the one hand, the young nation was feeding on the boundless hope for progress, and on the other, congenial to the technocratic spirit, America was discovering the unimportance and helplessness of man in an indifferent universe. The feeling of despair, brought about by science, can be found both in Europe and in America. The great works of Balzac and Zola, however, would not have been written without the scientific tradition. In America, too, the works of the naturalists were facilitated by the same tradition that had been carried over from Europe and developed further in native soil. Wherever we look, the transplanting of naturalism from Europe to the United States was thus inevitable.

But such a congenial literary development might not have taken place in another culture with an entirely different social and intellectual background. We know, for instance, that the same literary movement spread all over the world at the time and made some impact upon the Japanese novels. In Japan, however, the influence of naturalism was much less marked. One may conjecture that the Japanese tradition, unlike that of a Western nation, lacked not only a Pascal, a Bernard, a Pasteur, and a Darwin but also philosophers such as Comte, Taine, and Spencer who interpreted the works of scientists for literary men. This is perhaps why, for example, Natsume Soseki (1867–1916), an eminent Japanese novelist, felt no objection to the naturalists' detailed and objective treatment of material but was not at all convinced of the effect of the overpowering forces of heredity and environment on man. Soseki could not believe at the dawn of the Enlightenment in Japan that a good novel was to be made of the misery and littleness of man; what could enrich the spirit of the new era, he thought, was the rediscovery of aesthetic and humanistic values in tradition.

It can be easily seen that the equation of the intellectual climate and background between cultures would not be the only criterion for defining the genesis of American naturalism. Indeed, it would be difficult to see how such concepts as abstract forces, social Darwinism, and environmental and hereditary determinism, as well as a realistic and scientific mode of description, could have taken root in a new nation without the previous conditioning of these ideas and methods. The importation of French naturalism to the United States, though generally recognized, is far from obvious. Many American novelists came under the sway of French naturalism not only because of their desire to break the provincial chains of the American culture but also because the French positivist and literary aims were, simply put, in the air.

Although Crane and Norris began the naturalistic experiment in the 1890s, voices were heard before that decade that discussed the impact of heredity and environment upon man's fate.[10] In the *Atlantic Monthly* of January 1860, the first installment of Oliver Wendell Holmes' ''The Professor's Story'' appeared. When the installments were collected and published as the novel *Elsie Venner* (1861), Holmes included a preface in which he declared his uncertainty about the theory of heredity that constituted the ''machinery'' of his plot. He explained:

> Through all the disguise of fiction a grave scientific doctrine may be detected lying beneath some of the delineations of character. He [the author] has used this doctrine as a part of the machinery of his story without pledging his absolute belief in it to the extent to which it is asserted or implied. It was adopted as a convenient medium of truth rather than as an accepted scientific conclusion.[11]

Twenty-five years later, Holmes had effaced his doubts, and in a ''Second Preface'' claimed:

> The real aim of the story was to test the doctrine of ''original sin'' and human responsibility for the disordered volition coming under that technical denomination. Was Elsie Venner, poisoned . . . before she was born . . . morally responsible for the ''volitional'' aberrations, which translated into acts became what is known as sin; and, it may be, what is punished as crime? (p. vi)

Between the dates of the first and second editions, Holmes had read

Despine's *Psychologie Naturelle* (1868), and in an essay entitled "Crime and Automatism" Holmes had seconded Despine's contention that in "most cases crime can be shown to run in the blood."[12] The human will was "anything but free," and Holmes attributed its bondage to internal organic conditions and external surroundings.

The first of Holmes' "medicated novels," *Elsie Venner*, was an inquiry into the pathology of the will. The eponymous heroine was poisoned by snake venom *in utero*, and as she matured, her actions became serpentine. Frequenting snake-infested caves, hissing, and hypnotizing people by gazing into their eyes, Elsie was unable to control her actions. Representing the authorial viewpoint, a physician forcefully argued that the girl's volition was subjected to forces beyond her immediate control. Claiming that Elsie must be understood, not condemned, the physician unsuccessfully tried to remedy her plight. The novel interpreted the fable of man's fall in secular terms; like Eve, Elsie succumbed to the serpent and her death not only forced the community to realize that theological dogma must yield to scientific knowledge but also signaled the end of the Edenic town; an avalanche destroyed part of the village. The secular moral of the story can be found in "Crime and Automatism," for Holmes suggested: "In place of considering man as a creature so utterly perverted from birth that the poles of his nature must be reversed, the tendency is to look upon him rather as subject to attractions and repulsions which are to be taken advantage of in education" (p. 328).

Richard Dugdale's *The Jukes* (1877) also charted the environmental and hereditary conditions that shaped man's will. Dugdale's terminology—"degenerating stocks," "redeeming influence of virtuous aspiration," "social defilement," and "primitive tendency"—reminds us not only of Darwin's *The Descent of Man* but also of Zola's novels in which there are atavisms, crosses, and throwbacks. In fact, Dugdale's method of inquiry was fairly close to Zola's outline of the Rougon-Macquart series. As Dugdale put it, his approach was

one of historico-biographical synthesis united to statistical analysis, enabling us to estimate the cumulative effect of any condition which has operated through successive generations; heredity giving us those elements of character which are derived from the parent as a birthright, environment all the events and conditions occurring after birth which have contributed to shape the individual career or deflect its primitive tendency.[13]

Tracking down the members and ancestors of a given family pseudo-nymously named the "Jukes," Dugdale charted the frequency of arrest and the age of the defendant; then he plotted a genealogy that demonstrated the relationship between crime and family character. His conclusion was that man's fate was determined; the individual could not struggle unaided against the powers of heredity and environment. But Dugdale suggested that once the laws of behavioral causation were known, man's destiny could be controlled, an argument that foreshadows Zola's own conclusions in *The Experimental Novel*.

Clearly, there was a trend—no matter how slight—in American thought before the 1890s that suggested the limits of man's capacity to make moral choices and to control his life. American literary naturalism reflected the growing strength of this intellectual disposition, gaining impetus from a steady acceptance of social Darwinism, and if we turn to our well-known writers such as Garland, Crane, and Norris, the origins of literary naturalism are thrown into relief.

The following examples are suggestive enough of this hypothesis. Although it may be difficult to call Garland a confirmed and thoroughgoing naturalist, his notebooks indicate that he was familiar with the works of George Sand before 1890. According to Thomas Beer, Crane's reading of a translation of *La Débâcle* influenced his writing of *The Red Badge of Courage*. Even before Crane wrote *Maggie*, he must have had his heroine in mind when he called Zola's *Nana* "a real street walker." "You must pardon me," he wrote, "if I cannot agree that every painted woman on the streets of New York was brought there by some evil man. Nana, in the story, is honest."[14] Norris' debt to Zola has been meticulously traced by Lars Åhnebrink in *The Beginnings of Naturalism in American Fiction*, but Norris' own works such as *McTeague* and *Vandover and the Brute* and his statements in *The Responsibilities of the Novelist* are by themselves clear evidence of this influence. Although Dreiser said he had never read a line of Zola before he wrote *Sister Carrie*, he had heard about several French writers including Balzac and Zola from newspapermen in St. Louis as early as 1893.[15]

Even such casual evidence for the connection between French and American literary naturalism suggests that the influence was not limited to one author or to one aspect of the movement. Norris was most impressed with Zola's romanticism and the epic sweep of his works.

What was lacking in Howellsian realism, Norris thought, was "the unplumbed depths of the human heart, and the mystery of sex, and the problems of life, and the black, unsearched penetralia of the soul of man" that was so vividly depicted by the French master.[16] The ambience of Zola's *oeuvre* thus suited Norris' expansive mood in creating ambitious epics like *The Octopus* and *The Pit*, and sharpened his sense of modern bourgeois tragedy in *McTeague*. Dreiser may differ from Zola in technique, but both were stern moralists who never ceased using the tools of positivism to challenge convention. Dreiser's fascination with Balzac had more than an ideological basis. *The Great Man from the Provinces* (published in *Harper's* in 1894), Dreiser tells us, "seemed to connect itself with my own life"—that is, the discomfort of being unable to support a wife (*Book*, p. 422).

Thus American novelists who came of age in the 1890s strained against the conventional, formal aesthetic and social amenities of their literary tradition, change demanded by a host of complex factors that often merged—personal, social, and political convictions. Many of them felt that the genteel restraints of realism were bourgeois, that they smothered crisis, replacing diversity with a felicitous social norm. Consequently, French naturalism would not only place these writers in the avant-garde—a convenient position that challenges all aesthetic, political, and social relationships—but also provide them with a tradition for experimentation that would point out the inadequacies of realism.

Therefore, the dispute that remains unsettled in our own day over the naturalistic movement rests not only upon our vision of man but upon the way we believe literature functions as an educative, political instrument. The genuine vitality and legacy of the naturalistic vision reside within the concrete depictions of man's relationship to his environment and genetic endowment. In this manner, the naturalistic author mirrors the observable interpenetrations of self and society; he translates data and theory about human nature and conduct into their most comprehensible and observable form. That such a movement is varied and multiform is an asset. Crane, Norris, and Dreiser, each a distinctive individual talent, developed differently. But there is also a pervasive similarity of philosophic suppositions that binds together the works of all such writers. Whether for its diversity or identity in the character of naturalistic writing in the United States, there needs to be a variety of approaches for our understanding of the movement.

The growing critical concern with the content, form, and meaning of

American naturalism has resulted in several books that deal with the philosophical and aesthetic suppositions as well as theories of the movement, its major figures, and its genuine depth. Among them, Charles C. Walcutt's *American Literary Naturalism, A Divided Stream* has stirred a great controversy over the origin and meaning of naturalism. Lars Åhnebrink's *The Beginnings of Naturalism in American Fiction*, a pioneering and meticulous work, is a historical survey larded with comparative textual analysis that stops short of Dreiser and fails to penetrate the heart of ideas that animates the movement. *Essays on Determinism in American Literature*, edited by Sydney J. Krause, marks the beginning of a dialogue on this topic, but the collection is concerned, by definition, with determinism and not naturalism as a whole. And Donald Pizer's *Realism and Naturalism in Nineteenth-Century American Literature* does not, of course, address itself with the later naturalists.

American literary naturalism, therefore, is a highly complex subject matter, and the case of Dreiser serves to mark the controversy that still envelops its problems. Dreiser's relationship to this important literary and intellectual heritage is hardly simple or direct as we are often led to believe. When we deal with Dreiser, not only do we have to define precisely the nature of the naturalistic influences on him, which is essential in interpreting his work, but we must also explore in depth his personal experience as an individual and social being. For Dreiser was an original, albeit inconsistent thinker. He has been passionately supported by those whom his ideals and convictions inspired; he has been totally rejected by those who were prejudiced against him. Consequently, in the controversy that has ever plagued his criticism, Dreiser's stature as artist has been unfairly judged. Dreiser should also be recognized as an important social historian. Though at various stages of his development he was sympathetic toward Darwin and Spencer, and the naturalistic philosophy in general, Dreiser never dealt with those ideas without the context of American society. He is the one writer of his generation to whom we can today turn to reassess in perspective the genesis and development of twentieth-century America.

2 French Naturalists

Whether or not the young Dreiser was influenced by French naturalists remains an intriguing question. Many of his early critics who placed Dreiser in the tradition of American naturalism saw in his work primarily a literary influence, especially that of Balzac and Zola. Dreiser is frequently treated as the American champion who challenged the genteel tradition at home and successfully used his own experience to write fiction through the methods of these French writers. Those who argue that young Dreiser learned much from the manner and temperament with which Balzac constructed his Paris world in *The Human Comedy* find support in Dreiser's account of his first acquaintance with Balzac in *A Book About Myself*. Those who believe that Dreiser followed the manner of Zola rely on the assumption that Dreiser, entering the American literary world at the turn of the century, must have heard from Norris of Zola's *The Experimental Novel*, first published in English in 1893.

At the turn of the century naturalism was, indeed, the literary zeitgeist, and it is reasonable to assume that Dreiser would not have avoided those powerful influences from the French sources. Alfred Kazin correctly says in *On Native Grounds*:

> It was by a curious irony that Dreiser's early career became the battleground of naturalism in America. He stumbled into the naturalist novel as he has stumbled through life. It is doubtful that he would have become a novelist if the fight for realism in American letters had not been won before he arrived on the scene; but when he did, he assumed as a matter of course that a tragic novel so indifferent to conventional shibboleths as *Sister Carrie* was possible.[1]

Dreiser was, then, certainly indebted to Norris because the latter sent Dreiser's first novel to the critics with great enthusiasm.[2]

Having written *The Responsibilities of the Novelist* in an obvious echo of *The Experimental Novel*, Norris perhaps became the closest American counterpart of Zola. Most readers agree that Norris imitated Zola's method in his early novels, such as *Vandover and the Brute*, both in theme and treatment. When Norris exclaimed toward the end of *The Octopus*, "Men were nothings, mere animalcules, mere ephemerides that fluttered and fell and were forgotten between dawn and dusk,''[3] he was faithfully following Zola's principle of observing human life in terms of chemistry and biology. Stephen Crane, with the private publication of *Maggie: A Girl of the Streets* in 1893, had also pointed the way for the later naturalists. Merely on the basis of Crane's pessimism, however, it would be difficult to prove that he followed Zola's naturalism. His work seems to elude the precise category of "naturalist."

But the influence of these American predecessors of Dreiser, no matter how accurately they mirrored French naturalism in their own works, will not justify the assertion that Dreiser was really indebted to French naturalists. The timing of his arrival on the American scene tends to lead us astray in assaying the French influence on Dreiser. Moreover, as David Brion Davis has written, "it was too easy to ignore what he actually wrote and classify him as a Zola-type materialist who occasionally showed inconsistent emotional lapses of pity and sympathy."[4] The early critics of Dreiser were so busy pigeonholing Dreiser's work into the tradition of French naturalism that they virtually neglected what Dreiser had to say on that relationship. There is indeed such a record, in Dreiser's own words, to which we must now turn.

We are not always on safe ground when we accept without further examination what a writer mentions in a casual essay. We are compelled, nonetheless, to look into Dreiser's accounts of himself before he wrote *Sister Carrie*. His first acquaintance with the names of certain French writers took place in St. Louis in 1893, when Dreiser was working for the *Republic* under that paper's city editor, H. B. Wandell. In the time-honored advice of city-room editors to fledgling reporters, Wandell often urged young Dreiser to stick to "bare facts" in relating the day's catastrophe. Fascinated by French writers, especially by Balzac and Zola, Wandell constantly repeated the names of these French writers to Dreiser.[5] Not until much later, however, did Dreiser first read Zola; in 1894 at the Carnegie Library in Pittsburgh he read his first French novel, Balzac's *The Wild Ass's Skin*, in translation. Dreiser confesses he was electrified (*Book,* pp. 410–11). "This experience of Dreiser's," Malcolm Cowley says, "brings to light a curious phenomenon connected with the whole stream of foreign influence."[6] Cowley further implies that this experience of Dreiser's, gained in Pittsburgh, is substantial evidence that accounts not only for Dreiser's but for his generation's acquisition of the literary methods of the European naturalists.

Two integrated approaches have been used to determine the literary influences of French naturalists on Dreiser. One is the assumption based on the literary situation that existed around the turn of the century both in America and in Europe; the other is the reliance placed on whatever Dreiser says about French writers in an autobiography such as his *A Book About Myself*.

These arguments, however, present numerous problems, and it behooves us first to define clearly the principal criteria of the French doctrines in question. While Howells was working as a "springboard," presenting his version of scientific realism in conflict with the genteel idealism and romanticism of New England, a school of intensified realism had been founded in France. As literary realism intensified into the naturalism of Zola, the works of Balzac and Flaubert began to seem picturesque, idealistic, and even "romantic." Balzac's chief interest was in delineating every aspect of human life that was rich, beautiful, and meaningful. When Dreiser first read Balzac's *The Wild Ass's Skin* and other works from *The Human Comedy*, he was immensely fascinated by Balzac's manner of depicting his backgrounds, which were, in Dreiser's words, "abundant, picturesque, gorgeous" (*Book*, p. 411).

To Zola the voice of nineteenth-century science and thought conveyed the ultimate truth, and he attempted to apply its laws to his writing. Zola accepted only the so-called scientism, in which his treatment of characters and their milieu is identical with a scientist's treatment of materials and their conditions, or a physiologist's treatment of animals and their surroundings. Zola gives this conclusion in *The Experimental Novel*:

> If I were to define the experimental novel I should not say, as Claude Bernard says, that a literary work lies entirely in the personal feeling, for the reason that in my opinion the personal feeling is but the first impulse. Later nature, being there, makes itself felt, or at least that part of nature of which we have no longer any right to romance. The experimental novelist is therefore the one who accepts proven facts, who points out in man and in society the mechanism of the phenomena over which science is mistress, and who does not interpose his personal sentiments, except in the phenomena whose determinism is not yet settled, and who tries to test, as much as he can, this personal sentiment, this idea *a priori*, by observation and experiment.[7]

Zola even declared further: "The metaphysical man is dead." He believed that, however eternal the beauty of Achilles' anger and Dido's love might be, the modern novelist would have to analyze love and anger, to which metaphysicians had given only "irrational and supernatural" explanations (*Experimental Novel*, p. 54).

The whole stream of French naturalism is thus diversified. Yet, if we stick to the portion represented by Zola, we can note several of the criteria of naturalism—even though they were not necessarily put into practice by Zola himself as pointed out earlier. Zola and his followers insisted on objectivity and frankness; they believed in the influence of heredity and environment on the individual; they preferred proletarian, animalistic, or neurotic characters; their views were deterministic, pessimistic, and often annihilative; they were skeptical of traditional morality.

If, then, we were to establish the assumption that Dreiser was an American naturalist after the manner of Zola, we would have to prove that the same criteria are reflected in Dreiser's fiction. If the term *French naturalism* means objectivity and frankness, it can be applied to a description of most of Dreiser's works. If it means a faithful adherence to the development of science, it can also be accepted. If it means an attack on traditional moral standards, it can certainly be accepted. If it means that environment crucially influences character, it can still be accepted. As far as the hereditary influence on character is concerned, however, this is not even an issue in Dreiser's novels. Where is his treatment of familial or ancestral traits for the characterization of Hurstwood, Carrie, Jennie, Cowperwood, Eugene, or even Clyde? There are some such references in the works of Crane, Norris, and London, but American naturalistic writers may not be really concerned with the hereditary elements as European novelists such as Zola and Hardy. Furthermore, when the view of the world of Dreiser's characters is often confined to daydreams, his method appears least "objective": for example, Hurstwood's dreams and delusions are all the life left to him as he sits on park benches and in his sordid rooms. When many of Dreiser's characters are physically weak rather than strong and animalistic, they are scarcely like Zola's. Although Eugene Witla goes through a struggle brought on directly by his nervous breakdown which follows the dashing success of his first paintings, he is not a neurotic character; he is just physically exhausted and weak. And when we analyze Dreiser's view of life in his novels, we find that his views are not always pessimistic. In *The Bulwark*, Solon's faith, although assailed by many disasters, triumphs in the end. After Angel's death, Eugene is not at all pessimistic or annihilative. If the term *naturalism* has the effect of limiting our view of the scope of Dreiser's emotional creative power, it must be rejected.

One can easily recognize the fact that throughout his career Dreiser remained an independent thinker and practitioner. He did not go to Harvard, where Norris wrote *Vandover and the Brute* for Professor Lewis E. Gates' class of creative writing. Dreiser did not spend his formative years in Paris, as did Norris; it is inconceivable that Norris did not read Zola's work there. Dreiser never retreated an inch in insisting that Doubleday agree to publish *Sister Carrie*. When the Cincinnati Anti-Vice Society demanded that the U. S. Post Office authorities ban *The "Genius"* on the grounds that the book was "lewd" and "profane," he became extraordinarily defiant not only in the defense of his book but in his fierce attack on this society.[8]

Even to H. L. Mencken, his closest friend and ally, Dreiser in 1922 flatly spoke about matters of critical judgment: "In regard to the critic as artist—you never were a critic really. You have as you say—a definite point of view & a philosophy & you have used the critical role to put it over[.] Your comments on life have always been vastly more diverting to me than your more intensive comment on books" (*Letters*, 2: 405–6). After discussing his own play, *The Hand of the Potter*, with Mencken, Dreiser frankly told Mencken: "You may be well within your critical rights [concerning the American stage] but my answer is that I have more respect for my own judgement in this matter than I have for yours" (*Letters*, 1: 241). As late as 1938 Dreiser warned us: "It is very unlikely, in my opinion, that any examination of fictional theory ... is going to help anyone, writer or reader to understand creative writing, and least of all, enable anyone to better undertake it. It is just as well to remember that all critical and aesthetic theories arose after the fact" (*Letters*, 3: 794–95).

The fundamental originality of Dreiser, his honesty and truthfulness to his own experience, must be recalled when we argue over the literary influences on him. The last statement quoted even goes so far as to suggest that the basic influences on Dreiser were, indeed, extraliterary. It also presents his American experience as being more vital than the movements of thoughts and theories he might have received from the French naturalists.

☆ ☆ ☆ ☆

We have yet to classify the movements of thoughts and theories for their possible influences before Dreiser established his own creed. On the American scene, the fact remains that Dreiser had read Darwin before he became acquainted with Zola's work. In a letter of 1916 to Mencken, Dreiser says that as early as 1894 he had discovered Spencer, Huxley, and Tyndall, at the same time he discovered Balzac (*Letters*, 1: 211). Interestingly, this reading of Balzac's novels in 1894 in Pittsburgh while he was still a young reporter marks the beginning of Dreiser's serious interest in creative writing.

Although Dreiser was introduced to the French novelist "quite by accident" (*Letters*, 1: 211), several factors were not purely accidental. The immediate motive had been present in his mind over two years since he met the newspaper editor Wandell in St. Louis, but there was another far more significant reason for his discovery of Balzac. Few American writers really interested Dreiser at that time. He had long brooded over the aridity of American letters, as he said later. While he served as drama editor of the *Globe-Democrat* in St. Louis, he was amazed how unreal and fanciful the plays he saw were. According to what he had experienced and known in his childhood and youth, "the dreary humdrum of actual life was carefully shut out from these pieces; the simple delights of ordinary living, if they were used at all, were exaggerated beyond sensible belief." What made young Dreiser feel inferior in those days was not only a world of unreality and untruth then prevailing on the stage but a treatment of life elsewhere. It was not in Warsaw, Indiana, or even in Chicago and St. Louis where life to the young Dreiser was real. To him, "the East, New York, London, Paris, Vienna, St. Petersburg—were all the things that were worth while" (*Book*, p. 179). When Dreiser first saw the Paris world and its life through Balzac, *The Great Man from the Provinces* struck him as "a knockout. It was. I was quite beside myself and read three others without stopping," as he later told Mencken (*Letters*, 1: 211–12).

Even as late as 1911 Dreiser admired only a few American literary works, which included *The Red Badge of Courage, Main-Travelled Roads, With the Procession* (H. B. Fuller), *McTeague, The 13th District* (Brand Whitlock), *The Story of Eva* (Will Payne), *Quicksand* (Harvey White), and *Their Wedding Journey*. "When I go abroad," he wrote, "it is very different. Balzac, Zola, de Maupassant, Daudet,

Flaubert and Anatole France are great towering statues to me—the best in France.'' He further lists a number of celebrities in Russia, England, Germany, and Italy (*Letters*, 1: 121). This attitude is again illustrated by Dreiser's letter to Mencken in 1915, in which he asked for a comprehensive list of ''fugitive realistic Works of import'' in American literature (*Letters*, 1: 185).

Dreiser's experience in St. Louis as a drama critic thus forced him to react against the American literary scene. The young critic secretly felt that to be happy and fulfilled in his career as a journalist he had to go eventually to those cultural cities (*Book*, pp. 179–80). In the following year, when he first discovered Balzac, ''a new and inviting door to life had been suddenly thrown open to [him]'' (*Book*, p. 411). He describes Balzac with great affection:

> Here was one who saw, thought, felt. Through him I saw a prospect so wide that it left me breathless—all Paris, all France, all life through French eyes. Here was one who had a tremendous and sensitive grasp of life, philosophic, tolerant, patient, amused . . . . I knew his characters as well as he did, so magical was his skill. His grand and somewhat pompous philosophical deductions, his easy and offhand disposition of all manner of critical, social, political, historical, religious problems, the manner in which he assumed as by right of genius intimate and irrefutable knowledge of all subjects, fascinated and captured me as the true method of the seer and the genius . . . . (*Book*, pp. 411–12)

What impressed Dreiser in Balzac's novels is not only the French writer's prolific Paris world but essentially his insight and skill in conveying life experience. Whether or not Dreiser himself would be able to gain this kind of insight and skill was a question to be solved in the future. Naturally, he compared Balzac's Paris with his Pittsburgh. However, ''Pittsburgh was not Paris, America was not France, but in truth they were something, and Pittsburgh at least had aspects which somehow suggested Paris.'' He also wrote, ''I marveled at the physical similarity of the two cities as I conceived it, at the chance for pictures here as well as there'' (*Book*, p. 412).

Dreiser's effort and success to equate these two physical worlds and the two lives (his and Balzac's) were a means to an end. Although the means may have been useful in formulating a theory of fiction in his early career, it would not be regarded as a distinct literary influence. Rather it was then, more accurately, a ''joy'' as he confessed later. To the sentimentalist of twenty-three years, Balzac's *The Great Man from the Provinces* and du Maurier's *Trilby* (published in *Harper's* in the spring and summer of 1894), as Dreiser remembered, "had a strange psychologic effect on me at the time, as indeed [they] appeared to have on most of the intelligentsia of America" (*Book*, pp. 412–22).

That was in 1894. As late as 1897, as he wrote to Mencken, Dreiser had not had the slightest idea that he would become a novelist, but the inspirational and psychological effect of these European authors perhaps marked a turning point between his career as a newspaperman and that as a writer. He realized at that time that he had already accumulated a great amount of life experience behind him. It was certainly neither in Paris nor in London; it was in America and its great cities, which he discovered and by which he was fascinated "enough." "But because of the preponderant influence of foreign letters on American life," he wrote, "it seemed that Paris and London must be so much better since everyone wrote about them" (*Book*, p. 422).

But why not American life, and what he saw in his backyard? Though the beginning of his career appeared slow and tedious, as Dreiser later reflected,

the Spring time, Balzac, the very picturesque city itself, my own idling and yet reflective disposition, caused me finally to attempt a series of mood or word pictures about the most trivial matters—a summer storm, a spring day, a visit to a hospital, the death of an old switchman's dog, the arrival of the first mosquito—which gave me my first taste of what it means to be a creative writer. (*Book*, p. 413)

With the publication of *Sister Carrie*, Dreiser's interest in appraising modern American life was further extended. On the surface, he sought to describe all kinds and all patterns of American experience; underneath it, however, he was constantly moved by his subjective mind. His deep personal involvement with each character is a reflection of this mind. The suicide of a prominent saloon keeper, George Hurstwood; the theatrical success of a poor country girl, Carrie Meeber; the chance and fate of an innocent, lovable woman, Jennie Gerhardt; the stormy life of a temperamental artist, Eugene Witla; the materialistic pursuit by a bank clerk, Frank Cowperwood; the crime and punishment of a feeble-minded youth, Clyde Griffiths; the search for faith by a Quaker, Solon

Barnes—all these life experiences were derived from the facts that Dreiser himself knew. It is not surprising that he always displayed sympathy and compassion for his characters.

Dreiser did not always become a pessimist; like Balzac, he tried to find in this precarious life of man "a sweet welter . . . how rich, how tender, how grim, how like a colorful symphony."[9] To him this was none other than a genius' attitude, and he carried it throughout his life. When a reader asked him in 1940 if he believed in God and the immortality of the soul, Dreiser could only tell the reader: "I am thrilled by life's endless grandeur and genius as it presents itself in time and space."[10] This statement echoes exactly what the earlier Dreiser said about Eugene Witla toward the end of *The "Genius"*: "Great art dreams welled up into his soul as he viewed the sparkling deeps of space" (*The "Genius,"* p. 736).

This was his deepest conviction about life and fiction, whereas what he saw and how he saw life were diversified. His motives in his creative work are thus extensive; those of Balzac's world view and Zola's scientific treatment of man are intensive. Answering the question as to what motive was most important in his fiction, Dreiser said in 1938: "From time to time I have had all the motives you list and many variations of the same. In connection with a work of any length, such as a novel, I don't see how a person would have a single motivation; at least I never have had" (*Letters*, 3: 793–95).

The diversity of Dreiser's motivation in his novels does not fully account for an adherence to the method of the experimental novel. Yet he always referred to his long-held belief that man is the victim of forces over which he has no control. And he often called these forces nothing but "chemical" phenomena. As late as 1936 Dreiser still held a Zola-esque attitude toward the advancement of science. Dr. Hull, a professor of Yale's Institute of Human Relations and president of the American Psychological Association, had told a meeting of psychologists that the mind was not a psychic thing but something that physical facts could explain. Dreiser, fascinated by this statement, wrote him: "I want to ask you if you would be good enough to let me see this machine. I am very much inclined to believe in a mechanistic conception of things in general, and I have often thought that such a machine as you describe would some day be developed" (*Letters*, 3: 778–79). Again, Zola's scientism echoes in the following statement by Dreiser: "My studies of life cause me to conclude that individuality is a myth,—there is no such thing any more than there is an individual automobile, aeroplane, typewriter or suit of clothes. There are always slight differences but the construction and operating principles are sufficiently alike to make so called individuality a compliment—not a fact. So too with a turnip, a tree, a rose, a bee."[11]

But Dreiser's presumed indebtedness to Zola's view was, as he says, "hardly even a conscious process."[12] Its unconscious nature is moreover demonstrated by one of Dreiser's letters to Mencken written in 1916, in which he says that he had never read a line of Zola before he wrote *Sister Carrie* (*Letters*, 1: 215). Even the existence of Norris was yet unknown to him. "*Sister Carrie*," Dreiser tells us, "was written in the fall, winter and spring of 1899–1900. I never saw or heard of *McTeague* or Norris until after the novel had been written and turned in to Harper and Brothers who promptly rejected it with a sharp slap" (*Letters*, 1: 210).

We come up, then, against an obstacle in completing our parallel between Dreiser's theory and Zola's naturalism. And this is apparent in our evaluation of such a novel as *The Bulwark*. The book shows, to an extent, Dreiser's basic philosophy in his earlier writings, but it is surely not based on Zola's doctrine. Dreiser's interest in *The Bulwark* and *The Stoic*, his last novels, lies in religion. In *The Bulwark*, Solon himself suffers from cancer; but saved by his strong faith, he eventually conquers all the difficulties. The plot is not, in any way, an attempt to observe life merely in terms of chemical and physical phenomena. Earlier in his career Dreiser's stand on religion was unequivocal. He cautioned in a letter to Frank Harris (author of *Contemporary Portraits*) in 1918: "Kindly remember that I have absolutely no place in my philosophy for a religious or one-sided, so-called ethical, interpretation of life. My God if I have one, is dual—a compendium of so called *evil* as well as 'good' and a user of both for purposes which man as yet may not comprehend" (*Letters*, 1: 254). Again, in criticizing Johan Bojer's *The Great Hunger*, Dreiser said that a novel should not be a religious tract. In proof of this view, Dreiser had the book set side by side with Saltykov's *A Family of Noblemen*, Flaubert's *Madame Bovary*, Balzac's *Cousin Bette* and *Father Goriot*, and Danilevskaya's *Michail Gourakin*.[13]

The apparent inconsistency in Dreiser's thought is not necessarily a problem when we treat his entire work as a history of various emotions and points of view. At one time in his youth he received evolutionary knowledge from Darwin and from other English naturalists. At another time he was greatly moved by the novels of Balzac. Later he read Zola and the theory of the experimental novel. But throughout his life Dreiser was a harsh, stubborn practitioner of the experience he gained during his early development. Even before his emergence in the literary world, he had already been formulating his theory of fiction. When "The Shining Slave Makers," one of his earliest stories, was rejected by the *Century Magazine*, Dreiser took a fierce, opprobrious attitude toward the editor:

> I submit, if scientific fact can at all be bothered about in this connection, that the thing is scientifically correct according to Lubbock [author of *Ants, Bees and Wasps, a Record of Observations on the Habits of the Social Hymenoptera*, 2nd ed. (London, 1872)] and I have the volume and page to show for it . . . . It has had nothing more than a scientific reading for the purpose of establishing the scientific correctness of fictional points.

He then argued that "no man called upon to judge a thing from its scientific side should be allowed to establish the merit of a story as a piece of fiction" (*Letters*, 1: 46).

This attitude toward the editor of one of the most prestigious and influential literary magazines in 1900 represents, in a way, Dreiser's attitude toward his work throughout his entire career. He did not easily conform to any theory, any thought, or any knowledge. By the same token he cannot in any way be called merely a disciple of French naturalists. Instead, he worked hard and honestly to create fiction out of the powerful sentiments and ideals he cherished in his own observation of life. "We like sentiment, we like humor, we like realism," Dreiser as editor of the *Delineator* stated its policies, "but it must be tinged with sufficient idealism to make it all of a truly uplifting character. . . . Things which point a new way or provide a new method of handling or arranging the affairs of this world and the affairs of the individual in regard to his personal advance and improvement" (*Letters*, 1: 94–95).

What Dreiser had to say about his own writing and others' would not make his process of writing so simple as to be classified as one of mere influence—from the French or any other sources. He was always motivated by the instincts within him. His treatment of characters and events is decidedly far more personal, and often more subjective, than that of a literary naturalist. Zola theorized that there should be no room for personal sentiments and ideals on the part of the novelist. On the contrary, Dreiser was much of an idealist. He was honest and told the truth like any literary naturalist; however, his honesty and truth were not always rendered in terms of science but in terms of himself. In his later correspondence he stated his view on the relationship between a writer's feelings and a writer's material:

> In the first place, I think creative writing has more to do with emotion than any other single factor. Generalized and intensified feeling for life is what is expressed. When a writer traces the course of a complete emotional cycle, what you might call a selected causal chain, one view of it, or whatever, he has his work laid out, and the name by which it is called, novel, short story, play or poem, or whatever, really comes after the fact. It is the amount of material which is involved in the feeling which determines the form of the work. (*Letters*, 3: 793–94)

The personal feeling of Dreiser appears in various forms. It is often a strong compassion, but it may appear ugly if it is looked at through the eyes of convention. The book reviewer of the New York *Globe* commented:

> *The "Genius"* is probably Mr. Dreiser's most subjective work— and it is the ugliest . . . . Professor William Lyon Phelps, endeavoring to distinguish between "realism" and life and reality, has illustrated by saying that when Zola gazed upon a dunghill he saw and described a dunghill and nothing more; while Rostand, looking at the same unlovely object, beheld the vision of Chantecler. But Dreiser would never see Chantecler; only the dung—and the Hens![14]

But Dreiser saw America. He saw his native land as Balzac and Zola did theirs. To Dreiser this was a painful observation, yet he could not avoid it. There was no agreement, no compromise, no retreat. He did not even hesitate to reprove his mentor: "Norris wrote *McTeague* and *The Octopus*. Then he fell into the hands of the noble Doubleday who converted him completely to *The Pit*, a bastard bit of romance of the best seller variety" (*Letters*, 1: 329).

Although Dreiser read numerous books that made a deep impression, his theory had long before been determined in his mind. After Balzac, he read Hardy in 1896 and then Sienkiewicz in the same year—especially *Quo Vadis*, a novel that impressed the young Dreiser immensely at the time. For the following decade, his reading included Tolstoy, Stevenson, Barrie, and Dumas. Between 1906 and 1916 he read Turgenev, Dostoevski, de Maupassant, Flaubert, Strindberg, and Hauptmann; but he tells us these writers cannot be called influences. "They came too late," he says. "Actually I should put Hardy and Balzac first in that respect though I seriously doubt whether I was influenced for in St. Louis (1892) I was already building plays of a semi-tragic character. My mind just naturally worked that way . . . ."[15]

On Dreiser's own evidence, we must now explore thoroughly his early life in order to determine his development as an artist. After such a study we shall see that only the most facile critic could attribute the distinguishing characteristics of his writing to the French naturalists. To Dreiser the literary influences were hardly a conscious process. And his process of creating fiction was not slow or cold; it was passionate and emotional, and was intimately tied to his own life.

3 Youth

The maturing vision of Dreiser's youth before he became a newspaper reporter in 1892 is amply shown in his nonfiction—notably *Dawn*, the autobiography of his youth. But this development of the young Dreiser received only scant treatment in relation to his social and intellectual environment. His critics agree that the young Dreiser was not exposed to the kind of environment in which Henry Adams or Edith Wharton grew up. Dreiser is often bluntly called uneducated, uncultivated, unrefined, and even confused. The labeling even goes so far as to suggest that he simply had the wrong background for a novelist and that he was crude in his ideas as well as in his idiom. These critics say that Dreiser was handicapped, to begin with, in transcribing the sensibilities of ''good'' Americans. Lionel Trilling, for instance, wrote in attacking the liberal critics who defended Dreiser's style:

> No doubt Dreiser was an organic artist in the sense that he wrote what he knew and what he was, but so, I suppose, is every artist; the question for criticism comes down to *what* he knew and *what* he was. That he was a child of his time and class is also true, but this can be said of everyone without exception; the question for criticism is how he transcended the imposed limitations of his time and class. As for the defense made on the ground of his particular class, it can only be said that liberal thought has come to a strange pass when it assumes that a plebeian origin is accountable for a writer's faults through all his intellectual life.[1]

These critics are not so much hostile to Dreiser's intellectual and cultural background as they are repelled by his stubbornness in describing one kind of experience and one kind of philosophy. The impressive unity of effect in Dreiser's novels, as Stuart P. Sherman, an early critic, argued, ''is due to the fact that they are all illustrations of a crude and naively simple naturalistic philosophy, such as we find in the mouths of exponents of the new *Real-Politik*.''[2] Dreiser's interpretation of life, upon which we assume he developed his theory of fiction, is clear enough. There is, certainly, evidence indicating that he was, in most of his career, a naturalistic thinker. Throughout his writing, both autobiographical and fictional, Dreiser reiterated that man and his life are a complicated mechanism of chemical and physical reactions. The critics almost unanimously agree that he was a determinist.

But beyond this there are disagreements. To H. L. Mencken, Dreiser was not capable of emotional detachment as was Conrad, who was an aristocrat by birth and training:

> The lures of facile doctrine do not move him [Conrad]. In his irony there is a disdain which plays about even the ironist himself. Dreiser is a product of far different forces and traditions, and is capable of no such escapement. Struggle as he may, and fume and protest as he may, he can no more shake off the chains of his intellectual and cultural heritage than he can change the shape of his nose.... One-half of the man's brain, so to speak, wars with the other half. He is intelligent, he is thoughtful, he is a sound artist—but there come moments when a dead hand falls upon him, and he is once more the Indiana peasant, snuffing absurdly over imbecile sentimentalities, giving a grave ear to quackeries, snorting and eye-rolling with the best of them.[3]

The early defenders of Dreiser concluded that he was often a sentimentalist. He was "at once a sort of a poet and sort of grizzly bear, with a skin as tough as an elephant's and a heart as soft as butter. He is a romantic, a realist and a mystic all in one."[4] Most of his later critics maintained that Dreiser had subscribed to the mechanistic theory of Darwinism. Yet in the back of their minds these critics believed that Dreiser's constant betrayal of "the suspicion that will not down in him, that there is an inward, impelling force, pushing mankind upward as well as onward."[5]

Dreiser has been variously classified by critics who are not necessarily referring to the same qualities of his mind. As a novelist he appeared to have a discrepancy in his thought. Dreiser was often a sentimentalist, but in technique he was, indeed, a realist. At heart he was a passionate romanticist whereas in his intellectual heritage he was a stern naturalist in the sense of Darwin and Spencer. The Dreiser criticism has a tendency of continually classifying his literary heritage and neglecting the immediate surroundings in his boyhood. Charles Shapiro, in his critical study of Dreiser's novels, aptly reproves us for this neglect.[6] In recent years, ever since Robert Elias edited Dreiser's important letters, a revival and reevaluation of Dreiser's biographical works, especially *Dawn*, has been called for. Francis Hodgins, Jr., reviewing Dreiser's published letters, remarked:

They will not substantially alter the standard biographical configuration. Nor will they reduce the importance of Dreiser's own protracted effort to tell the story of his life in *Dawn*, *Newspaper Days*, *A Traveller at Forty*, and *A Hoosier Holiday*; but they make clear with a new intensity the almost total dissociation from any cultural or literary tradition that underlay Dreiser's compulsion to explain himself to his times. This, in fact, may suggest their clearest value: they may prove not so much an addition to the factual record as a better explanation of the one we already have, a body of evidence in the writer's own words that will allow us finer discriminations of emphasis and importance.[7]

Now that the storm of controversy that swirled around Dreiser has subsided, we can accept his words calmly. The conclusion that Dreiser gave to his account of his early youth, for instance, cannot be interpreted otherwise. At the age of sixty Dreiser reflected:

In considering all I have written here [*Dawn*], I suddenly become deeply aware of the fact that educationally speaking, where any sensitive and properly interpretive mind is concerned, experience is the only true teacher—that education, which is little more than a selective presentation of certain stored or canned phases of experience, is at best an elucidative, or at its poorest, a polishing process offered to experience which is always basic.[8]

This experience had always been with him. Inside Dreiser the novelist, there is always the wandering, wide-eyed youth who grew up in a pious German family in small towns in Indiana. He could have been a newspaperman for the rest of his life, made love to hundreds of women, or strolled the dark corners of American cities. And yet he could never be thoroughly sophisticated. When Dreiser tells us how excessive masturbation at one time in his boyhood almost ruined his health, or how stealing twenty-five dollars from a cashier's drawer caused him to lose a job, the revelation not only embarrasses us but takes us to the heart of the matter about this youth and novelist to be. Admitting that some organizing mind and methods are useful, Dreiser believed it more necessary for youth to be left to free experiences and to those natural deductions based on them. Freshness and ingenuousness were always in his view of life; he never became weary of it. Dreiser was always discovering things he had never known before, and they fascinated him even though they disgusted him. This ambivalence is, at least, part of what has puzzled his critics.

☆ ☆ ☆ ☆

Like any child, Dreiser seems to have formulated his interpretation of life by observing his own family. He was one of the ten surviving of the thirteen children of John Paul Dreiser (1821–1900), who was born in Germany and came to America when young, and Sarah Schänäb Dreiser (1833–1890), who had eloped with her husband. The Dreiser children were somehow kept together by their self-sacrificing and idealistic mother who was of Pennsylvania Dutch origin and of the Mennonite faith. The young Dreiser naturally became more sympathetic with his mother's discipline than his father's Catholicism, which was as steady as it was fanatical. Dreiser always felt an affinity to his mother's strangely nebulous and optimistic view of life. When his sister Theresa (to whom Dreiser refers as Ruth in *Dawn*) was pursued by a wealthy Chicago manufacturer, his mother was not capable of advising Theresa shrewdly in the matter. She did not even think it important to advise her daughter. Being dubious of life and its mysterious manifestations, Mrs. Dreiser thought it best to let her daughters cope with their own problems. Dreiser was in complete agreement with his mother's attitude. Interestingly, her predilection for a rocking chair, reminiscent of that of Carrie at the end of the novel, became a symbol for Dreiser's own dreamy nature.

Besides his sympathy with his mother's approach to life's problems, Dreiser was also influenced by his sisters and brothers. Dreiser's sisters as described in *Dawn* (named fictitiously and arranged without regard to the order of their birth because they were clearly the prototypes in his novels) had widely different personalities. Theresa had an artistic temperament, a trait that, in Dreiser's opinion, was her weakness. A second sister, Emma (whom Dreiser called Janet in *Dawn*), was a simple, affectionate girl who was motherly, unambitious, and impractical. The sister who brought some misery for the family with her illegitimate child was a sensual, sensitive, and selfish girl called Sylvia (Amy in *Dawn*). Sylvia was always criticized for being convinced of her superiority despite the fact that she was by no means intelligent. In contrast to Sylvia, Claire (Trina in *Dawn*), who was closest to Dreiser's age, was really intelligent and practical but lacked human compassion. His oldest sister—born in 1861, ten years before Dreiser—was baptized Mary Frances and called Mame (Eleanor in *Dawn*). Mame was a social climber and had a real penchant for interfering and imposing advice on the family, an attitude most of her younger brothers and sisters resented. Dreiser thought that her success in capturing a wealthy man gave her ideas far beyond her real insight and set her to lecturing, criticizing, and dictating.

Although Dreiser was conscious of his sisters' characteristics, he was dimly aware of certain emotional activities in which they were involved. A middle-aged widower named Joseph H. Bull, who admired Theresa, used to appear to take her out for an afternoon drive or evening engagement. A young man named Austin Brennan, stopping at a local hotel, would invite Mame, Theresa, and their mutual friends for dinner. The three younger sisters, too, before they came of age, eagerly accepted attentions of boys and men alike. As Dreiser recognized, Mame, who always inclined toward acquiring a higher social and economic status, went to Chicago where she met the aristocratic Brennan. But how Mame had had the audacity to introduce Theresa to Mr. Bull, who traveled to Evansville to see Theresa, was beyond Dreiser's comprehension. (In fact, Brennan had earlier introduced Mame to Bull; when she turned down Bull's marriage proposal and married Brennan, Mr. Bull now turned his attention to Theresa.) It was a great shock to young Dreiser later when he happened to enter the apartment one day in the absence of the family and witnessed Theresa in the arms of Bull. Dreiser could not understand by what arrangement the man and his sister chanced to be there. Similarly, Emma, whom her father used to call a "bad" girl but who later turned out to be a good wife, came to Chicago to live with an old well-to-do architect in a fancy hotel. Dreiser recalls Emma giving him and one of his brothers meal tickets for a restaurant attached to the hotel. At that time Dreiser was more concerned with the amount of money he earned by selling newspapers and running errands for a caramel man down the street than his sisters' love affairs. As Dreiser wrote later, he attempted to disentangle this "knot or network of emotions and interests, all relating to the particular love life of each, but [he] would fail for lack of any real knowledge of the underlying subtleties and beauties—as, of course, beauties and subtleties there were" (*Dawn*, p. 172).

Dreiser later effectively used these patterns of family experience for the basis of some of his novels. The events surrounding Emma's life, for example, closely parallel those of Carrie. Emma went from the architect to L. A. Hopkins, a clerk at a Chicago tavern called Chapin and Gore (the Fitzgerald and Moy's of the novel). Hopkins stole

$3,500 from the safe at the tavern, taking Emma with him, and later returned all but $800, begging the tavern owners not to prosecute him (Hurstwood stole $10,000 and also returned most of it). The newspapers in Chicago at that time reported that Emma (identified as "Mamie Tracey Treigh," a dashing blonde), unlike Carrie, did not allow herself to be deceived into leaving Chicago but rather went of her own free will. She and Hopkins went to New York by way of Montreal (instead of Toronto as in the novel).[9]

The elder Dreiser, of course, boiled with anger every time such an incident befell the family. He always disapproved of the conduct of his daughters, but the youthful and obedient Dreiser at the time was perplexed by his father's attitude. That his sisters were not behaving respectably, according to the accepted social standards, and that men were exploiting his sisters as mere "playthings" were Dreiser's first reaction. But he gradually began to realize that they were their own mistresses, who, in fact, seemed to enjoy being playthings. "And through it all ran the feeling that good, bad, or indifferent as individuals or things might be, life was a splendid surge, a rich sensation, and that it was fine to be alive" (*Dawn*, p. 173).

But it was his family's economic and social status that influenced Dreiser's mind most strongly and later imparted a characteristic tone to his fiction. The elder Dreiser imposed on his children a constant urge toward the genteel and respectable, but his discipline was always defeated by poverty. What young Dreiser saw in his family is exactly what Clyde Griffiths sees in Kansas City. Dreiser later wrote in *An American Tragedy*:

> Indeed the home life of which this boy found himself a part and the various contacts, material and psychic, which thus far had been his, did not tend to convince him of the reality and force of all that his mother and father seemed so certainly to believe and say . . . . Yet the family was always "hard up," never very well clothed, and deprived of many comforts and pleasures which seemed common enough to others. And his father and mother were constantly proclaiming the love and mercy and care of God for him and for all. Plainly there was something wrong somewhere. He could not get it all straight . . .[10]

The Dreiser family, moreover, never identified itself with any fixed social class. The Dreiser children, trying to break away from the conventional standards of their parents, felt strongly the urge to climb the next higher social ladder. To them it meant money, clothes, and the society of the hotel lobby. Dreiser observed his sisters Emma and Sylvia escape the poverty-stricken household into the world of "long, blinking lines of gas-lamps," "large plates of window glass," "genteel business men in 'nobby' suits." [11] This is, indeed, the great moment of Dreiser's creative crystallization, for in it were born Sister Carrie and Jennie Gerhardt. The fear of poverty is the central motive behind his entire career as a writer; this consciousness stuck in the mind of the boy Dreiser and remained for the rest of his life. And yet he was not obsessed by gross material ambitions, as his letters well testify. Needless to say, Dreiser himself had the usual desire to get ahead like anyone else; as an artist, however, he came to possess a stronger desire to observe and understand the complicated mechanism of social life.

One aspect of this mechanism of which Dreiser became aware was class distinction. In *Dawn*, Dreiser illustrates such distinction between his own family and the "aristocratic" Brennan (fictitiously called Harahan) family. Mame, as mentioned earlier, married a member of the Brennan family, but young Dreiser failed to understand why the socially and intellectually superior Brennan was attracted to her in the first place. Dreiser knew that social class in America was largely determined by the degree of wealth. He noticed this immediately with his sister Emma, as he says, "I was filled with wonder at her clothes, furniture and the like, which seemed to contrast more than favorably with our own. Her boudoir dressing-table, for instance, was piled with bright silver toilet articles and a closet into which I peered was plentifully supplied with clothes. Janet [Emma] herself looked prosperous and cheerful" (*Dawn*, p. 173). The recurring use of clothing as symbols in his writing, both autobiographical and fictional, is often pointed out. Carrie's constant reference to clothes, as F. O. Matthiessen says, signifies her "craving for pleasure" and "the constant drag to something better." [12]

Another sister, Sylvia, much like Jennie Gerhardt, was clearly a victim of class discrimination. Trusting the sweet words of Don Ashley, the son of a prominent family in Warsaw, Indiana, Sylvia yielded to him. When Sylvia realized her pregnancy, she appealed in vain to Ashley to marry her. She was really little more than a street girl to Ashley, and he fled town without leaving his address. When Sylvia finally attempted to explain to Ashley's mother that he had seduced her under the pretext of marriage, the lady coldly replied, "My son couldn't marry you if he wanted to. He has other obligations. Besides, how do I know you weren't bad long before you met him?'' (*Dawn*, pp. 260–61). Dreiser later learned that the local physicians and politicians suppressed Mrs. Dreiser's legal action against the seducer to protect the interests and prestige of the Ashley family.

This event became a basic plot for the Lester Kane–Jennie Gerhardt affair in Dreiser's second novel. In real life, the scandal was the source for a town gossip for weeks. Emma, who had earlier eloped with Hopkins to New York, where she was well settled (unlike Carrie, who becomes a stage actress, Emma was running a brothel), wanted to help her pregnant sister. Sylvia went to New York to have her baby delivered and remained there, sending the child back to her parents in Warsaw, Indiana. This became a pattern in Dreiser novels: the parents in *Jennie Gerhardt* take custody of Jennie's illegitimate child; in *An American Tragedy*, Esta returns home with her illegitimate child Russel. In both cases, the girl's mother is more sympathetic and understanding toward such a crisis than the father. In fact, the whole incident infuriated the elder Dreiser, a religious fanatic. In *Jennie Gerhardt*, the daughter's shame enraged her father, whereas in *An American Tragedy* it was kept from Esta's father for a long time. As Dreiser poignantly describes in his last novel, *The Bulwark*, the Dreiser children were all rebellious against the moral scruples constantly dictated by their father.

During the series of disgraceful events taking place in the Dreiser family, the mother was the one who withstood the ordeal and held the family together. In one of the most desperate periods, when the elder Dreiser was out of work and the family had little money, the oldest daughter Mame, aged sixteen, gladly accepted ten dollars for her intimacy with one ''Colonel Silsby,'' a prominent Terre Haute attorney. Like Senator Brander in *Jennie Gerhardt*, Silsby wanted to send Mame to a private school, but made her pregnant instead. Unlike Brander, who dies before he can marry Jennie, the lawyer deserted Mame, giving her a hundred dollars and the address of an old country doctor (fictitiously named Dr. Dinsmore) who would perform abortions. (Dreiser used some of these details in describing Roberta's search for an abortionist in *An American Tragedy*.) After Mame learned of the doctor's death, she confided her problem in her mother. Her mother kept Mame home where Mame had a stillborn child delivered. In the published version of *Dawn*, Dreiser, apparently having changed Mame to her closest friend named Kitty Costigan, says that he heard this story years later from Mame herself. Dreiser discusses Mame's pregnancy at length in both versions of the autobiography and confesses that "the events which followed contribute one of those pathetic episodes which might well employ the art of the novelist" (*Dawn*, p. 73). "I remember so well," Dreiser continues, "how mother, in that soft, caressing way of hers, took care of this girl [Kitty Costigan]. I remember her putting her arms around her, after she first heard the story, and saying to her: 'Well, never mind, I will see you through. You will be all right; don't cry. Perhaps you will be a better girl for it'" (*Dawn*, p. 75). The last sentence is exactly what Mrs. Gerhardt speaks to Jennie in the novel.

In all these traumatic experiences the Dreiser family went through, Dreiser was convinced more than ever that money was the root of all evils. If the family had been well to do, his sisters would not have had their troubles. If the family had not been discriminated against socially, they would all have been saved from the further embarrassment they suffered. To young Dreiser, however, the power of money seemed to operate in a mysterious way. When the family's financial situation deteriorated, the beneficences of Mame's lawyer lover were readily accepted. Mrs. Dreiser kept quiet and her husband never learned of this. When Dreiser's oldest brother Paul was in jail for forging a bank note in his father's name, it was this same lawyer and politician who helped to get Paul out of jail. For young Dreiser it was thus difficult to divide the world naively into good and evil.

As a boy Dreiser was always curious about the pattern of life a man ought to follow in order to succeed. Naturally he tried to visualize such a pattern in the lives of the male members of the family. In this respect, the elder Dreiser was not, of course, a good model; between what he preached to his children and what they had in life existed a wide gap that the young Dreiser could hardly overlook. During Dreiser's first seven years his father did not have steady employment; nevertheless, the elder Dreiser clung to his authoritative role as head of the family. In retrospect, Dreiser thought that one "needed to know him neither long nor intimately to learn that to him God was a blazing reality, with the Son and Blessed Virgin to the right and left and the Holy Spirit, in the shape of a dove, hovering over all" (*Dawn*, p. 5). The endless vagaries and complications of his father's mood and conduct finally impressed Dreiser as not only fantastic but pathetic.

There was evidently another life beyond the gloomy Dreiser household. Whispers from another world drifted in and caught the ear of the visionary child. He distinctly remembered his first dream of "beautiful red, green, blue, and yellow marbles floating about in the air, and of nickels, dimes and quarters lying everywhere on the ground! What disappointment, what despair, to wake at morn and find that a seeming reality was not!" (*Dawn*, pp. 17–18). He looked around him—at his sullen, unsuccessful, "God-fooled" father, and at his mother with her sorrowful, enduring face and work-worn fingers. There was imprinted in the mind of the child the desire to arrive, to be famous and rich and admired, companion to the masters of the world.

There must be also another America beyond the quiet streets of Warsaw—an America of success, adventure, laughter, and power. Dreiser sought this vision in the lives of his older brothers. Rome (Marcus Romanus) was an adventurous vagabond who constantly grieved his mother. He was a self-sufficient man who thought that the world was made for him. The only good thing that Dreiser remembered about this brother was his ability to travel somehow in various faraway places—Mexico, Honduras, and California. Rome would arrive home after one, two, three, and, in one instance, four years. A postcard would be received from him from some strange town on which was scribbled: "En route to Cheyenne (or Dallas) (or Matamoras). All right with me. Don't worry. See you Christmas" (*Dawn*, p. 152). But soon Rome's adventure proved to be one of an unpromising kind. He would relate to his friends and his family successful projects in the copper and lumber camps of northern Michigan, and profitable ventures in railroading in western Kansas, southern Canada, and Vancouver. Even the naive, dreamy boy, as Dreiser was, gradually came to suspect that "he rode in box cars at times, slept in lumber yards and jails." Yet Rome, "resplendent in good clothing, a cane, a watch and some jewelry ... paraded the more showy spots of the world" (*Dawn*, p. 222).

Whereas his older sisters embarrassed young Dreiser, Rome worried him. In *Dawn*, Dreiser describes Rome's returning home after a long absence and at once borrowing money by advertising himself as Paul's brother. As Mrs. Dreiser tenderly cared for her daughters so did she love this prodigal son of hers. Despite a wayward life he was leading,

Rome kept feeling a strong affection for his mother. When he was told by Dreiser that his mother had been dead for some time, Rome broke down hysterically: "And she asked me in the dream why I didn't come home .... I knew it! I knew it! The only friend I ever had, the only friend. And she always wanted me to do better!" In reality, Rome was the vainest member of the family. As Dreiser recalls, Rome used to lounge in style in front of the Terre Haute House on Wabash Avenue and pick his teeth, pretending he had just eaten there. Toward the end of *Dawn*, Dreiser gives the impression that Rome met a drunkard's death in a lonely city after a long period of wandering, reforming, and becoming depressed (p. 522).

Unlike a woman who might be kept by her lover, a man like Rome could drown in a cold canal while drunk or be left dying in a dark alley of a large city. Dreiser, as did his brother, feared such a destiny. Rome's later life suggested what happens to Hurstwood, who dies a beggar's death in the New York slums. While *Sister Carrie* was being suppressed, Dreiser wrote short articles, "The Loneliness of the City," in which he lamented living among strangers, and "The Track Walker," in which he mourned the accidental death of a railroad worker who was nothing more than a "human nine-pin." Rome's later life also foreshadowed what actually happened to Dreiser himself during the lowest period after his first novel: suffering from a severe depression, he contemplated suicide in the East River, as he later told Mencken (*Letters*, 3: 980). During the same period, Dreiser published another magazine article, "The Rivers of the Nameless Dead," where he contrasted the unidentified body of a man floating in the North River at Twenty-fifth Street against its beautiful and wealthy background.[13] Fortunately, however, by the time *Dawn* was finally published in 1931, Rome had been found in a nursing home for men in Chicago and was brought to New York under the care of Mame and Dreiser, who by then had become an established novelist.

In contrast to Rome, Dreiser's oldest brother, John Paul, Jr., turned out to be a successful man. When he was young, however, Paul was a jailbird and vexed his father, who intended Paul for the priesthood, as related in Dreiser's affectionate portrait, "My Brother Paul," in *Twelve Men*.[14] To the young Dreiser, Paul was a generous and sympathetic man who always had a good sense of humor. Paul lacked any deep understanding of life, but he was nevertheless always constructive and creative. Dreiser's first recollection of this brother is of himself as a boy of ten and Paul, a man of twenty-five. Six or seven years earlier Paul had left home without any explanation of where he was going. Thus, the arrival of this brother was like that of a total stranger—"or nearly so—and yet, fascinatingly enough, a stranger who was more like a fairy godfather or the well known occidental Santa Clause." Unlike Rome, who gave his family nothing but trouble whenever he returned, Paul came home like the sun giving warmth to the earth. Paul gave Dreiser and Ed, another younger brother, copies of *The Paul Dresser Songster* with his picture on the cover just above the price (ten cents) and a copyright notice by Willis, Woodward and Company, New York, N. Y. To Dreiser this was a proof that his brother was unmistakably connected with that big city and the wide world.[15]

Dreiser was not only learning the difference between success and failure from the two brothers but he was also trying to understand the mysterious reality of success. He soon recognized that Paul's triumphant return home was related to a prosperous local madam with jet-black hair—Annie Brace. Known by the name of Sallie Walker, she ran a high-class brothel on Main Street in Evansville. Dreiser as a young boy often witnessed a quarrel arising from the affectionate difference between the two. Paul was a man of decidedly promiscuous and variable disposition, and Sallie accused him of being unfaithful. Dreiser had never known, as he wrote,

> a man more interested in women from the sex point of view (unless perchance it might be myself), nor one to whom women were more attracted. Amazingly attractive, the women of the world in which he moved as well as others of different levels were constantly on his trail with proffers of diversion and support. He began early and, like Jack Falstaff, died unregenerate.

Dreiser concluded years later that Paul was a genial and lovable Lothario who devoted his whole energy, thought, and money to this unquenchable sexual desire (*Dawn*, p. 154).

Paul was then living in New York as a songwriter for Howley, Haviland, and Company. He wrote and composed such popular songs as "The Letter That Never Came," "Pardon Came Too Late," "I Believe It for My Mother Told Me So," and "Just Tell Them That You Saw Me." The official state song of Indiana, "On the Banks of the Wabash," was originally composed by Paul with part of its lyrics written by Dreiser himself when he was editor of *Ev'ry Month*, a music and literary magazine.[16] Paul was the only member of the family who helped Dreiser from the beginning as he did the other Dreisers. It was Paul who rescued Dreiser from his newspaper drudgery in the middle 1890s and introduced him to the world of Broadway. A few years later Dreiser wrote about these experiences in a magazine article, "Whence the Song."[17] Carrie Meeber's search for a stage career and her ultimate success were based on this intimate knowledge that Dreiser had acquired through Paul.

More than the success story with which Paul imbued Dreiser, his young mind was influenced by his brother's character. Paul, though a good Catholic, possessed little understanding of the social virtues; in fact, he had little or no knowledge of social organization or government. It was useless to talk to Paul about the welfare of the state or patriotism. Dreiser was, nevertheless, profoundly fascinated by his brother's unorthodox, but successful life. Dreiser then realized that by reason of criticism on the part of others—taboos and the like—man does not prefer to contemplate his own idiosyncrasies, either in real life or in literature. At least, Paul never worried about his unnaturally voracious sexual appetite. It is at this stage of Dreiser's development, when he was merely fourteen years old, that he began to reject the traditional clear-cut dualism of good and evil, fact and fancy, reality and appearance.

This rebellion against the traditional sanctions of life was precipitated by the awakening of his own sexual desire. Young Dreiser was shy, innocent, and emotional; he was always in a misty dream, which scarcely dispersed until he had passed out of his teens. Very early, however, he was much disconcerted and at times prepossessed with the mystery of sex, though his shyness long kept him virginal:

> How the hot fire nature had lighted in my body was driving me to almost frantic efforts at self-satiation! And how, for the next two or three years (to say nothing of the next twenty-five) it harried me from hell to hell! Although my mother and father and the pleasant father confessor of our church were constantly counselling me to keep pure in thought and feeling, yet my proper nature was gratifying itself with insistent thoughts and emotions that concerned girls and this sex function. (*Dawn*, p. 209)

He was poor; he was without friends who could give him authoritative advice on the matter of sex and love; he thought himself unattractive to women. And yet he was poignantly conscious of the great and sensuous flow of human passion that was swirling all about him. ''I was so hungry,'' Dreiser cries out, ''for life and love!'' At another time in his adolescence, he recalls, ''I tried to think that I could get along without them, or that other boys and girls were not having as good a time as I thought, but life always gave the lie to my imaginings'' (*Dawn*, p. 266).

His brother Paul was the first to pose the problem of sex to the twelve-year-old Dreiser, who, at that time, was not old enough and mature enough to appreciate the problem. But somewhat later, after the wakening of his own sexual instinct, Dreiser became more sympathetic to Paul's amorous escapades. Dreiser recalls himself being thrust into the very center of the ''den of iniquity,'' the place where Paul and his mistress Annie Brace stayed:

> . . . It was hot and bright in this semi-southern world, and there was Paul, in the trousers of a light, summery suit and a silk shirt, making his morning toilet. With him was his Annie, in a pink and white, heavily beflounced dressing gown, and surveying me with an amused if not very much interested eye. The rooms—living-room, bedroom and bath—were not yet made up for the day, but to my uninformed eyes they were beautiful, everything in them rich and wonderful, a marvelous place . . . .
> . . . I can see her now, in chemisette, her arms and breast exposed, 'making up' her cheeks and eyes. The bedding in every case, as I noted, was tumbled, the garments of the occupant strewn about in an indifferent and (to me even then) blood-tingling way. In a flash, and without being told, a full appreciation of the utility of the male as such came to me. I wished that I might stay and see more, even that one of these women would take a fancy to me. Yet I also knew quite well that such things were still in the dim, distant future for me, if at all. But these pink-meated sirens, however vulgar they might have been in their physical as well as mental texture, were wonderful to me as forms, that spirometric formula that appears not only to control but compel desire in the male. (*Dawn*, p. 142)

Brooding over the mystery of this orgiastic life, Dreiser lamented that this life had fallen to so low a state in the modern world, and yet he was utterly convinced of the value of the house of prostitution. In *Dawn* he argues that nature knows better than man what it needs. ''Its flare of self-expression,'' Dreiser maintains, ''indicates a keener logic than all

man's petty and spindling fumbling with ethics and morals.'' For
Dreiser, neither Venus nor Ashtoreth was dead, their shrines illumined
by eternal fires. He questioned why the traditional moral standard did
not prevail if it were so important and essential; or if the immorality in
human society was so destructive, why had it not destroyed the world?
(pp. 143–44, 444).

All this questioning about sex was not, at first, the yearning of the
artist. Dreiser did not want so much to picture the whirling scenes—
moral or immoral—he saw about him as to play a part in them. But
young Dreiser, being extremely shy and hesitant, felt uneasy in the
presence of girls. It is only natural that Dreiser's first love should have
been Platonic. The girl was a dark-haired, pale-faced, rather shy child
who studied in the next room at school. Sensuality in connection with
this girl appeared forbidden and unrealistic; only adoration and yearning and kissing her maiden lips in his imagination were the extent of
his role. Then one evening in the springtime Dreiser was to experience
his first sexual intercourse with a baker's daughter, suddenly and unexpectedly (*Dawn*, pp. 247–49).

It was at this time that he fell into autoerotic practice to gratify his
''blazing'' sexual impulse. Although he would be able to have a sexual
contact with the baker's daughter again, he would not be quite content
with such a ''common'' girl. Yet he felt unable to front ''the elusive
subtlety of the more attractive girls of the town.'' Thus he substituted:
''For weeks and months,'' confesses the sixty-year-old Dreiser, ''every two or three days at the most, I now indulged myself in a kind of
fury of passion. I would run to my room or any secret place I had
appointed, and there in a kind of excess of passion and delight, give
myself over to this form of self-abuse.'' He would combine it with
passionate imaginations of one of the girls he most admired but failed
to have relations with. He would visualize such girls in his act and yet
make resolutions not to do the act again. But the resolutions were
broken over and over again. In fact, his first Platonic love, ''Myrtle
Trego,'' was never visualized in the practice (*Dawn*, pp. 268–72).

The natural result of this behavior was a radical change in Dreiser's
point of view about sex, as well as a change in his physical condition,
though he learned later that the physical change was not a result of this
act. He was afraid that people would notice his face blotched and
marred by pimples and that he would become a weak man for the rest
of his life. He was seriously thinking of those innumerable advertisements addressed to ''Weak Men'' or ''Victims of Self-Abuse.'' There

were, in fact, on the market a number of pills prescribed by physicians in Buffalo or Scranton, Pennsylvania. Later he realized that there was no more the matter with him at that time than there is with any healthy, normal boy who indulges in such a practice:

> Poor, ignorant humanity! I wish that all of the religious and moral piffle and nonsense from which I suffered in connection with this matter could be undone completely for the rest of the world by merely writing about it. What tons of rot have been written and published concerning the spiritual and moral degradation of this practice! . . . Doctors, more religionistic than medical, writing endless silly books on hearsay or because of early asinine terrors of their own! (*Dawn*, p. 272)

In his own thinking Dreiser discovered that his erotic fantasies and his imagined fulfillment were not abnormal; rather they were part of the texture of life. To the adolescent Dreiser, his brother Ed, who was close to him in age, seemed to like girls, but in so simple or animalistic a manner as to contrast sharply with the blood-and-brain fury they set up in him. In Dreiser, if not in Ed, the sexual awakening signaled more than mere physical desire. It was as if Dreiser shed the chrysalis of his youth; he was already conscious of a wild flaming enthusiasm for the color of life. The flowers, trees, birds, sky, houses, stores, music, clothing—all combined to present an indestructible harmony that echoed one thing: love. His idea of love is not that poetic abstraction celebrated by religious poets, nor the gutteral sensuality professed by the materialist. "My dreams," he defines, "were a blend of each: the diaphanous radiance of the morning, plus a suggestion of the dark, harsh sensuality of the lecher and the libertine—a suggestion merely, none the less a potent one which gave to all beauty and all reality a meaning" (*Dawn*, p. 210).

The last years of his adolescence, however, witnessed neither the libertine's sensuality nor the artist's beauty. After the family turmoils from which he had desperately tried to extricate himself, Dreiser was now enslaved by the commercial life he had to struggle with in Chicago. In those days he was not even conscious of the intense sexual feeling that had earlier harrowed him:

> There I had been rising at five thirty, eating an almost impossible breakfast (often the condition of my stomach would not permit me to eat at all), taking a slow, long distance horse car to the business

heart, working from seven to six with an hour for lunch, in a crowded, foreman bossed loft, and then taking the car home again to eat, and because I was always very tired, to go to bed almost at once. Only Saturday afternoons in summer (the Saturday half holiday idea was then becoming known in America) and Sunday in winter offered sufficient time for me to recuperate and see a little of the world to make life somewhat endurable for me,—a situation which I greatly resented. It was most exasperating.[18]

With great hopes not only academically but socially as well, Dreiser arrived at Bloomington to attend the State University in the fall of 1889. The beauty of the college town—vines laden with blue grapes, flowers blooming even in late December, grass stretching "like balm to my soul"—inspired in him once again a yearning for love. In the first week at the university, sitting in his room in an old house, Dreiser looked at a window across the yard and noticed a small blonde, blue-eyed girl spying on him. Whenever he tried to concentrate on his studies, this girl loosened her hair and let it fall over her book, making a halo on her face. Dreiser was at once enchanted by the beauty of it. A few days later "this artful Circe" introduced herself to him through his landlady and asked him to help her with her Latin and English grammar. With little knowledge of the subjects and with his innate shyness, though ecstatic with her hair brushing his cheek, Dreiser was literally frozen at his chair. Embarrassed by his "swollen" tongue and blushed face, she finally said, "Oh, well, I think I can get along now. I'm so much obliged to you," and departed. He almost cried. Dreiser started worrying about his own inadequacies with girls the next day, when his roommate Bill Yakey (a football star and later a state senator) arrived and chased this girl around the yard, exclaiming, "Say, she's a cute little bitch, that" (Holiday, pp. 489–93; Dawn, pp. 382–86).

In spite of this failure, Dreiser kept on his search. He was not unsociable, and he was not unattractive, but somehow opportunities to meet girls came and went. At one time he was determined to get acquainted with a high school girl living across the street from him. In her, Dreiser found Dante's Beatrice, confessing his adoration of this maiden at sight: "a slim, delicate, tenuous type, her black hair smoothed back from her brow, her thin, slender white hands holding a few books, a long cape or mackintosh hung loosely about her shoulders." But, when this girl received a letter containing Dreiser's passionate expressions of love, she became frightened and vanished from his sight (Holiday, pp. 493–95).

At another time, a sophomore law student named Day Allen Willy (David Ben O'Connor in *Dawn*), the son of a wealthy upstate judge, arranged a double date for Dreiser and him at Willy's apartment. While the evening conversation went smoothly among the four present, Dreiser felt at ease. But as soon as Willy and his companion left and went to a bedroom, Dreiser's old anxiety returned. His blind date, Eva Casper, was stunning, he thought; she even made an overture for intimacy that Dreiser perfectly understood. But all this while an inferiority complex was stifling his head:

> My hands and knees were really shaking, the more so since directed by her, and seemingly unconsciously, first her knee was touching mine and next, about her waist and over one breast was one of my arms and its hand. She had been willing it, and so it came to pass. Devil! Beast! Also her face was so close to mine, one girlish cheek pressed against my own, that kisses were unescapable. From that it was but a step to the other room. (I was even thinking of the baker's daughter and her methods at the time.) But instead of heartening me as that might have (since I came off well enough at that time), I was now reduced by that lunatic word or thought: *impotence*, which I had read in so many of those driving ads relating to "lost manhood." And all because of some night emissions, the only reasonable explanation of which should have been potence of the first order. Can you imagine! And I was insisting on the direct contrary! (*Dawn*, pp. 429–30)

His worst fear was now realized: once the contract was made, Dreiser says, "I was instantly finished." And he saw Eva unsatisfied. He even worried that Eva would tell the story to Willy's girl and she to Willy, so that eventually his impotence might be exposed (*Dawn*, pp. 430–33).

With this adolescent consciousness of love and sex, beauty and frustration, Dreiser was also much concerned with his intellectual training. His earliest education was provided at a small German parochial school in Terre Haute. At the age of six, Dreiser remembers, he was taken to the church school by his eight-year-old sister Claire. He was terrified by the nuns dressed in black with their flaring white bonnets; he felt strange in articulating the alphabet—"a long line of curious-looking German symbols" (*Dawn*, p. 27). A few years later, his family moved to Evansville, and Claire, Ed, and Dreiser were placed in a school attached to "Heilige Dreifaltigkeit Kirche" on Vine Street. For a sensitive child, the church was dignified, interesting, and impressive, but the school was as poor a shift for an institution of the kind as he had known. He remembers only one Herr Professor Ludwig von Valkenburg as a young man, "whiskered like Michaelangelo's Moses, and a Vulcan for size and energy, functioning here as principal of this school and devoting all of his time to those pupils who were too old, too unruly or too advanced in their studies . . . to be taught by the nuns." There was no curriculum worthy of the name: a mixed gibberish of minor arithmetic, beginner's grammar, reading, Bible history, spelling, and catechism. The children, at twelve or older, must begin the work of making a living and planning their careers. But the teaching entirely neglected American history, geography, algebra, geometry, zoology, and botany, let alone the arts and literature. The school started and ended with prayers (*Dawn*, pp. 129–31).

In the fall of 1884, the Dreiser family arrived in Warsaw, Indiana. Despite the pious protests from her husband, Mrs. Dreiser immediately sent the three children to the free public school. Dreiser was enrolled in the seventh-grade class at West Ward School where he fell in love with the young teacher, May Calvert, with "her sunny smile . . . soft, kind eyes . . . friendly voice," who, unlike the nuns, took a special interest in him. He had some trouble with arithmetic, and with grammar he "could gain no least inkling of what it was all about. Why nouns and verbs and participles, anyhow? What was the good of them? When it came to the Fifth Reader, geography, spelling, [he] felt more or less at home. These interested [him], especially geography." Miss Calvert used to say: "But, Theodore dear, you write good English. Your longest sentences and paragraphs are correct and orderly. I don't understand." "Neither did I," Dreiser recalls, "although I flushed with some mystical vicarious pride. I myself wondered—and very much so—how it was that I did it, for I could not say how" (*Dawn*, pp. 192–93). Perhaps, what his seventh-grade teacher and Dreiser himself noticed in his writing was to determine his prose style for the rest of his life.

In the midst of family problems, Dreiser somehow managed to have an interesting, inspirational life at school. He owed it, of course, to Miss Calvert, who gave him not only an incentive for self-expression but love itself:

And somehow, with all this, a growing something that was very close or akin to affection—love, even. Her eyes, her pretty mouth, her hair, her pink cheeks! Her face at all close to mine, I trembled and felt what . . . actually that *she* would put her arm around me and hold me, rather than that I might put my arm around her and hold her. Had words come, they would have been "Love me; love me, love me, please!" And so often her soft eyes looked as though that were true.[19]

Later in high school Dreiser had another teacher, Mildred Fielding, who made a great impact on his intellectual training. She suggested that since Dreiser was of German extraction, he should study German literature, particularly the works of Schiller, Goethe, and Heine. At the same time he became interested in physiology, botany, astronomy, and zoology. Natural objects—the sea, the stars, the earth, the blood—fascinated him. "Very sensitive," Miss Fielding would tell him. "Your mind is very different. You understand well enough where you are interested. It is only where you aren't that you do so poorly. But you mustn't let that worry you. You must study and go on, for your mind will find its way" (*Dawn*, p. 275). His enthusiasm suddenly extended to the reading of history—Caesar, Napoleon, Washington, and Lincoln taking a strong grip on his fancy. Then he developed an interest in novels, plays, poems, which seemed to him rich in their suggestions of the varied and far-flung world.

Despite Miss Fielding's sympathy for his family disgrace (Sylvia's infant had been sent to Mrs. Dreiser from New York), Dreiser left Warsaw for Chicago in the summer of 1887. For two years, unlike Carrie in Chicago, Dreiser struggled to maintain a steady job. But at the end of this period he was on his way out again at the hardware firm of Hibbard, Spencer, Bartlett and Company at Wabash and Lake Streets, when his savior—none other than Miss Fielding, now the principal of a Chicago high school—suddenly appeared at the company. "Theodore," she told him, "work of this kind isn't meant for you, really. It will injure your spirit. I want you to let me help you go to school again." She wanted to send him to Indiana University for one year at her expense, and pleaded with him: "You may never learn anything directly there, Theodore . . . but something will come to you indirectly. You will see what education means, what its aim is, and that will be worth a great deal. Just go one year, at least, and then you can decide for yourself what you want to do after that." Recalling this dramatic moment in his youth, Dreiser wrote years later: "She was an old maid, with a set of false upper teeth, and a heavenly, irradiating smile. She had led a very hard life herself and did not wish me to." Dreiser learned that in 1893, only four years later, Miss Fielding, having eventually married, died in childbirth (*Holiday*, p. 483).

In the summer of 1889 Miss Fielding wrote to Indiana University and asked for his admission although he had only one year of high school work. In the fall Dreiser was accepted as a special student with the permission of the university's president, David Starr Jordan. Once Dreiser arrived at the campus, he decided to follow the degree requirements and, in the first term, he chose Anglo-Saxon, Elementary Latin, and Preparatory Geometry. The university records show that because Dreiser did not take the examination in Anglo-Saxon, he passed the course without a grade and that he received a grade of "1" (Passing) in the other courses. In the winter term he continued to study Latin and Geometry and replaced Anglo-Saxon with Philology, receiving a passing grade only in Geometry. In the spring term he took courses in Virgil's *Aeneid*, the Study of Words, a Freshman Algebra, doing particularly well in the Study of Words. The *Indiana Student* (the campus magazine) reported that after two months at the university, Dreiser took part in its major literary club, *Philomathean*, and was elected secretary of the club. At the end of the first year he left the campus, but the *Indiana Student* for the January, 1891, issue says: "Theodore Dreiser, though Freshman last year, is working in Chicago at present, where his home is. He expects to return to I. U. next year."[20]

These records clearly indicate that whereas Dreiser had an interest in literature, he was not at all enthusiastic about his academic subjects. In fact, his own recollections of college life show that his professors only convinced him of the shallowness and futility of academic learning. One of his professors, Walter Deming Willikus, Ph. D., Litt. D., though impressive and known as author of articles in *The Ladies' Home Journal* and *The Atlantic Monthly*, struck Dreiser as scholastic and intellectual in traditional learning, but lacking in originality, strangeness, power, and revelation. In short, Willikus' work was plainly as he was—exotic, insubstantial, full of the mere repetition of great thoughts. Another professor, of Greek and Latin, appeared to Dreiser to be preternaturally solemn, without a trace of humor; as for ideas, this man had none—the mere echo of older ways and approaches. Bill Yakey (Dreiser's roommate and classmate) once inquired about the professor's attitude toward the story of Jonah and the whale and the gourd vine, whether the Bible as translated could be accepted literally. "Literally!" he replied. "Every portion has a direct or a mystic meaning which faith and prayer will make clear." Dreiser pondered for a moment and asked himself, "Faith and prayer! What questioning could go beyond that?" Yakey's opinion of the teacher— "and I always liked Levitt's [Yakey's] opinions because they were so ribald, middle-class and American"—was that he was "a damned old fool." Then and there Dreiser's trust in *la vie academique* vanished— "not with an arresting detonation but as mist vanishes before heat and light, the light and heat of the strong, ordinary, creeping, grinding life that I had come to know" (*Dawn*, pp. 412–16; *Holiday*, pp. 486–95).

Scholars tend to agree that Dreiser was a self-taught man. Expecting little significance in any possible literary influences on him at this stage of his development, they give no attention to the pattern of reading in his youth. Although Dreiser gained little from his schoolwork, he took the suggestions of others about what books he should read. By the time he left for Chicago when he was sixteen, Dreiser had already read variously and widely. Some of the books that Dreiser read he chose himself, but many were suggested by his teachers and friends. Because of the kind of family in which he grew up, his reading was, for a long time, haphazard—without classification and discrimination. But this was significant in considering his intellectual development. He soon realized for himself what was real and what was superficial. At one time Dreiser was immersed in romantic literature, because he was always tempted to imagine that which he could not get in his experience. When he became involved in the real life about him, he sought out the kind of images in literature that corresponded to reality, and eventually came to reject his nostalgia for romantic stories.

The earliest reading that Dreiser remembered took place at home when he was a little over ten. In the loft of their new house Dreiser discovered Ouida's *Wanda*, Lytton's *Ernest Maltravers*, and books of poetry containing Gray's "Elegy Written in a Country Churchyard," Goldsmith's "The Traveller" and "The Deserted Village." Dreiser tells us that though he did not know all of the words and did not look them up in a dictionary, he enjoyed reading these books. Dreiser says he loved and understood the worlds described in these books. About the same time young Dreiser had access to some of the romantic periodicals that each week were thrown over the fence of his house. In the next issue of such a magazine as *The Family Story Paper, The Fireside Companion*, or *The New York Weekly*, published in the 1880s, he would anxiously wait to find out "what became of the poor but beautiful working-girl who was seized by thugs on her way to work and driven, gagged and blindfolded, to a wretched shanty far out on the Hackensack meadows, where she was confronted by her lustful and immoral pursuer" (*Dawn*, p. 125). Being introduced now to fairy tales such as "Diamond Dick," "Brave and Bold," "Pluck and Luck," "Work and Win," and those other predecessors of the later "Nick Carters" and "Frank Merriwells," Dreiser tried to visualize a colorful but impossible world. With the freedom of action as in dreams, he would ride over the plains of Africa, Australia, or Asia with the heroes of these tales.

Then one day a dandified book salesman appeared at the door, selling *Hill's Manual of Etiquette and Social and Commercial Forms*. This was, Dreiser clearly wants us to note, the first book that influenced him. Dreiser's interest in such a book seems far more credible than his early inclination to metaphysical speculation (though such a tendency characterizes the later Dreiser as his *Notes on Life* demonstrates). Years later he recalls his enthusiasm for *Hill's Manual*:

> A to me fascinating and, as I shall now testify, highly illuminating volume! To this hour I hark back to it in fancy at times, not to any particular item of its contents but to the wonderful sense of strangeness and mystery and beauty and delight which the most inane things in it evoked in me. There is fire and there is tow, but without tow, however humble, no fire, and without this book, its delicious, suggestive commonplaces....
> ...Pictures of how and how not to rise from or sit down to a table; how and how not to hold the knife and fork at meals; and how and how not to eat soup from a spoon. (*Dawn*, pp. 104–5)

Dreiser regarded *Hill's Manual* as if it were a courtesy book like the medieval *Babees Book* or John Russell's *Boke of Nurture*. But more importantly he was fascinated by the *Manual*'s doctrine of success about the "men who began as nothing in this great sad world but rose by honesty and industry and thrift and kind thoughts and deeds to be great" (*Dawn*, p. 105)—a doctrine that was not only to color his own adult life but to shape the theme of success and failure of the American Dream in his writings. Dreiser as a free-lance writer contributed his own accounts of successful men to a magazine entitled *Success* in the late 1890s. Beginning with the January 1898, issue, Dreiser published a series of interview articles called "Life Stories of Successful Men," in which he dealt with the men who appeared to have a firmer control over their destiny than he himself could ever hope for.

In speaking of his omnivorous reading, Dreiser also tells us that in his late youth he read *The Scarlet Letter, The House of the Seven Gables, The Alhambra, The Sketch Book, The Conquest of Granada*, and *Water Babies*. He recalls reading "Evangeline" and thinking it wonderful, and many of the other poems of Longfellow, Bryant, and Whittier caught his fancy. He liked Poe's "Raven," "Annabel Lee," and "The Bells," and he was recommended to read Cooper's *The Pathfinder* and *The Deerslayer*. Dreiser wants us to believe that, of all these readings, no books made a deeper impression on him than *Water Babies* and *The House of the Seven Gables*. One can, however, hardly detect in his mind or fiction the influence of either Kingsley or Hawthorne. At that time some phase of impossible sentimentalism must have haunted Dreiser's mind, and he would turn to romanticists such as Ouida and Laura Jean Libby. Dreiser was convinced then that though life itself seemed precarious, cruel, and insatiate, it was nonetheless generous, merciful, and forgiving. And he concludes:

> Yet never would I say of any picture of it, realistic or otherwise, that so much as fragmentarily suggests its variety or force, that it is dull. The individual himself—the writer, I mean—might well be a fool, and therefore all that he attempts to convey would taste of his foolishness or lack of wisdom or drama, but life, true life, by whomsoever set forth or discussed, cannot want utterly of romance or drama, and realism in its most artistic and forceful form is the very substance of both. It is only the ignorant or insensitive who fail to perceive it. (*Dawn*, p. 199)

Even his father, convinced that Dreiser had distinct intellectual tendencies, approved of the purchase of sets of Irving, Dickens, Thackeray, and Scott, and somehow managed to provide the money for it. Besides these volumes, Dreiser at the age of fifteen and sixteen enjoyed reading works by Carlyle, Bunyan, Fielding, Dryden, and Pope, and also liked Thoreau, Emerson, Twain, and Lew Wallace, the author of *Ben-Hur*. Dreiser in 1911 wrote to William C. Lengel (one of his former editorial assistants on the *Delineator* and then a reporter for the Kansas City *Post*) that among all the American books he had read as a boy, *Uncle Tom's Cabin, Huckleberry Finn, Roughing It,* and *Ben-Hur* were the only works he really enjoyed (*Letters*, 1: 121). Whatever recollections he may have had about his reading, Dreiser as a boy was fond of romantic literature; and life outside looked to him then "so lush, full and sweet, a veritable youth-dream of lotus land" (*Dawn*, p. 252).

This was the last sign of young Dreiser's inclination to romanticism. Even on occasion some vague notion of writing in imitation of Dickens or Thackeray occurred to him—in the same way he dreamed of becoming a general or judge as any ambitious youth would. In fact, he was at the time preoccupied with Dickens' novels; Thackeray, despite his clearer logic, seemed to him to be much inferior to Dickens. At this point his high school teacher recommended two fields for his reading: the rise of the German empire and Shakespeare. Dreiser thought that the teacher was just trying to cheer him up out of his depressing family circumstances. In any event, Dreiser secured somebody's copy of *Rise of the German Empire*, Carlyle's *French Revolution*, which he failed to understand; Shakespeare's *Julius Caesar, Macbeth, Antony and Cleopatra, Hamlet,* and *Merchant of Venice*; and Goethe's *Wilhelm Meister*. After these readings, Dreiser's passion for Dickens weakened, and his interest in Thackeray somehow became greater than that in Dickens. Before Dreiser in his boyhood encountered the work of Herbert Spencer (which apparently made an impact on him when he read it again in the middle 1890s) he still read both realistic and romantic writers. Dreiser even read the works of Whitman and Marlowe, recommended by a friend of one of his sisters, but he says that he did not appreciate their value until years later. Dreiser regretted that he was not at that time introduced to Balzac (*Dawn*, p. 279).

While Dreiser was in Chicago, he was rather happy now that he was away from home. But he was bored with his work at the hardware firm; he disliked his boss and despised most of the workers there who knew nothing but sorting pots and pans. The only person he liked was a fellow worker named Christian Aaberg, a forty-five-year-old Danish immigrant, who made a lasting influence on young Dreiser's intellectual training. A romantic and a libertine, Aaberg would arrive on Monday morning, exclaiming "My Gott! My Gott, how drunk I was yesterday... Oh, these women! These devils of women!'' Aaberg once shocked Dreiser, who was still attending church in those days, by saying that the cross was originally a phallic symbol. The Dane used to lecture Dreiser on the philosophy that mind alone makes the essential difference between the masses and the classes. Aaberg spoke authoritatively about Goethe, Ibsen, Wagner, Grieg, Andersen, and Strindberg, and this later led to Dreiser's reading of Stevenson, Crockett, Barrie, and Jerome.[21]

Dreiser's former teacher, Mildred Fielding, again initiated his interest in Spencer while he was still in Chicago. Before Dreiser left for Bloomington she told him:

> "[The] world is full of half-concealed shames and tragedies. But they are not really important here, there, or anywhere. What I want you to do is to study and develop your mind. Read philosophy and history. You will see how life works and how mistaken or untrue most beliefs are. Read Spencer. Read a life of Socrates. Read Marcus Aurelius and Emerson." (*Dawn*, p. 370)

The suggestion was a revolution in Dreiser's intellectual history. When he went to college, despite his reluctance to become seriously involved in class instruction, he confidently discussed Darwin's evolutionary theory with his friends. About the same time, he says, he also became acquainted with the works of Nietzsche.

All this time a compelling force seems to have driven this sensitive but somberly dignified observer to achieve such an understanding of life. For Dreiser says in reflection, "I can feel sorry for him who is so fearful of life and so poorly grounded in an understanding of things that he is terrorized lest someone discover that his uncle was a horse thief or his sister a prostitute or his father a bank-wrecker, but I cannot sympathize with his point of view" (*Dawn*, p. 3). Man cannot, Dreiser argues, produce his relatives or manipulate himself or the world. The only thing, and the wisest thing man can do, is to observe as accurately as he can with his own pair of eyes.

Once Dreiser sat down again to read, Robert Louis Stevenson and Mrs. Humphry Ward still charmed him, but his impressions of them failed to stay. Then Tolstoy's *Kreutzer Sonata* and "The Death of Ivan Ilyitch" struck him not as sociological interpretations of life but as stories that mirrored life itself. Tolstoy's world astounded him and thrilled him with a sudden manifestation that it would be wonderful to be a writer.[22] In all these years, writers such as Tolstoy seemed to have taught Dreiser that the artist must see life as a whole, not transcribe nature in its detail. Dreiser was learning to observe life from a retiring perspective where all life seemed beautiful. He was seeking and was to find a new voice, one which, detached from life, would echo through it. And by the time he reached his adulthood, Dreiser had learned to see beauty in the sordid, and meaning in the simple—a vision that later characterized his art.

4 Newspaper Days

Despite the influence on him of various intellectual and philosophical teachings during his youth, Dreiser at the threshold of his newspaper career was still naive, conventional, and somewhat romantic. The objective observation of life that he believed he had acquired—the very note on which *Dawn* ends—was yet to have a further test in his work as a reporter. In fact, the realist-romanticist ambivalence in the young Dreiser persisted for a long time. But, by the time he had accumulated enough experience in journalism, the battle had gradually been won for the realist. Dreiser's experience with American journalism in the 1890s was clearly crucial in formulating his vision of life, his selection of theme, and perhaps even his technique of fiction. Unlike *Dawn*, Dreiser's *Newspaper Days* (which appeared in its first edition as *A Book About Myself*, the publisher's title) is thus a story of his initiation—of challenge, of battle, and of revelation.[1]

During this period Dreiser began to aspire to write creatively, and the work of reporting appealed to him as a career of glory. He sought, struggled with, and succeeded in the newspaper world. In the end, the world he was involved in would prove to be the same world he knew in his childhood—a world without moral principles, without liberality, and without disinterested concern for human values. The world he learned about believed in nothing and nobody:

> Most of these young men [newspapermen] looked upon life as a fierce, grim struggle in which no quarter was either given or taken, and in which all men laid traps, lied, squandered, erred through illusion: a conclusion with which I now most heartily agree. The one thing I would now add is that the brigandage of the world is in the main genial and that in our hour of success we are all inclined to be more or less liberal and warm-hearted. (*Book*, p. 70)

Yet, in remembering this conclusion, Dreiser would hasten to add that he "was still sniffing about the Sermon on the Mount and the Beatitudes, expecting ordinary human flesh and blood to do and be those things." Therefore, the point of view of these newspapermen seemed to him "at times a little horrific, at other times most tonic" (p. 70).

If the real world were made of horror and tension, it would not be the kind of the world in which the young Dreiser would be delighted to live. Now and then he would look back with sorrowful disappointment to the idyllic world he once lived and believed in. When he visited the home of Sara White, his fiancée, he suddenly became nostalgic: "We Americans have home traditions or ideals, created as much by song and romance as anything else: *My Old Kentucky Home, Suwanee River*. Despite any willing on my part, this home [Sara White's] seemed to fulfill the spirit of those songs. There was something so sadly romantic about it" (p. 425). Dreiser had this flare for romantic feelings during his stay in Pittsburgh in 1894, a period considerably later in his newspaper career. His mind shuttled between the industrial city of the East and the rural region of the Midwest. Missouri, to him, abounded with America's "idealism, its dreams, the passion of a Brown, the courage and patience and sadness of a Lincoln, the dreams and courage of a Lee or a Jackson" (p. 426). But, to the Dreiser who had seen the struggle of the poor workers, and the degradation of the street girls, in Pittsburgh, it was impossible to share in the "fixedness in sentimental and purely imaginative American tradition" (p. 426). Although the mature anti-Puritan might have affected to delight in disillusionment, the discovery that life was unlike his boyhood dreams was a serious business for the young man. And this revelation was indeed the most important turning point in his life.

James L. Ford, one of the most professional of newspapermen in the nineties, commented on the significance of newspaper experience for a novelist. "There are," Ford wrote in 1894, "young men working in newspaper offices now who will one of these days draw true and vivid pictures of modern New York as it appears in the eyes and brains of those who know it thoroughly, and very interesting fiction it will be, too."[2] Ford went on to complain about the "literary quarantine" of the lower-class section of New York City where one might find a richer and more significant variety of human life than he himself knew. To encourage young fledgling writers, Ford wrote:

> The enduring novel of New York will be written not by the man who, knowing his audience of editors rather than his subject, is content with a thin coating of that literary varnish known as "local color," but by this very young man from Park Row or Herald Square . . . . When this young man sits down to write that novel, it will be because he is so full of his subjects, so thoroughly in sym-

pathy with his characters—no matter whether he takes them from an opium-joint in Mott Street or a ball at Delmonico's—and so familiar with the various influences which have shaped their destinies, that he will set about his task with the firm conviction that he has a story to tell to the world. (Ford, pp. 127–28)

Ford's comments were prophetic, for these novels that were demanding to be written were exactly the novels that writers such as Stephen Crane and Dreiser were ultimately to produce. But ironically these were the same novels that Crane and Dreiser in the nineties and later had trouble publishing—the stories of Maggie, and of Carrie and Hurstwood.

Dreiser took the words of Ford seriously. There was then a hole in the dike of Dreiser's optimism, and the rest was but a matter of time. In the four years 1892–95, it was everything or nothing with him. If this was not altogether a world of rosy virtue and joy, then it was ignoble, inane, an object to be tolerated with a kind of weary distaste. Regardless of the consequences, Dreiser at the age of twenty-one launched his apprenticeship in writing. In Chicago, in St. Louis, in Pittsburgh, and finally in New York, he was to observe and scrutinize corruption in politics, venality of the press, immorality in upper-class society, dishonesty in the financial world, and debauchery of the slums—a wide variety of American experience that gave Dreiserian fiction a sense of truth.

How would Dreiser with his style of writing be able to make the grade as a newspaperman? However acute an observer young Dreiser might have been, he was not at all prepared for the form of writing the trade of journalism demanded. Fortunately the journalism of the nineties, unlike that of today, was not uniform in style. Whereas factual news items were reported strictly in a simple and objective manner, most of the feature stories thrived on the personal styles of individual reporters. Dreiser's rambling style was not necessarily detrimental to his success; the poetic mood he brought in from his youth became an asset. Though irritatingly sentimental at times, this style distinguished him from his fellow novices. Dreiser steadily climbed the ladder of success just as many of his fictional characters did. Despite some setbacks along the way, he always had the will to promote himself; he enjoyed working as a journalist and he was fairly good at it.

Chicago was Dreiser's home base as a writer. He had often visited there as a boy with dreams of success in the world. Unlike Bloomington where he had a year's college work, the Chicago of the late eighties and early nineties gave Dreiser what he needed to be the novelist he later became—life in the raw with its spectacle of ferocity. Like Sister Carrie, Dreiser plunged into that world, struggled in it, and came out not only unscathed but initiated. He secured his foothold in the profession; he got his work printed.

Dreiser had previously lived in Chicago for a short period when his mother took the family from Evansville, Indiana, in 1884. When he returned to Chicago three years later, his sisters Mame and Theresa were still living there. For two years, in the midst of his sisters' complicated love affairs, he worked hard at one job after another. In the early summer of 1890 he went directly to Chicago from Bloomington, this time to test his independence from his family. Being poor, he still had to live in a small apartment with Ed and Claire, who were both working in the city. Since his mother was now dead, and his two older sisters, Emma and Sylvia, had gone to New York, his aging father was left with Mame, Theresa, and Al, who lived a few blocks away. His brother Paul was busy on the road and Rome was on the tramp's trail; the disintegration of the Dreiser family was virtually complete.

With this background Dreiser was still delivering laundry the following summer. But this job came to an end after a few months because the owner of the laundry discovered that Dreiser had held out twenty-five dollars of his collection money. Dreiser was terribly worried that he might be arrested, but as in Hurstwood's theft in *Sister Carrie*, he was spared from prosecution. Then, seeing an advertisement that the Chicago *Herald* wanted help in its business department for handing out free toys for poor children during the Christmas holidays, he applied for and got the job, hoping it might lead to a reporting job. He could not stay on the *Herald* after the Christmas holidays, but his urge to land a job on a newspaper was strong as ever. He was thrilled to catch a glimpse of Eugene Field at the prestigious *Daily News*, but he could not even reach the assistant editor. Finally Dreiser became determined to get a position with the fourth-rate *Daily Globe* on Fifth Avenue. Although the city editor at the *Globe* told him, "Nothing today. There's not a thing in sight," he was encouraged by the tone and returned to the *Globe* office daily. After two weeks the copyreader with a keen, cynical eye (John Maxwell) asked him, "Why do you pick the *Globe*? Don't you know it's the poorest paper in Chicago?" Dreiser replied innocently, "That's why I pick it . . . I thought I might get a chance here." Maxwell laughed. "Hang around," he said, and added that he might find him a spot in their coverage of the National Democratic Convention, which was to open in June. Dreiser was hired temporarily at fifteen dollars a week (*Book*, pp. 36–39, 47).

Even before he started working with the *Globe*, Dreiser had been reading Eugene Field's "Sharps and Flats," a column that made the *Daily News* famous. Though sometimes highly imaginative, Field's writing was filled with descriptions of various phases of city life. Dreiser had earlier read mostly descriptions of foreign scenes, and of New York, which sounded like a foreign city to him, but Field's Chicago was typically American, and Dreiser decided that he wanted to imitate him. Like Whitman, Dreiser wanted to sing and dance to the rhythms of American life. Dreiser imagined himself an orator with a huge audience before him. To him Chicago at that time seethed with an especially human atmosphere. Walking from palce to place, he began to compose vaguely formulated word-pictures—free verse, he says— which concerned everything and nothing but somehow echoed the poetic outbursts of his jubilant mood. "Indeed," he says, "I was crazy with life, a little demented or frenzied with romance and hope" (p. 3).

In this mood Dreiser gained an impetus to write. He had an enormous urge to express himself and put down his whirling thoughts, as he had in the past. But he was afraid that his practical experience in writing was slight; he thought that he was a man of slow and uncertain response to anything practical. He was inclined to see only color, romance, beauty; he thought he was only a half-baked poet, romancer, dreamer. But he distinctly remembered the writings of Emerson, Carlyle, Macaulay, Froude, and John Stuart Mill. He was also aware of the existence of Nietzsche in Germany, and Darwin, Spencer, Wallace, and Tyndall in England. But, in the midst of a bustling midwestern metropolis, these philosophers meant little to Dreiser. Instead he recalled, "Chicago was like a great orchestra in a tumult of noble harmonies. I was like a guest at a feast, eating and drinking in a delirium of ecstasy" (p. 20). Regarding book reading as cheating, he went out and immersed himself in the events of the city—the attitude that qualified him for a cub reporter just in time.

One thing Dreiser learned from his Chicago experience was that a writer's value was determined by the ability to observe as well as by the ability to cultivate techniques for rendering his vision. One of the early feature stories he wrote in Chicago was based on facts he uncovered in the city's South Side. The story was a slum romance involving a girl who had run away from a most miserable family. Her mother spoke in tears to Dreiser about the death of her husband, the injury of her only son which crippled him and made him unable to find work, and this disappearance of the only daughter—her last hope. After the girl had left her home she met a youth and decided to elope with him. From a journalistic point of view there was nothing much to the story, but Dreiser had an eye for detail in this kind of episode, which was all so familiar to him in his own family. The parents of the boy were simple working people, who were little concerned about their son's whereabouts. Dreiser touched on the wretched little homes of both families, the condition of the run-down neighborhoods, and the poverty and privation that ill became a young, pretty, and sensuous girl (*Book*, p. 74). By this time Dreiser himself had cut his last tie with his family, leaving Ed and Claire and taking a room for himself on Ogden Place overlooking Union Park—where he later placed Carrie in the novel.

The story impressed the city editor John T. McEnnis, who believed that a reporter must make something out of an incident whether or not its had news value. Dreiser owed a part of his first success to the man who had given him a chance—John Maxwell, his copyreader. Maxwell told him during one of the earliest days of his work: "Life is a God-damned stinking, treacherous game, and nine hundred and ninety-nine men out of every thousand are bastards" (p. 59). Maxwell talked about the phases of Chicago he knew intimately and contrasted them with those of San Francisco, where he had worked when he was a young man. He assured Dreiser: "A hell of a fine novel is going to be written about some of these things one of these days" (p. 68). Through this mentor, Dreiser managed to articulate a new vision of life that surprised and impressed even Maxwell, the more experienced reporter, who told Drieser: "You're one of the damnedest crack-brained loons I ever saw . . . but you seem to know how to get the news just the same, and you're going to be able to write" (p. 59).

Another thing Dreiser learned in Chicago was the fact that life was not orderly and genuinely beautiful as books had led him to believe. He had long suspected that an enormous difference existed between the wealthy, courteous, and so-called good people, and the poor, degraded, and bad people. As a boy from the other side of the tracks, Dreiser had always looked into the clean, well-lighted places of wealth and power. Yet sobriety or virtue, control or abandon, appeared to have nothing to do with becoming either rich or poor, a success or a failure, in America. Dreiser began to suspect that man succeeded for some reason that had little to do with any of these factors. He was beginning to realize that people invented laws for other people to live by and in order to protect themselves in what they had achieved. He appreciated Maxwell's accusation that people did not intend those laws to apply to themselves or to prevent them from doing anything they wished to do. Standing now on the very tracks dividing society, Dreiser continued to see the miseries, scandals, corruptions, and crimes, of the rich and the poor alike. Who was to blame for these problems became the overwhelming question for Dreiser. He never grew weary of this question, but he never found a solution to it. But he began to suspect even then that "man is the victim of forces over which he has no control" (p. 65).

This speculative tendency helped Dreiser form one of his important concepts of life. However derivative and rigidly formulated Dreiser's statement might sound in the light of naturalism, it nevertheless came from his own work as a reporter. But, in those days, journalism was not yet ready to accept such a view as Dreiser's, for nearly all news stories were distorted reality in order to heighten color and romance. Most of the well-received feature articles were written, by the current fashion in fiction, in imitation of a Victorian writer such as Dickens. Even the successful feature that Dreiser wrote was tinged with undue pathos and sentiment. It was Maxwell again who cautioned Dreiser not to let his youthful romantic flair take the best of his writing, and gave him an antidote: "Read Schopenhauer, Spencer, Voltaire. Then you'll get a line on this scheme of things."[3]

The real feel of newspaper work in Chicago now encouraged Dreiser to get more experience. When Maxwell and McEnnis advised him to find a better position in St. Louis, not only was Dreiser flattered but he felt he was to satisfy his long-awaited dreams. At that time St. Louis was famous for many literary men it had produced. Augustus Thomas (a St. Louis *Star* reporter who became a nationally known columnist), Henry Blossom (once a society editor who made his reputation in the literary circle), and W. C. Brann (a former *Globe-Democrat* man who was now editor of the *Iconoclast*)—all were impressive enough. In addition, Eugene Field, William Marion Reedy, and Mark Twain, who had worked as reporters in the city at one time or another, were, of course, also towering figures of success. Their achievements sounded forbidding, but Dreiser was comforted by the knowledge that even "Mark Twain had idled about here for a time, drunk and hopeless" (*Book*, p. 130). To become a literary man, Dreiser believed, a cub reporter must survive the necessary groundwork. Only after that could one leap the chasm of journalism and literature as his predecessors had obviously done.

Unexpectedly, however, Dreiser found St. Louis unexciting. Years later in the first issue of the *Esquire* magazine he wrote:

> St. Louis at that time, and to me at least, was so infernally dull.
> The drowsy, muddy, sleepy Mississippi River. The dry and often intense and unbroken summer heat. The dull and commonplace business activities—shoes, dry goods, hardware, beer. And the inane and meaningless social groups: French, German, Irish, Old South American, with their ridiculous money, family or religious standards, their large houses, brainless teas, dances, receptions or "at home": their marriages, deaths, births, anniversaries, as opposed to the dreadful slums, veritably sties and warrens along the waterfronts and elsewhere and in which dwelt thousands upon thousands as socially forgotten as though they were dead![4]

In *A Book About Myself*, Dreiser gives the same impression: "St. Louis, I said to myself, was not as good as Chicago. Chicago was rough, powerful, active; St. Louis was sleepy and slow . . . . But on that evening how dull and commonplace it seemed—how slow after the wave-like pulsation of energy that appeared to shake the very air of Chicago" (p. 88).

What, instead, stimulated Dreiser's interest in St. Louis was his discovery of a diversity in human conditions. He was regularly assigned to cover a murder, a suicide, a failure, a defalcation as well as an important wedding, a business or political banquet, a ball or a club function. His most memorable assignment in St. Louis was to visit the police station in North Side. It was a gold mine for the raw material a realist must have: rapes, riots, murders, fantastic family complications of various kinds. Of that section of the city, quite appalling to him even years later, Dreiser later reflected:

> It was all so dirty, so poor, so stuffy, so starveling. There were in it all sorts of streets—Jewish, negro, and run-down American, or plain slum, the first crowded with long-bearded Jews and their fat wives, so greasy, smelly and generally offensive that they sickened me: rag-pickers, chicken-dealers and feather-sorters all. In their streets the smell of these things, picked or crated chickens, many of them partially decayed, decayed meats and vegetables, half-sorted dirty feathers and rags and I know not what else, was sickening in hot weather.... In these hot days of June, July and August they [Negroes] seemed to do little save sit or lie in the shade of buildings in this vicinity and swap yarns or contemplate the world with laughter or in silence. Occasionally there was a fight, a murder or a low love affair among them which justified my time here. (*Book*, pp. 219–20)

As in Chicago, Dreiser was amazed by the color of existence however sordid and at times hopelessly tragic it may have been. When he served as a drama critic on the *Globe-Democrat*, he was puzzled by the distorted scenes he saw on the stage. Why couldn't such real life as he saw in the city be shown? The audience liked the splendor of the Orient; the high societies of New York, London, and Paris; the decadent world of Dumas *fils*, Oscar Wilde, Henry Authur Jones, and Arthur Wing Pinero. Dreiser would complain: "There were the really fine clothes and the superior personalities (physically and socially), and vice and poverty (painted in such peculiar colors that they were always divinely sad or repellent) existed only in those great cities" (p. 180). On his assignments he would report a crime of a lurid character that compelled him to think, and on the same day he would cover a lecture on transmigration and Nirvana.

All this hustle made his vision kaleidoscopic for the first time, an invaluable quality of Dreiser's early writing. He still tended to brood, but the scene widened, bearing a spectacle, as he saw it through the eyes of his fellow reporters. Dreiser indeed acknowledged their influences, as he wrote in 1919: "Nearly every turning point in my career has been signalized by my meeting some man of great force, to whom I owe some of the most ecstatic intellectual hours of my life, hours in which life seemed to bloom forth into new aspects, glowed as with the radiance of a gorgeous tropic day."[5] Peter McCord, an illustrator with the *Globe-Democrat*, was such a man, through whom, Dreiser tells us, "I was destined to achieve some of my sanest conceptions of life" (*Book*, p. 121). To McCord, life was a magnificent mystery, often absurd and yet beautiful. "A thief was a thief," McCord exclaimed, "but he had his place. Ditto the murderer. Ditto the saint. Not man but Nature was planning, or at least doing, something which man could not understand, of which very likely he was a mere tool" (*Twelve Men*, p. 3). McCord would untiringly continue his discourse on the Negroes, the ancient Romans, the Egyptians, the Chinese, the grotesque Dark Ages, the vile slums and evil quarters in America. Dreiser was awestruck when McCord urged upon him what Dreiser then regarded as a list for a scholar—books by Maspero, Froude, Huxley, Darwin, Wallace, Rawlinson, Froissart, Hallam, Taine, and Avebury. Even at this point of Dreiser's intellectual development, McCord succinctly stated the naturalistic theory: "It's all good to me, whatever happens. We're here. We're not running it. Why be afraid to look at it? The chemistry of a man's body isn't any worse than the chemistry of anything else, and we're eating the dead things we've killed all the time. A little more or a little less in any direction—what difference?" (*Twelve Men*, p. 32).

The diversity of human conditions still puzzled Dreiser, and when he returned to his room at night he often brooded over what McCord had said. Dreiser would wonder alone at the inscrutability of nature, his idea that everything in nature—even the prostitutes on Chestnut Street—played a role in a grand scheme man could not yet understand. On one assignment he interviewed Annie Besant, a popular theosophist, who came to St. Louis to give a lecture. "You do not recognize, then," Dreiser asked her, "a controlling principle—a God?" She replied with an air of mysticism:

> No, we do not. If there is a God, the order of this life is then manifestly unjust. Some beings are born with ability and strength, some with dulled senses, with weaknesses and with deformities. If you say that a just being has sent a weakling into the world to battle on equal terms with strength and ability, then you simply admit that the controlling influence is unjust. Instead of accusing a divine being with being partial, we turn to the individual himself and find a solution of the apparent discrepancy in reincarnation.[6]

But Dreiser was not entirely convinced, reasoning that the discrepancy in human existence was not the result of the absence of God but rather of man's inability to comprehend God.

By this time Dreiser was not at all afraid of looking at life's every facet. When a train accident occurred, for instance, he was eager to give a fuller account than he would have previously given. After seeing an oil tank explode he rushed to the morgue of the hospital, where the naked bodies of the victims were laid out. He would ask himself, "Who were they?... The nothingness of man! They looked so commonplace, so unimportant, so like dead flies or beetles." Later he was sent out to interview a group of bandits responsible for a train robbery. Owing to his insight and skill he detected a train carrying the gang to the county jail before the reporter from the rival paper. To get on the train Dreiser ran across the field and even paid the railroad agent for stopping the train. All his efforts came to little avail because the other reporter, taking advantage of the situation, also got on the train, succeeded in getting an interview before Dreiser, and took the robbers to the office of the other paper to be photographed. Most significantly, this incident dramatized what had been growing in Dreiser's thinking—the impotence of man's will and mind in the face of perverse and haphazard circumstances. The implication was grave, for the incident proved to him once and for all "the weakness of the human mind as a directing organ." Both incidents fixed his thoughts permanently on the understanding that life is cruel and that luck comes to many who sleep and flies from those who try (*Book*, pp. 163, 307).[7]

Another influential reporter in Dreiser's St. Louis days was Robert Hazard. Hazard and another friend of Dreiser's collaborated on a novel in which the main characters are an actress and a newspaperman, her lover. In the story a treacherous murder takes place. The newspaperman, himself innocent, is arrested and convicted. The actress, who is in love with the newspaperman, attempts to save him but fails. After reading the novel in manuscript, Dreiser was impressed, not by the book but by the fact that it could not be published because of its subject matter and the puritanical character of the American mind. "How queer," Dreiser thought. "Yet these two incipient artists had already encountered it [the American moral standard]. They had been overawed to the extent of thinking it necessary to write of French, not American life in terms of fact. Such things as they felt called upon to relate occurred only in France, never here—or at least such things, if done here, were never spoken of" (p. 132). And yet it was amazing that the news columns in those days carried accounts of the most horrible crimes side by side with stories of the sweet inanities of love. Often the news columns gave distorted pictures of men and women: all men were honest, all women virtuous, all mothers gentle and self-sacrificing, all fathers kind and industrious. However, when describing "actual facts" for news, one was not permitted to indicate what one actually saw, much less what one actually felt.

This suppressed novel made an impact on Dreiser personally because he had been involved in one love affair after another since the day he arrived at Poplar Street Station. Both the published and unpublished versions of *A Book About Myself* have the theme of Dreiser's blazing sexual urge ever since he left Bloomington. In the midst of his reporting duties he still tried to correspond with a Chicago girl named Lois (Alice in *A Book About Myself*). At one point he was shocked by a letter from her complaining that he had forsaken her because he had moved up to a better job in another city. She asked him to return all the letters she had written him, and for a postscript wrote:

> I stood by the window last night and looked out on the street. The moon was shining and those dead trees over the way were waving in the wind. I saw the moon on that little pool of water over in the field. It looked like silver. Oh, Theo, I wish I were dead. (p. 127)

Dreiser was so moved by this letter that he used it almost verbatim in *The "Genius"*, published twenty-three years later:

> "Dear Eugene:" she wrote, "I got your note several weeks ago, but I could not bring myself to answer it before this. I know everything is over between us and that is all right, for I suppose it has to be. You couldn't love any woman long, I think. I know what you say about your having to go to New York to broaden your field is true. You ought to, but I'm sorry you didn't come out. You might have. Still I don't blame you, Eugene. It isn't much different from what has been going on for some time. I have cared but I'll get over that, I know, and I won't ever think hard of you. Won't you return me the notes I have sent you from time to time and my pictures? You won't want them now.["]
>
> "RUBY."
>
> There was a little blank space on the paper and then:—
> "I stood by the window last night and looked out on the street. The moon was shining and those dead trees were waving in the

wind. I saw the moon on that pool of water over in the field. It looked like silver. Oh, Eugene, I wish I were dead."[8]

While Lois was still on his mind, Dreiser met a girl one night when he was covering a church function. He was still apprehensive about his own sexual ability when he persuaded her to stay overnight in his room. Dreiser apparently succeeded this time, describing it as "a delicious contest, made all the more so by a real or assumed bashfulness."[9] On the next morning Mrs. Zernouse, his landlady, discovering several hairpins in the room or in the bed, grew suspicious. An account of this experience is discreetly omitted from the published version of *A Book About Myself*. "As I recall it," Dreiser wrote in the manuscript,

> it followed rather swiftly for . . . she made such pointed comments and seemed to take it as so very natural and desirable even, that I felt called upon to trifle with her, and in a very few moments she had surrendered, and in the same place, though in by no means so tempting a way. . . . The point that impressed me was that her transports, although vigorous and noisy, decidedly so, were yet very quick to end. She seemed to see nothing awry in her brief blazing orgasms and over and over congratulated me enthusiastically, in the moments of action of course, on my sex power. (*Book* ms., ch. 13, p. 2)

Soon Dreiser became her lover; she waited for his return from his reporting rounds often until after midnight. Although he was relieved of his doubts about his sexual prowess, he was disappointed by the differences between himself and the woman. "By degrees," Dreiser recalled, "but rather swiftly at that, owing to the growing feeling that she was gross and very much beneath me mentally and in every other way, I began to tire of her" (ibid, ch. 13, p. 2). He finally cut his entanglement with her by simply moving to another roominghouse. Such accounts in the manuscript version of *A Book About Myself* were not fictional, since one Globe-Democrat reporter later recorded:

> Theodore Dreiser, in his *A Book About Myself*, tells of his two years on the staff of the *Globe-Democrat*. A rough-tongued "Tobe" Mitchell was the city editor during those two years (1892–93) of Dreiser's stay, and Dreiser handles him savagely in his book. But office gossip had it in 1896 that Dreiser had been active in obtaining feminine relaxation for Mitchell . . .[10]

Yearning to be a writer himself someday, Dreiser always wished to portray life as he knew it but did not know how to undertake such a task. Unfortunately his serious interest in fiction took the form of drama, clearly inspired by the current fashion on the stage. When he was on the *Globe-Democrat*, he reviewed plays shown in the St. Louis area. With a lack of experience in criticism and a sentimental inclination still remaining in him, Dreiser was easily carried away by the love scene in a totally spurious play. His reviews were enthusiastic at best, and often embarrassed his editorial staff. At one time, merely wanting to cover as many plays shown in an evening as he could, Dreiser wrote on one production: "A large and enthusiastic audience received Mr. Sol Smith Russel." To his horror, the *Republic*, the rival paper, made the announcement in the morning edition that because of the flood that production had not arrived in town the night before.[11]

As an unsuccessful drama critic Dreiser even tried his hand at a play of his own. Encouraged by McCord, he wrote a draft of a comic opera entitled *Jeremiah I*. The story was about an old Indiana farmer who accidentally struck a mythical Aztec stone on his farm, was taken back to Mexico of the Aztec dynasty, and was hailed as a despot by the natives. An Aztec maiden with whom the farmer later fell in love persuaded him to transform the form of government from a despotism to a republic, and the farmer became a candidate for president. McCord was so enchanted by the whole idea that he even suggested costumes and settings for its production and volunteered to act the part of Jeremiah I. Dreiser was obviously interested in the glamour of politics and sex, but he "mistrusted the reality of it all. Fate could not be that kind, not so swift." And he thought that a play of this kind would never be produced even at a high school (*Book*, pp. 194–95).

Although Dreiser felt his limitations in judgment and taste, he never tried to hide them. Whenever he saw something he thought was genuinely beautiful, he would not hesitate to express his judgment with superlatives. When the black singer Sissieretta Jones, billed as "the black Patti," gave a superb performance at Exposition Entertainment Hall one night, he wrote in a review entitled "The Black Diva's Concert": "Her singing reminds one of the beauty of nature and brings back visions of the still, glassy water and soft swaying branches of some drowsy nook in summer time. She trills the chromatic scale to perfection, and varies it in a manner too rich to describe."[12] The *Globe-Democrat*, in spite of its name, was a morning Republican paper with the largest circulation in the area, and its famous editor

Joseph B. McCullagh was known for using a sharp tongue in his editorials. Negroes were not publicly acclaimed in St. Louis in those days, and rival papers seized the opportunity of Dreiser's review to get even with McCullagh, calling him a "nigger-lover."

In St. Louis, Dreiser also detected the conventional attitude toward news material in another influential man, H. B. Wandell (city editor of the *Republic*, to which Dreiser later transferred). From Wandell he learned more about the use of details in news articles. Wandell told him:

> Ah, it was a terrible thing, was it? He killed her in cold blood, you say? There was a great crowd out there, was there? Well, well, write it all up. Write it all up . . . . Write a good strong introduction for it, you know, all the facts in the first paragraph, and then go on and tell your story. You can have as much space for it as you want—a column, a column and a half, two—just as it runs. (*Book*, p. 212)

It was Wandell who first mentioned the significance of Zola and Balzac to Dreiser, as pointed out earlier. Wandell told Dreiser on his first assignment: "Bare facts are what are needed in cases like this, with lots of color as to the scenery or atmosphere, the room, the other people, the street, and all that" (p. 211). At the same time, however, Dreiser was strongly aware that "there was a sneaking bending of the knee to the middle West conventions of which he [Wandell] was a part" (p. 207). Dreiser was told to present all the facts he could find, just so far as they would not invite any libel suits.

Under Wandell Dreiser became a trusted feature correspondent for the *Republic* and was sent to the Columbian Exposition at Chicago in 1893. Dreiser's assignment was to accompany twenty Missouri schoolteachers—who had won a popularity contest, the paper's promotion gimmick—to the fair and report on the teachers' activities on the trip. The young bachelor was delighted at the opportunity to travel with these girls and to return home with them. He saw the exposition; and yet, unlike Henry Adams, who was awed by the dynamo and other scientific exhibits, Dreiser was only busy shepherding the twenty homely spinsters.

The conservatism of the Midwest took a toll in Dreiser's private affair which began on this journey to Chicago. Once he got on the train in St. Louis, his lustful eye (just like Drouet's in *Sister Carrie*) fell on a red-haired girl, Sara (Sallie) Osborne White—his wife to be.

"You've never been to Chicago, then?" Dreiser asked. "Oh no," she said. "I've never been anywhere really. I'm just a simple country girl, you know" (*Book*, p. 241). Her direct, unpretentious attitude fascinated Dreiser, and he talked to her as an old Chicagoan. He took Sallie around in the city (as Drouet does Carrie in the novel). They went to Lincoln Park to see a colored fountain given by C. T. Yerkes, Frank Cowperwood's prototype; to the newly built "Alley L"; and to the recently opened Siegel, Cooper and Company, a huge department store (p. 264). His courtship of Sallie resumed after he returned from the Chicago trip. But, unlike Carrie, Sallie (known as Jug since childhood) was two years older than Dreiser. She was a conventional, "shy little school teacher,"[13] and she ducked all his attempts to seduce her. Some of those who knew of Dreiser's courtship in St. Louis called him "a big silly"; he was always "gawking and mooning" (Lengel, p. 120). He brought Sallie roses, and bought her expensive clothes. He put on a Stetson hat, wore pleated shirts, and carried a cane, and, as thus attired, he took her to theaters. But, unlike Drouet with Carrie, he stole only a few kisses from Sallie. The busy schedule of his daily rounds for the newspaper exhausted him. Before he left St. Louis, however, he proposed to Sallie, spending his last cent on a diamond ring, and they became engaged. But Jug was persistently a virginal Methodist, and he was too poor to marry; Dreiser was continuously sexually frustrated.

Under these circumstances, the most meaningful statement on human existence he had ever heard came from a fellow journalist named Mathewson. In a socially dull atmosphere of the city at the time, Mathewson's vision struck sharply into Dreiser's naiveté. The impression crystallized when he read Mathewson's review article in a Sunday paper. Mathewson displayed a great rapport with the novelist whom every intellectual in town was talking about—Émile Zola—and with Zola's method of conveying "gutter" life. In America, Dreiser knew, such life surfaced only in the police court, the jail, the bawdy section, and the morgue. Dreiser later wrote:

> Indeed, in sleek, almost wholly inaesthetic and material minded St. Louis, there was life quite as efflorescent with lechery and gluttony as ever in Paris, only here glazed over with an outward and better-than-thou pretence which compelled thousands to denounce this man Zola with a moral fervor only equaled by their secret vices. Unclean! Unclean! Unclean! He and all his works![14]

Although Zola and his novels were French, Zola was dealing with exactly the same greeds, lusts, ambitions, successes, and failures that Dreiser was facing daily in St. Louis and in American life. To Dreiser, the difference between American and French novels was obvious; in the deliberate art of a French writer such as Zola, people were stripped bare of that pretense which, like a London fog, enveloped the Anglo-Saxon world—in contrast to the clear Mediterranean sky—and made people see themselves through a glass darkly. Not only did this article acclaim the iron courage of Zola the man but it made Dreiser feel as if he were immersed in the world of *Thérèse Raquin, L'Assommoir*, and *Nana* even though he had not read a work of Zola.

The peculiar effect of Mathewson's article on Dreiser at the time was not brought by his discovery of Zola but rather by Dreiser's perplexity over the character of Mathewson himself. Dreiser remembered that Mathewson in his office was frail, pale, and totally inactive whereas in print he came out forceful and penetrating with a tremendous mental power and acumen. Once Dreiser saw Mathewson completely drunk with his delicate finger pointing to the street. Mathewson would rave against the middle class and their blatant hypocrisy:

> "Look at 'em! Look at 'em" (And once more waving a feeble hand). "Ignorant! Dirty! Useless! Eating and drinking and loafing, and, and, reproducing themselves. For what? For what? So's there'll be more of 'em to eat and drink an' loaf an' reproduce. An' they're supposed to be sober. An' I'm drunk. An' everybody else that wants to eat and drink and . . . reproduce themselves in St. Louis an' everywhere. You're sober. An' I'm drunk. An' you want to reproduce. An' I don't. An' I want to think. An' they don't—or can't. An' they're sober. An' you're sober. An' I'm drunk. Ha! Ha!" (*Esquire* 1: 125)

Mathewson stared at the wretched cobbled street, its low, old buildings, its nondescript population of blacks and whites, its degraded and, if not evil, plainly dull and humdrum masses, their stores, rooms, brothels, bars, and their hot, smelly bodies. Drieser realized how true it was that people, including Mathewson, were indeed enacting a human drama he wanted to write about. He thought that these people "were dreaming—a wild, bitter, troublesome and yet colorful and exciting dream . . . . Here in this drab, decayed, out-at-seat, down-at-heel, poverty-limited street, with its dirty children, black and white, and its stray cats and dogs, I was swelling with an excess of sympathy, wonder, respect, even awe. Drunkenness? Drunkenness? Who was really drunk?'' (ibid, 125).

Dreiser understood that Mathewson was talking about the forces of life itself with which man had nothing to do. Gradually Dreiser began to realize that Mathewson's solution to the dilemma was to escape these forces entirely. Dreiser believed that Mathewson felt himself physically and mentally unfit, and perhaps out of key with life. To Mathewson, life—its noise, its notions, its people, their ambitions, and even love—meant nothing, sound and fury signifying nothing. He could not and would not cope with life; he was a simple nihilist. Mathewson later committed suicide and Dreiser wrote an epitaph: ''The struggle to live without violence is a dream; to live by violence is aesthetic death'' (*Esquire* 2: 114).

However meaningful Mathewson's death was to him at the time, Dreiser went on a quest for his version of aesthetic life. He sought beauty in the ugliness, believing that heroic drama went on in the dark alleys of the city. When he covered the case of a Negro stevedore on the Mississippi who slashed his unfaithful mistress with a razor, Dreiser turned it into a somber romance and published it in the *Republic*, while the rival *Globe-Democrat* reported it as ''a low dive cutting affray'' (*Book*, p. 283). Dreiser's story described ''the hot river waterfronts of the different cities which the lover had visited, the crowded negro quarters of Memphis, New Orleans, Cairo, the bold negro life which two truants such as the false mistress and her lover might enjoy'' (pp. 283–84). He also tried to suggest ''the sing-song sleepiness of the levee boat-landings, the stevedores at their lazy labors, the idle, dreamy character of the slow-moving boats'' (p. 284)—the identical scene Dreiser used several years later in a magazine article, ''The Trade of the Mississippi.''[15] The old black refrain of laborers and the rhythmic vernacular of old black mammies, Dreiser tells us, ''moved me to a poetic frenzy'' (*Book*, p. 284).

Unlike Mark Twain—to whom such scenes in the region had been so familiar—Dreiser came upon these scenes as a stranger under a spell. But he devoured them and made them part of his permanent vision of American life. True, Dreiser produced nothing like the romantic *Adventures of Huckleberry Finn* or even the bitter social criticism of the region in Twain's *Pudd'nhead Wilson*. Yet, with these two awestricken years in the region, Dreiser had the full potentialities to turn himself into another Twain. Dreiser used some of the experience in dramatizing the tragedy of a rapist he so effectively portrayed in "Nigger Jeff," one of his first attempts at fiction.[16] Dreiser, of course, appeared on the scene decades later than Twain; perhaps, the kind of social problems Dreiser faced in St. Louis could be more meaningfully compared to what a writer such as Faulkner was later to seize upon in his novels. In any event, Dreiser's work in St. Louis was the longest and the most impressionable in his journalistic career. At least the experience made him grapple with the texture of life he had never known in Chicago, let alone the small towns of Indiana.

When he left St. Louis early in March 1894, Dreiser traveled east, eventually taking a job in Pittsburgh. Although he was to settle down to a relatively permanent newspaper position there, he first went to Grand Rapids, Ohio, twenty-five miles southwest of Toledo. He had hoped to become a partner in the *Wood County Herald* (circulation 500), but once he saw the dusty printing machine in the loft of a feed store, he exclaimed to himself, "It's horrible. I should die" (*Book*, p. 366). Then he drifted to Toledo, where he met Arthur Henry, who later encouraged him to write fiction and to whom *Sister Carrie* was to be dedicated. Henry helped him get four days' work reporting a streetcar strike for the Toledo *Blade*. Dreiser rode on the car the company attempted to run, and reported the scenes along the track. He had courage, and like Hurstwood, he took a risk of being attacked by the strikers, but there was actually no violence.[17]

Because there was no permanent position for Dreiser on the *Blade*, he had to move on. In Cleveland, the gorgeous mansions of Rockefeller, Tom Johnson, and Henry Flagler along Euclid Avenue raised his high hopes, but he earned only $7.50 for some Sunday feature work for the Cleveland *Leader* during a two weeks' stay. Dreiser then took a train to Buffalo, where he tried all the newspapers but in vain. Though his supply of money was dangerously low, he took the trolley to Niagara Falls. Dreiser envied the honeymooners he saw there and thought of Jug he left behind. After ten days he moved down to Pittsburgh, seeing mountains for the first time in his life.

On the fourth day of his stay in Pittsburgh, Dreiser received a telegram from Arthur Henry in Toledo offering him a position as a

reporter with the *Blade* at a salary of eighteen dollars a week. Elated,
Dreiser hastily erased the figure to read twenty-five dollars and showed
the telegram to the city editor of the *Dispatch*. Dreiser was hired by the
Dispatch on the spot at a weekly salary of twenty-five dollars and
began to work there on the next day. It was in April 1894, only two years
after the great Homestead steel strike, and Dreiser became ever more
conscious of the life struggle, vividly embodied in labor strife. The
details of the strike were fresh in his mind; he was excited over the news
that reported the industrial drama of America. He heard, for instance,
that the three hundred Pinkerton guards who had been introduced into
the steel plant in Homestead for its protection had killed several workers
and injured many more. The steel company, after letting the strikers
starve for six months, imported East European peasants, whom the
company referred to as Hunkies, Polacks, Lits, and Croats.

Dreiser took the workers' struggle as his own. What he saw in
Pittsburgh at that time helped him visualize for the first time what he
had long suspected: that the strong eventually overpower the weak.
"Like huge ribbons of fire," he wrote, "these [Phipps and Carnegie]
and other names of powerful steel men—the Olivers, Thaws, Fricks,
Thompsons—seemed to rise and band the sky. It seemed astonishing to
me that some men could thus rise and soar about the heavens like
eagles, while others, drab sparrows all, could only pick among the
offal of the hot ways below" (*Book*, p. 393). Never before did Dreiser
see such a wide gulf dividing the rich and the poor. Not only did he feel
a surge of sympathy for the poor and the oppressed but he also saw the
shame behind the often professed principle of equality of opportunity.
The fact that all men did not have the same capability, he then assumed, resulted in the lack of equality of opportunity. But those endowed with strength and power should not be arrogant and forget the
mere chance by which they happened to become powerful. Dreiser saw
that the poor, particularly the very poor day laborers, were exploited
and misused, and yet he was unable to find any solution to change their
conditions. "The mill-owners," his fellow reporter Martyn astutely
observed, "pay them the lowest wages, the landlords exploit these
boardinghouse keepers as well as their boarders, and the community
which they make by their work don't give a damn for them, and yet
they are happy, and I'll be hanged if they don't make me happy. It
must be that just work is happiness" (p. 405). Dreiser understood
Martyn as saying that a worker would be happier if he had a heavy load

of work to occupy himself with, that the work itself enabled the worker to avoid the ennui of useless and futile thought. Not surprisingly, Dreiser recognized that the prostitutes (whom he saw walking behind the press building and along the Monongahela River) posed a situation parallel with the laborers. The police who were supposedly protecting vice were really preying upon it.

As a young reporter who felt a constant urge to write about such a matter as class warfare, Dreiser was frustrated in any attempts to express the truth as he saw it. His city editor, though cool and speculative, instructed him specifically as to the value and the limitations of news. Dreiser was told not to touch on labor conditions, because this subject was assigned to the specialist who was to make prescribed reports. Dreiser was not allowed to detract from the rich or the religious, for they were considered "all right" as far as the city desk was concerned. He was told not to cover scandals in high society. The editor's explanation was that the "big steel men here just about own the place, so we can't. Some papers out West and down in New York go in for sensationalism, but we don't" (p. 406).

Dreiser was once sent out to interview Andrew Carnegie—the arch-industrialist—who had just returned from his latest travel abroad and was to speak to the city elite at the Duquesne Club. Dreiser was only allowed to stand in the back of the room, and note taking was prohibited. Dreiser was later handed a copy of the speech addressed to the people of Pittsburgh, and was informed that the *Dispatch* could publish it. Carnegie, "short, stocky, bandy-legged," struck him as having "a grand air of authority investing him." Going out on assignments, Dreiser would collect material on the lives of Carnegie, Phipps, and Frick; their homes, retreats, clubs, local condescensions, and superiorities. "The people of Pittsburgh," he remembered, "were looked upon as vassals by some of these, and their interviews on returning from the seashore or the mountains partook of the nature of a royal return" (p. 416). Dreiser was appalled by the obvious threat of these industrialists to move their industries to another city unless their economic policy was supported and protected. It was preposterous to Dreiser that they acted as if the life of Pittsburgh depended entirely upon them.

Carnegie's machinations, for example, disturbed Dreiser's conscience so much that a few years later he wrote a magazine article (reprinted twice) on the man's character.[18] In the article version Dreiser satirized Carnegie's appearance of generosity in contributing part of his huge fortunes to various libraries. In reality, Dreiser subtly noted, Carnegie was, like the Chicago industrialist Charles T. Yerkes, an egocentric public figure. "Selfish wealth," Dreiser remarked with a bit of sarcasm, "stands surprised, amazed, almost indignant, at the announcement that Andrew Carnegie, instead of resting in Olympian luxury on the millions he has earned, and going to the grave with gold tightly clutched in his stiffening fingers, proposes to expend the bulk of his riches, during his lifetime, for the benefit of his fellow men" (*Success* 2: 453). Both Yerkes and Carnegie, Dreiser perhaps thought, respected no law but the self-decreed in remolding the economic lives of American cities to realize their own grandiose schemes.

Dreiser was equally unsympathetic with American politicians. At one time Dreiser had an opportunity to interview Thomas B. Reed, recent Speaker of the House of Representatives and the probable Republican presidential nominee, who was favored by industry. Dreiser questioned the Speaker on his reactions to the organization of Jacob S. Coxey's "hobo" army, which had planned to march to the Capitol in protest against the dictatorial trusts. Reed was indignant about the marchers' motive, which to him meant revolution, and he was utterly unheeding of their complaints against monopoly. Sympathetic to the marchers' cause, Dreiser was convinced that the rapidly developing financial oligarchy in the country was intended to enslave the workers. For the interests of industry and trust organizers hiding behind a huge tariff wall, Reed was one of the chief protectors of the steel plutocrats such as Carnegie and Phipps. A few years later, however, Dreiser wrote, surprisingly, a sympathetic article—"Thomas Brackett Reed: The Story of a Great Career"—for *Success* magazine.[19] Dreiser's change of heart was, perhaps, the result of pressure from its editor Orison Swett Marden, who had commissioned Dreiser to write thirty such articles on various national figures.

Dreiser was greatly disappointed by the uncritical, almost worshipful reception of the exploiters by members of the press and public officials. Nor were certain members of the clergy, as Dreiser found out, completely free from the influence of the industrialists. Thus Dreiser's activities as a journalist were severely restricted. He was not allowed to report the facts he found, let alone his own views. He was instead assigned a mild task "to do city hall and police," and was asked only to write feature stories on what he considered to be the most trivial matters.

Between May and November 1894, Dreiser wrote one or two such pieces every week for the *Dispatch*. He described, for example, how two cats in the neighborhood lived together; how farmers reaped a field; what kinds of melody were heard on midsummer nights in the city; and what kinds of danger dogcatchers must face.[20] Occasionally he turned into his characteristic brooding. In writing about Potter's Field, he would feel how lonely the "friendless" dead must have been, and yet he reasoned: "It's blessed not to be able to feel the desolateness of that mound of the future, which shall be one's own and over which the elements shall sweep in their varying moods, as though we had never been."[21] Death always fascinated Dreiser as much as it did Emily Dickinson, and his reflective mood now enabled him to capture its peculiar moment. In describing an old man's death on a hospital bed, Dreiser noted that even while the man's eyes "were yet strained the glassiness crept into them, and the watching attendant closed the lids. Then the loosened jaw was bound shut, the arms folded and the body wrapt in rough linen." [22] Dreiser was not here acquiring an eye for detail, which the city editor would require, but was instead learning how to convey a sense of continuity, contrast, or paradox that such a topic as death suggested in his mind.

Because of his light assignments, Dreiser habitually crossed the Allegheny River into the suburbs and often made his way to the Carnegie Library, where he read Balzac for the first time—the novelist his fellow reporters and editors in St. Louis used to talk about. While reading the *Human Comedy*, Dreiser identified himself with Balzac's characters—Raphael, Rastignac, Bixiou, Bianchon. "With Raphael," he recalled, "I entered the gaming-house in the Palais Royal, looked despairingly down into the waters of the Seine from the Pont Royal, turned from it to the shop of the dealer in antiques, was ignored by the perfect young lady before the shop of the print-seller, attended the Taillefer banquet, suffered horrors over the shrinking skin" (*Book*, p. 411). Dreiser's own experience with the heartless woman was all too realistically portrayed. Balzac's *Wild Ass's Skin* contained Dreiser's own childhood's struggle with Catholicism, his shyness over women, and his yearning for sex and fame. Balzac's portrait of Raphael echoed his own dreams as he devoured the novelist's words: "How often, mute and motionless, have I not admired the lady of my dreams . . . Have we not all of us, more or less, believed in the reality of a thing because we wished it? . . . I myself would often be a general, nay, emperor . . ."[23]

In his own life Dreiser continued to search for a consoling woman.

Unlike St. Louis, Pittsburgh gave him an easy access to prostitutes, and now that he had more free time and was away from Jug, he began to seek out their services. The manuscript version of *A Book About Myself* lists three such women he patronized and describes one of them as ''irretrievably lost, of course—but not I, who shared this sensual traffic with her'' (*Book* ms., ch. 60, p. 9). Another one was a beautiful woman whom Dreiser admired, but she was heartless and absent-minded. Shocked when he discovered that she was a drug addict, Dreiser started a sermon on the evils of such a habit. Remaining totally indifferent, the prostitute said, ''Oh, Great God! Why do you talk? What do you know about life?'' Like Raphael in Balzac's novel, Dreiser indeed knew so little about life! Dreiser wrote:

> My primary lust vanished on the instant. I sensed a kind of misery and hopelessness here, and for once in my life did a decent thing. I had not much for myself, but I took out three dollars, about all I had, and laid it on the nearby mantel. ''That's all right,'' I said when she looked at me oddly. ''I'm glad to give you this. You don't want me tonight, anyhow,'' and I went out in the rain and so on home, thinking of her and the old house and the bare room, and the punctured arm—and I have so thought of her since, if once a thousand times. And I never saw her after.'' (ibid, ch. 60, pp. 10–11)

The experience, however, did not depress his spirits, for he was convinced more than ever that only the prostitute and the debauchee would ultimately know the secret of life.

His own life experience, his writing of feature stories, and his reading of Balzac now went on concurrently. Whenever he came upon a possible topic, he tried to relate it to his own life. It is quite possible, as Robert Elias has speculated, that Balzac's interpolations on the comings and goings of an ant made near the end of *The Wild Ass's Skin*[24] influenced Dreiser's feature on a fly. Dreiser years later recalled how he developed the story at that time:

> Being young and ambitious, and having just crawled out of a breeding-pit somewhere, he alighted on the nearest fence or windowsill, brushed his head and wings reflectively and meditated on the chances of a livelihood or a career. What would be open to a young and ambitious fly in a world all too crowded with flies? There were barns, of course, and kitchens and horses and cows and pigs, but these fields were overrun, and this was a sensitive and cleanly

and meditative fly. Flying about here and there to inspect the world, he encountered within a modest and respectable home a shiny pate which seemed to offer a rather polished field of effort and so on. (*Book*, p. 413)

Obviously there is a close analogy between this fly and Dreiser, who was then still a cub in the newspaper "field." Dreiser moodily reflected upon the forces in nature and society that controlled him. He looked at the contrast between the conditions of the rich and the poor; he analyzed the struggle between management and labor. Dreiser, like the fly, had wandered rather aimlessly, observing life in its diverse facets of existence and recording the impressions in his mind.

The story somehow won an unexpectedly friendly reception by the assistant city editor who was fond of anything sentimental, and Dreiser attempted another piece. This time he dealt with man's existence in nature. On the day he wrote a draft of this piece, a spring rain was falling with huge clouds and magnificent lightning. Describing the conditions of the city—dry, smoky, dirty—he explained how the sudden storm, like an answer to a prayer, soothed the city lying panting in the deadening heat. He depicted how suddenly the city changed— shutters clapping, papers flowing, office windows and doors being shut, signs swinging with squeaks, and people rushing to cover. He touched on the homes of the rich and poor, the office buildings and factories, the hospitals and jails which all underwent a change. And he even cited specific incidents and images of animals and men.[25] To Dreiser this sketch illustrated how all-encompassing the effect of natural forces was and how swiftly the conditions of men changed under them. He felt that with this writing he had somehow hit upon a vein of his own thought, but the feature did not please the moods of the city editors; apparently it lacked the humor and optimism of the fly story. Recognizing that his "more serious attempts were not so popular as the lighter and sillier things" (*Book*, p. 415), Dreiser nevertheless continued to search for ideas in his wanderings into the countryside and bizarre neighborhoods.

The lack of harmony between his and the editors' views of existence eventually led Dreiser to decide to leave Pittsburgh for New York. His first serious reading of Huxley, Tyndall, and Spencer toward the end of his stay in Pittsburgh reinforced this decision. "I was daily facing a round of duties," Dreiser says, "which now more than ever verified all that I had suspected and that these books proved'' (p. 458). Before this reading he had never denied the existence of Christ and the soundness of Christian morality. But now his reading of *Science and Hebrew Tradition* and *Science and Christian Tradition* convinced him that the Old and New Testaments were merely records of erroneous religious experiences. Moreover, Spencer's *First Principles* made him discover that ''all I deemed substantial—man's place in nature, his importance in the universe, this too, too solid earth, man's very identity save as an infinitesimal speck of energy or a 'suspended equation' drawn or blown here and there by larger forces in which he moved quite unconsciously as an atom—all questioned and dissolved into other and less understandable things'' (pp. 457–58). Up to this time Dreiser had always believed in human will. But now Spencer made him believe that ''one got nowhere, that there was no hereafter, that one lived and had his being because one had to, and that it was of no importance.'' Dreiser now called man's ideals, struggles, sorrows, and joys merely ''chemic compulsions,'' and declared that man was ''a mechanism, undevised and uncreated, and a badly and carelessly driven one at that'' (p. 458). Thus, Spencer's principle brought out an ominous formula to account for the unsolvable disorder and cruelty of life that Dreiser had long suspected.

Dreiser applied the formula to his journalism, and began to watch how the chemical and mechanical forces were operating in and around man. Suicides seemed inevitable and helpless because these victims had given up the fight against the forces with which Dreiser himself felt often compelled to come to terms. He now saw that a scandal always existed in the care of prisoners in some jails. He witnessed how ''the hope of pleasure'' and ''the fear of pain'' caused jailers to cheat prisoners, to feed them rotten meat, and to torture them into silence and submission. One must recall that Dreiser later theorized Hurstwood's deterioration in the novel by using the same principle of pleasure and pain suggested here. Dreiser also observed in Pittsburgh how politics interfered—the hope of pleasure again and the fear of pain on someone's part—and concealed the facts from the public. The existence of poverty and wealth—arrogant property owners with ''rights'' and subservient citizens without them—all seemed glaringly real.

Dreiser's first reaction to all this was that, because nature would not help man, man must help himself. But Dreiser came to believe that self-help was impossible since man was precisely a product of the same incidental and indifferent forces. Since the whole phenomenon was hopeless, he thought he might as well forget it and let these forces work freely over him. Yet, lacking the temperament, he could not do that either. "All I could do," he says, "was think, and since no paper such as I knew was interested in any of the things about which I was thinking, I was hopeless indeed" (p. 459). Finally in late November 1894 after only seven months, Dreiser's career in journalism in Pittsburgh came to an end. With $240 saved, Dreiser was at least relieved of the dismal scene in town, and looked forward to the charm of the yet unconquered literary capital—New York.

Spencer's impact on Dreiser in Pittsburgh influenced Dreiser's course of action in two ways. On the one hand, he gained more confidence in his view of existence now that it found support in the foremost philosopher of the time. Dreiser did not find an outlet for such ideas in Pittsburgh, but he hoped that he might be able to do so in New York. In July 1894, a few months before he finally settled in New York, Dreiser went there to see his brother Paul. Paul took time out to show him the city, especially calling his attention to the extravagance of the rich. "The people out West," Paul told him, "don't know yet what's going on, but the rich are getting control. They'll own the country pretty soon. A writer like you could make 'em see that. You ought to show up some of these things so they'd know" (*Book*, p. 449). Although he did not believe, as Paul did, that transcribing life would ever change it, Dreiser accepted the suggestion as a challenge. Paul's encouragement, coinciding with his own reading of Spencer, inspired Dreiser to test his belief in the biggest city he was ever to encounter in his life.

On the other hand, Dreiser was now emotionally reacting against the Spencerian determinism that would make man a victim of forces. He felt that, despite these forces, man should not resign himself to the haphazard law of nature; man could challenge the law. Dreiser now attempted to apply this attitude to his own career. The ambivalent feeling about Spencer's philosophy at this point of Dreiser's life was, in short, responsible for much of the inconsistent and often contradictory thinking that was later revealed in his fiction. In any case, it was Paul who prompted Dreiser to leave Pittsburgh. Paul, romantic and optimistic, insisted that if his brother came to New York he would be a success. In fact, Paul had more faith in Dreiser's talents and potentialities than Dreiser himself did.

About this time Dreiser was reading of an Indo-English newspaperman, Rudyard Kipling, who had been making a great success with his novels and short stories. There were a host of others whose reputations Dreiser was not yet familiar with: Jacob Riis, a Dane who had made a study of the tenements in New York; Abraham Cahan, a Jewish immigrant who became a novelist; Richard Harding Davis, an editor who later worked as a foreign correspondent, sending back his famous exotic and romantic tales; Hamlin Garland, a midwesterner who later undertook a literary career in the East; and Stephen Crane, a free-lance New York newspaperman who had already published *Maggie* at his own expense. Indeed, New York in the mid-nineties served as a hotbed for turning reporters into writers, changing the whole course of American literature. Dreiser thus arrived at the scene at an opportune time.

Even after having had some setbacks and disappointments in the newspaper work in New York, Dreiser was not discouraged. The fact that he had succeeded elsewhere gave Dreiser the notion that he should somehow succeed here. His mood then was not that of one who shunned a grueling contest; he was determined to stay in New York whatever happened to him. And yet he was constantly speculating on what he should do when his money was gone.

Dreiser's apprehension had an adequate cause. The country was in the midst of the worst depression it had ever known, and New York, the financial capital then as now, was suffering the severest blow. Dreiser now remembered Speaker Reed and his opposition to Coxey's army which had marched against the Capitol. But now the headlines flashed all kinds of unrest in the city and the nation. Almost every business in town was reported to be failing. The price of agricultural products dropped to a record low in 1894, and so did wages. Strikes, numerous throughout the country, became increasingly bitter. In the following winter, streetcar drivers in Brooklyn staged a violent strike for nearly two months (which Dreiser later used most effectively and accurately in *Sister Carrie*). The economic depression naturally took the heaviest toll among the city dwellers. Jacob Riis had earlier reported that fourteen thousand men looked for shelter each night on the Bowery. At one time in the theater district there were over two thousand men lined up for a charity loaf of bread.[26] A few years later Dreiser poignantly described such wretchedness in two of his free-lance articles,[27] as well as in dramatizing Hurstwood's final plight in the novel.

Before the unknown journalist, New York loomed large like an ocean—''so huge and powerful and terrible'' (*Book*, p. 437). There was something about the city that always made him seem useless and trivial despite his high spirits. He would look upon the throng swirling on Broadway that made the nineties ''gay.'' He walked, open-mouthed, up fashionable Fifth Avenue to Central Park. He then went down to Wall Street, seeing the vast mass of people swarming upward from that district and crossing the plaza to the Brooklyn Bridge. At the plaza, known as Printing House Square, Dreiser looked up the soaring buildings. The high newspaper offices in the buildings formed the nerve center of the metropolis and the country as it was then. To the northwest lay Henry James' Washington Square; to the northeast lay the Bowery, the most famous slum that European immigrants had ever made on the continent.

Across a small park stood City Hall, where Theodore Roosevelt as police commissioner was busy working with journalists for urban reform. Dreiser stood in the park and once again stared at the newspaper buildings:

> There was about these papers an air of assurance and righteousness and authority and superiority which overawed and frightened me. To work on the *Sun*, the *Herald*, the *World*! How many cubs, from how many angles of our national life, were constantly and hopefully eying them from the very same sidewalks or benches in City Hall Park, as the ultimate solution of all their literary, commercial, social, political problems and ambitions. The thousands of pipe-smoking collegians who have essayed the *Sun* alone, the scullion Danas, embryo Greeleys and Bennetts! (pp. 456–57)

Besides James Bennett's *Herald*, Charles Dana's *Sun*, and Joseph Pulitzer's *World*, New York boasted a host of other equally famous papers: the *Tribune* (for which Stephen Crane became a full-time reporter after leaving college for lack of money), the *Press* (which William Randolph Hearst was making the most sensational of all), the *Post*, the *News*, the *Journal*, and the *Times*.

Casting his eyes downward, Dreiser now saw on the benches of the park ''even in this gray, chill December weather, that large company of bums, loafers, tramps, idlers, the flotsam and jetsam of the great city's whirl and strife." "I presume I looked at them," Dreiser wrote uncertainly years later. But the contrast between the dejected scene and the high offices above—which a young "tramp" as Dreiser was then saw—clinched "the idea of *Hurstwood*" (pp. 463–64). The story of the Bowery bum was hardly a new idea. The economic depression, the unemployment, the cold winter of New York, the indifference of the rich—all created his pathetic plight. What was unique about this was that every literary man in New York at that time, including journalists, talked about it and some tried to write about it. The decade saw Riis' *How the Other Half Lives* (1890) with a statistical analysis, as well as Josiah Flynt's *Tramping with Tramps* (1899) with a humorous yet serious sociological point of view.

Novelists were also interested in the subject: Howells was said to have suggested to Garland that "he go down and do a study of this midnight bread distribution which the papers are making so much of."[28] Garland, in turn, passed this suggestion along to Crane—of whom Howells had the highest opinion among the newcomers. Several months before Dreiser's arrival in the city, Crane, taking Garland's hint, made a sketch called "An Experiment in Misery," first published in the *Press*. This version opens with Garland's suggestion of the experiment to Crane himself:

> Two men stood regarding a tramp.
> "I wonder how he feels," said one [Crane], reflectively. "I suppose he is homeless, friendless, and has, at the most, only a few cents in his pocket. And if this is so, I wonder how he feels."
> The other [Garland] being the elder, spoke with an air of authoritative wisdom. "You can tell nothing of it unless you are in that condition yourself. It is idle to speculate about it from this distance."
> "I suppose so," said the younger man, and then he added as from an inspiration: "I think I'll try it. Rags and tatters, you know, a couple of dimes, and hungry, too, if possible. Perhaps I could discover his point of view or something near it."
> "Well, you might," said the other, and from those words begins this voracious narrative of an experiment in misery. (*New York Press*, 22 April 1894, part 3, p. 2)

After the experiment in which Crane, disguised as a bum, and a companion he picked up in the Bowery—a real bum—spent a night together in a flophouse, Crane reported in the story:

The people of the street hurrying hither and thither made a blend of black figures changing yet frieze-like. They walked in their good clothes as upon important missions, giving no gaze to the two wanderers seated upon the benches. They expressed to the young man his infinite distance from all that he valued. Social position, comfort, and pleasures of living, were unconquerable kingdoms. He felt a sudden awe.

And in the background a multitude of buildings, of pitiless hues and sternly high, were to him emblematic of a nation forcing its regal head into the clouds, throwing no downward glances; in the sublimity of its aspirations ignoring the wretches who may flounder at its feet. The roar of the city in his ear was to him the confusion of strange tongues, babbling heedlessly; it was the clink of coin, the voice of the city's hopes which were to him no hopes. (*The Portable Stephen Crane*, p. 165)

Despite the conclusion that Crane as narrator in the story "confessed himself an outcast" (p. 165), the story itself implied that "the root of Bowery life is a sort of cowardice."[29]

Dreiser, who also dealt with Bowery life, would never make such an implication; he would conclude unequivocally that misery was caused by uncontrollable forces. Unlike Crane's bum, Hurstwood was obviously not a coward. More importantly, however, Dreiser in 1894—a tramp of sorts because he was unemployed and desperate—was not to become Crane's tramp who was "to willingly be knocked flat and accept the licking" (Beer, p. 140). Dreiser, now twenty-three, was conscious of his past accomplishment. Although the newspaper world in New York literally terrified him, he was not to succumb to it. Yet he could not reach the editor at any of the newspapers he tried; he was often turned away by office boys who chewed gum and indifferently uttered, "No vacancies." Winter was setting in and Dreiser was gravely worried about how to gain a foothold in this world. At four o'clock in the afternoon, tired of running from office to office, Dreiser would dubiously turn his steps northward along bustling Broadway to Fifteenth Street, walking and staring into the shops. His wanderings had something in common with those of Sister Carrie (*Book*, p. 464). Paul was on the road again and would not be of any help until spring. Dreiser was then living with Emma and her lover, L. A. Hopkins, who had earlier eloped from Chicago. Hopkins, like Hurstwood, was unsuccessful in New York. But Emma constantly encouraged Dreiser: "You're wondering how you're going to get along. I know how you are.

We're all that way. But you mustn't worry. Paul says you can write wonderfully'' (p. 464).

Like Carrie (who was to be based on Emma), Dreiser somehow succeeded in getting a job. The city editor of the *World*, then America's largest newspaper, thought the applicant promising and exploitable. On the staff of the influential paper with such well-known journalists as James Creelman, Reginald De Koven, and David Graham Phillips, Dreiser felt satisfied on the first day of work. But this newspaper office turned out to be a sweatshop, and the city editor a slave master. Dreiser, working "on space," was paid $7.50 a column—which ran twenty-one inches as he himself measured—for his articles. As he remembered, Dreiser on his first day wrote a one-inch column, earning "a total of one dollar and eighty-six cents, or a little less than street-sweepers and snow-shovelers were receiving" (p. 474). Though Dreiser was not aware of it, most beginners knew that working on space meant they were at the lowest level of journalists. The next step up was the regular news story. If successful, he could sign it as his own. Then came the feature story, which would reveal his own style and philosophy. And finally the magazine article would be assigned to those reporters who proved their skills in the Sunday editions.[30] Indeed, Dreiser in 1894 found his battle far from having been won.

Now as a lowly reporter in New York he was obsessed with the image of the survival of the fittest. Fifth Avenue was an agglomeration of wealth that would solve all earthly ills. In search of beauty, dignity, and security—the most wonderful and yet elusive in life—which the mansions there displayed, he looked at them, felt them, admired them, and yet he resented them, because he himself was poor and seeking. On the same day, in his reporting rounds, he would once again come across the East Side; the Bowery; the Brooklyn waterfront with another concentration of poverty, dirt, and despair. In Wall Street the struggle presented itself on another level. The district was "a sea of financial trickery and legerdemain" (p. 480), crowded with sharklike financiers. How could one's little arithmetic intelligence fare in such a world? As Dreiser saw it, nothing but chance and luck could save the average man from the bottom of the sea. The street was vibrant with graft, greed, niggardliness, ruthlessness for some, and hopelessness, defeat, despair for others. If one had a tip or a little skill, one would become a millionaire like Cowperwood he was later to create; but one might very easily be torn to bits, and there was no mercy.

The pattern was the same as he came to view his own work at the *World*. Dreiser was conscious of the fact that the owner of the *World*, Joseph Pulitzer, like himself, got started in St. Louis. "An upstart Jew" (p. 469), as Dreiser thought at the time, Pulitzer was typically aggressive and restless. Pulitzer's ambition to mold American journalism in his own image was making the editorial room a battleground for the survival of the fittest. The men working under him looked like tortured animals. All of them were either writing frantically at their desks or scurrying in and out. They were concerned only with themselves. If one asked them a question or favor, they would stare at the questioner as if he were an idiot or a thief. Dreiser was appalled at the disillusioning gap between the facade of such a moralizing paper as the *World* and the mercilessness of its internal struggle. Dreiser found himself a mere machine or private in an army to be thrown into any breach. He was expected to contribute the results wanted, or resign; even if he did contribute, he would not be rewarded. One day he ran into an acquaintance of his and inquired about the whereabouts of a former St. Louis city editor who had come to New York. The man replied, "Oh, Cliff? Didn't you hear? Why, he committed suicide down here in a West Street hotel." "What was the trouble?" Dreiser persisted. "Tired of the game, I guess," he went on. "He didn't get along down here as well as he had out there. I guess he felt that he was going downhill" (pp. 487–88), a simple truth foreshadowing the destiny of Hurstwood in New York.

Dreiser's duties as a city reporter brought him to the scenes that were so depressing that he felt unable to write anything worthwhile even if he wanted to. In Bellevue Hospital he would discover not only the murder of helpless welfare patients but the open graft involving the food, clothes, and medicine that were donated to the patients through charity. Many of the alcoholics and obstreperous patients were doped, beaten, or even killed, and sometimes they were operated upon by incompetent and indifferent interns. Those cured but unable to afford their fees were sent off into the streets for new struggles to survive. They were supposed to compete with the well and strong; but they would come back to their former wards because they were still physically weak, harassed by the often miserable weather, and penniless. The hospital officials, doctors, and nurses, staying in the warm rooms, chatting, smoking, and flirting, were least concerned about the world of miseries. Dreiser heard one of them say, "Oh, that old nut? ... I knew he couldn't live. We couldn't give him the necessary attention here. He didn't have any money, and there's too many here as it is..." (p. 496). The most startling thing Dreiser ever recalled there was a betting among two young surgeons and a nurse in the receiving ward. He saw them wager fifty cents and patiently wait to find out whether the next person brought in by the ambulance would arrive dead or alive. Other forms of corruption in the government disgusted him, and his old brooding would inevitably return. Brothels, for example, were not only winked at but openly preyed upon by the patrolman, the captain, the inspector, the reporter, and the politician. The scene he had witnessed in Pittsburgh repeated itself here, more frequently and on a larger scale.

Dreiser soon recognized that the corruption he saw in the city was also infecting the lives of his own relatives. Some of his close relatives were already living in New York when he arrived there. To help the Hopkinses, Dreiser came as a boarder on whose steady payment they were largely dependent. When Hopkins earlier came to New York with Emma, he somehow managed to connect himself with politics, and Dreiser heard then that they were living comfortably with their two young children. But since then the Lexow Committee's investigations into corruption, which cost Tammany the election, had also cost Hopkins his sinecure as an inspector. "Now, having fallen from his success," Dreiser wrote, "he was tractable" (p. 439). Like Hurstwood, Hopkins was now mentally and physically deteriorating. The kinds of horror stories that Emma had told Dreiser about Hopkins had to be deleted from *Sister Carrie* and later from *A Book About Myself*—that Hopkins pressed her to turn their flat into a brothel and could get protection and patrons from the police for only fifty dollars a month; and that Hopkins threatened to leave her and their children on the pretext that "he was wrongly mated" (*Book* ms., ch. 75, pp. 7–13).

Ironically, Hopkins' problem in New York helped Dreiser gain a better understanding of his own problem as his days with the *World* were numbered. From the beginning Dreiser was eager to expose the scenes of injustice and immorality he was facing on his rounds. But his own contact with them gave him, "a look so harsh and indifferent at times as to leave me a little numb" (*Book*, p. 487). Moreover, if he came up with a good story to report, he had to let his superiors handle it. One Saturday afternoon, after only two months on the job, when he brought in his notes on a missing girl whose body had ended up at the morgue, he was told by an assistant editor to give the facts to another man to write the story. Dreiser summoned all his courage and protested: "I don't see why I should always have to do this. I'm not a beginner in this game. I wrote stories, and big ones, before ever I came to this paper." "Maybe you did," retorted the editor, "but we have the feeling that you haven't proved to be of much use to us" (p. 501). Young and hard working though he was, Dreiser "confessed himself an outcast," as Crane's disguised tramp in "An Experiment in Misery" admitted (*The Portable Stephen Crane*, p. 165). For the first time in his life, Dreiser directly felt the indifferent and awesome and often disgusting forces of life described in Spencer. He now felt as helpless as the sick men thrown out of the city hospital. He voluntarily quit the *World* before he could be fired rather than prolonging his useless struggle there.

But Dreiser was not to give in to such a terror of life, as Mathewson and Cliff did by ending their own lives. He was determined to pursue a career as a writer of fiction (*Book*, p. 489). Such writers as George Cary Eggleston, Rudyard Kipling, Richard Harding Davis, and Stephen Crane had once been newspapermen in New York and some of them were new arrivals in the literary scene—and Dreiser thought he could emulate them. Yet, how to write fiction, he confessed, was far beyond his knowledge at that time, only four short years before the writing of his first novel. His readings in Spencer and Huxley, Dreiser now thought, "in no wise tended to clarify and impel my mind in the direction of fiction, or even philosophy" (p. 490). Desperately he began to examine the fiction and articles published in such prestigious magazines as *The Century*, *Scribner's*, and *Harper's*. He was dismayed to find a serious breach between his own vision and what was depicted in these articles. The coarse, vulgar, and cruel aspects of life he had seen in journalism were not dealt with in the magazines; every one of the writers saw life in a happy, roseate vein. In *Harper's*, for example, Howells, Charles Dudley Warner, Frank R. Stockton, and Mrs. Humphry Ward were all writing about nobility of character, sacrifice, and the greatness of ideas and joy in simple things. Dreiser was quick to note:

Love was almost invariably rewarded in these tales. Almost invariably one's dreams came true . . . . Most of these bits of fiction, delicately phrased, flowed so easily, with such an air of assurance, omniscience and condescension, that I was quite put out by my own lacks and defects. They seemed to deal with phases of sweetness and beauty and success and goodness such as I rarely encountered. There were so many tales of the old South reeking with a poetry which was poetry and little more (George W. Cable; Thomas Nelson Page). (*Book*, p. 490)

Even if Dreiser had imagined he could write a worthwhile story from his life, it would not only have shocked the magazine editors but it would never have been printed. To have a story published, one must depict only our best selves and arrive at a happy ending—the accepted editorial policies everyone knew but Dreiser. And if the world of the evil and sordid must be referred to, it must be done with the charm of shadow, not the nightmare reality of fact. "When I think of the literary and social snobbery and bosh of that day," he reflected, "its utter futility and profound faith in its own goodness, as opposed to facts of its own visible life, I have to smile" (p. 500). Dreiser's contempt for the literary establishment of the nineties indicates, not a sense of jealousy, but a simple belief that writing must deal with facts of life— those awesome forces that haunted him and at times, as he admitted, would paralyze his zest. Granted he lost a game of journalism, but he won a true vision for the novelist-to-be in the coming century.

Ev'ry Month

4 EAST 20 - STREET
NEW YORK

THEODORE DREISER.
EDITOR

N.Y. May 20th .97

My Dear Henry:—

Behold I sent you 13 etchings, registered and the same are to select from for a discourse on the Philosophy of Hope. Now also behold that the said discourse has not shown up and I am waiting and a letter cometh and sayeth "I am too busy to finish it—

Now, witness O Lord! I am a peaceable and God-fearing citizen and have always given half of that which I had to my suffering fellow citizen — neither have I robbed any body, but this is too much

On this and the following pages appears the letter Dreiser wrote as editor of *Ev'ry Month* on May 20, 1897, to Arthur Henry of Toledo, who had become a close friend and a contributor. Dreiser was later inspired to write *Sister Carrie* by Henry, to whom the novel was dedicated. *Courtesy of the University of Pennsylvania Library.*

surely I am not to be thus thrown down in my hour of great need.

Verily the said paintings are fine paintings and appropriate and do represent strange philosophic things both hopeful and unhopeful. Yea they are hot stuff. They are fine and good and while they are duplicated in some instances (Oh Lord!) they are still suitable for selection. Therefore that this delay should come upon me is exceeding hard. It is difficult to bear. Yea, it is too much.

Be it vouchsafed me, Oh I'oh (latest revised spelling) that these paintings be at once selected from

and commented on and that
I be fully informed so that if
others and more may be needed
I may go forth and secure them.
And be it also vouchsafed that
the same be returned intact
and complete, and that all things
relative to this article be fulfilled
to me. By the words of Beardslee
this much is coming to me,
that I may have somer
reward for my long devotion.
Selah!

Verily then choose, and observe
that No. 6796 is Hero and Leander
likewise known as the despair
of Hero. Know also that I am
looking for Tantalus and will

probably find some and also Napoleon at St. Helena, which pictureth great-disdain indeed. Eschew that; smile, and be merry.

I have thanks to add for your kind invitation O, Henry and return and regards to send to your excellent Helpmeet If nothing interfereth in the early future time (or rather late) I will hie me to your nook on the Maumee. I have also a cheek which if nothing interfereth I will retain - forever and ever. Be not - idle then, but - bestir yourself for I shall await your answer in great- fear and trembling I am. Truly Dreiser

Thanks on behalf of him Sinicism.

5 Editorial Work

Readers, and even scholars, of Dreiser have hardly noted the significance of the writing he did before he wrote *Sister Carrie*. The period between 1895 and 1899, between his withdrawal from newspaper work and his first attempt at writing fiction, is quite different from the rest of Dreiser's career. During this period Dreiser firmly made up his mind to become a novelist, and whatever move he made during these years he was anxiously waiting for an opportunity to write as uninhibitedly as possible. It is, however, puzzling that the parts of his life before he resigned from the newspaper profession were specifically and minutely described in his two autobiographies, *Dawn* and *A Book About Myself*, whereas Dreiser did not describe his life during these years in any single work.

Why Dreiser did not discuss his experiences as an editor and contributor of magazine articles during the four years before he wrote his first novel is not known. Some facts concerning his account of the period, however, are known. Toward the end of *A Book About Myself*, Dreiser tells us that he might relate this part of his career under such a title as "Literary Experiences." It is, further, interesting to note that this project was announced in certain editions of his novels and in some trade publications as being "in preparation" and "ready for the publisher." But the fact remains that no such book was ever published. In reply to John F. Huth, Jr.'s inquiry, Dreiser's secretary wrote in 1936: "As to a book on his literary experiences, Mr. Dreiser is very very uncertain as to whether and when it will appear."[1] Dreiser was extremely reticent about his activities during these years. It is, therefore, difficult to say whether he thought that these four years were unimportant for his career as a novelist or that he preferred to remain silent about this period in his life for some other reasons.

At any rate, in May 1895 Dreiser found himself unemployed and destitute. It was his brother Paul who again saved him. Paul was a partner in the newly formed music firm of Howley, Haviland & Company in New York. Years later Dreiser recalled his first visit to the firm's Twentieth Street office:

The space this firm occupied was merely one square room, twenty by twenty, and in one corner of this was placed the free "try-out" piano. In another, between two windows, two tables stood back to back, piled high with correspondence. A longer table was along one side of a wall and was filled with published music, which was being wrapped and shipped. On the walls were some wooden racks or bins containing "stock," the few songs thus far published. Although only a year old, this firm already had several songs which were beginning to attract attention, one of them entitled *On the Sidewalks of New York*. By the following summer this song was being sung and played all over the country and in England, an international "hit." This office, in this very busy center, cost them only twenty dollars a month, and their "overhead expeenses," as Howley pronounced it, were "juist nexta nothin'." I could see that my good brother was in competent hands for once.[2]

On his second visit to the office during the summer, while Paul was on the road, Dreiser discovered that Howley and Haviland were thinking of starting a magazine to promote their music sales. Frederick B. Haviland—still a shareholder of another firm, the Ditson Company, which published a popular magazine called *Musical Record*—argued that another magazine in the field would sell. Although Dreiser knew practically nothing about music then, he concurred with Haviland and proposed that they let him edit the magazine.

Dreiser got the job, which paid him ten dollars a week through the summer while preparing the first issue, and fifteen dollars a week thereafter. The salary was very low, he felt, but it rescued him from destitution. Dreiser named the magazine *Ev'ry Month*,[3] and its first issue appeared on 1 October 1895 with a description on the cover, "Edited and Arranged by Theodore Dreiser." Not only was Dreiser proud but he thrived on the work at the office in the midst of a vaudevillian trying out a new song with piano as vividly described in his free-lance article "Whence the Song."

As his editing proceeded, however, Dreiser felt restricted by the publishers. When Arthur Henry asked him in the fall of 1897 whether he was succeeding as editor, he complained: "I am drawing a good salary. The things I am able to get the boss to publish that I believe in are very few. The rest must tickle the vanity or cater to the foibles and prejudices of readers. From my standpoint, I am not succeeding."[4] Evidently he had a disagreement with the publishers on the magazine's editorial policy, and as a result, he was forced to resign.[5] During the two short years as editor of the magazine Dreiser nonetheless achieved a sense of great responsibility as well as having opportunities to visit studios and other editorial offices in New York.

After he completed the issue of *Ev'ry Month* for September 1897, Dreiser worked as a free-lance magazine writer. Between November 1897 and the fall of 1899, when he started to write *Sister Carrie*, Dreiser published more than a hundred articles and poems, chiefly the former, which appeared in such periodicals as *Harper's, Cosmopolitan, Metropolitan, Munsey's, Ainslee's, Demorest's, Success, Truth, Puritan,* and *New Voice*. Unfortunately, Dreiser in his free-lance writing did not succeed in acquiring as much freedom of expression as he had wanted and expected. In fact, most of his articles, as discussed in the next chapter, dealt with factual information on successful men and women in various fields, historic places, factories, workers, and the poor and the wretched. And in his generalizations he was not so profound as in the reflections he presented in *Ev'ry Month*.

Both in editing *Ev'ry Month* and in writing free-lance articles Dreiser, nonetheless, enjoyed his work, as compared to his previous struggles as a newspaper reporter. The reasons for his decision to leave newspaper work are given in *A Book About Myself*, published twenty-five years later. But his earliest statement concerning his newspaper experience is found in the issue of *Ev'ry Month* for March 1897. At that time he wrote:

> Into what channel do you suppose such journalism as now prevails turns the minds of such innocents...? How quickly must bright conceptions of undefiled progress fade in the light of the actual experiences which young men and women are compelled to encounter in order to build up the great papers of to-day? The stories published, the plots and crimes unravelled, the functions most largely described—how do these operate upon and affect the minds engaged in the work of gathering the details? Surely, it cannot be said that they work the mind's advantage.[6]

In newspaper writing Dreiser would insert occasionally the idea that the world about him was not as roseate as his newspaper editors thought it was. But in his magazine articles he wrote as forcefully as he wished of the ideas that he had built up for many years. It is here that he found an outlet for writing on political, social, economic, and literary subjects. We can also discover in these writings a clearer definition of his philosophy of life, a vacillation between his pessimistic and optimistic attitudes toward man's life, and finally a glimpse of his fundamental theory of fiction.

In the fall of 1895, at the beginning of his magazine period, Dreiser achieved some sort of independence as a journalist, but he was greatly apprehensive about the responsibilities that went with editing an entire magazine by himself. He was only twenty-four and, unlike many of his former newspaper colleagues, he had never been published in a magazine. But now, not only was he going to learn how to express himself in a journal of his own but he had to learn from scratch how to solicit material from others and, above all, to put it together for others to enjoy reading. The task before him was indeed challenging, for none of the three partners had ever been responsible for administering a business of this kind.

Howley and Haviland, however, were not as ambitious as the editor since they wanted only to increase the sales of their music. The rise in circulation of *Ev'ry Month* to sixty-five thousand in two years[7] thus surprised everyone involved, including Dreiser. He was to resign from the editorship of the magazine at the height of its success, but the knowledge and experience he acquired during this period were to make a great impact on his future career. For during the next two years before writing *Sister Carrie*, Dreiser became one of the most prolific magazine writers ever known in America in that period. And, most importantly, during the suppression of his first novel, Dreiser resumed his editorial work, first with Hampton's *Broadway Magazine*, and eventually with the Butterick publications for women.

From the beginning of its publication, *Ev'ry Month* seemed to have scored a note that was quite different from the one that was originally intended by its publishers. The magazine was aimed at a general audience, particularly the whole family, but the most avid reader in the nineties was the woman. As Frank Luther Mott points out in *A History of American Magazines: 1885–1905*, there was a large audience for "women's magazines at some time or another in this period. Any hustling publisher could start such a journal 'on a shoestring'; he could get cheap literary help to write and clip miscellany for the household . . . ."[8] Dreiser thus followed suit. Because the magazine's major subject matter was music, the first issue of *Ev'ry Month* was subtitled "An Illustrated Magazine of Popular Music and Literature." But the April 1896 issue changed the subtitle to "An Illustrated Magazine of Literature and Popular Music," with a proper emphasis on literature since that subject increasingly attracted the female audience. Finally, in July 1896 *Ev'ry Month* was subtitled "The Woman's Magazine of Literature and Music," but Dreiser apparently was not permitted to keep the title for long. In June 1897, a few months before his resignation, *Ev'ry Month* merely carried the labels "Music" and "Literature" along with the contents on its cover.

During his editorship Dreiser tried his best to make the magazine his own. One of the essential ingredients of a popular magazine in the nineties was the use of colorful illustrations. Dreiser's interest in art and the artist—strongly reflected not only in his free-lance articles but also in his novels—goes back to his editorial days with *Ev'ry Month* in the winter of 1895. At that time, looking for striking illustrations of city life for the Christmas issue of the magazine, Dreiser paid a visit to the studio of a popular artist named William Louis Sonntag, Jr.[9] Dreiser had earlier been attracted to Sonntag not only by reputation but by his colored drawings depicting night scenes of New York that appeared in one of the Sunday newspapers. These pictures, in Dreiser's recollection, "represented the spectacular scenes which the citizen and the stranger most delight in—Madison Square in a drizzle; the Bowery lighted by a thousand lamps and crowded with 'L' and surface cars; Sixth Avenue looking north from Fourteenth Street."[10] Dreiser's interest in this artist—a member of the Ashcan School noted for street scenes—is demonstrated by Dreiser's later drawing of Eugene Witla in the novel *The "Genius"*. The characterization of Dreiser's hero in that novel derives as much from Sonntag as from Dreiser's friend Everett Shinn, another Ashcan School painter. In any event, in the mid-nineties Sonntag's reputation outweighed Dreiser's. Instead of getting realistic pictures from Sonntag, Dreiser received only the romantic ones—a serious looking woman with beautiful hair flowing on the one side of the page, and a pretty fur-coated girl caught in a snowstorm.

Dreiser also learned a great deal about the business end of the project. Howley and Haviland were eager to advertise their new songs, whereas Dreiser sought to bring in the needed revenue by putting advertisements for such items as Pears' Soup, Sapolio, bicycles, and furniture. In order to purchase illustrations cheaply, the magazine often carried a feature article that described the artist and his studio. The January 1897 issue thus began Authur Hoeber's series, "American Women in Art," which introduced new talents with illustrations. In the free-lance period following his editorial work, Dreiser wrote over twenty-five articles on various American painters and sculptors, an experience to which his earlier training with *Ev'ry Month* clearly bore fruit. As a drama critic Dreiser printed photographs of scenes from plays he was reviewing for *Ev'ry Month*. He also illustrated the various roles of his favorite actors through photographs voluntarily submitted to the magazine.

Politically, too, Dreiser was an active commentator. The "gay" nineties derived its name from the flourishing life-styles of the city, but the spirit of the decade suffered from the country's worst economic depression in the century. In 1896, Dreiser came to support the Populist demand for "free silver." McKinley and gold won the election over Bryan and silver, but Bryan was to remain Dreiser's hero for years to come. In the rivalry between Joseph Pulitzer's *World* and William Randolph Hearst's *Journal* over R.F. Outcault, creator of the Yellow Kid, Dreiser quickly sided with the *Journal* as if to avenge the *World*, which had wronged him the year before when he was on its staff. Echoing the *Journal*'s propaganda about Spanish atrocities in Cuba, Dreiser as editor of *Ev'ry Month* also urged the United States' intervention in Cuba.

The American 1890s witnessed an unprecedented involvement of journalism with politics and vice versa, and Dreiser's *Ev'ry Month*, though a minor periodical, did not remain aloof. Even after the *Journal* took away Outcault from the *World*, his reputation continued to soar. Dreiser, taking advantage of Outcault's change of position, was now able to solicit from him some photographs and newly drawn pictures of the famous Kid for *Ev'ry Month*. Dreiser also successfully approached the *Journal*'s political cartoonist Homer C. Davenport as indicated by a highly flattering feature article on Davenport that appeared in *Ev'ry Month*. Davenport, like Dreiser, was a product of the West, and no one in his day surpassed Davenport in satirizing the gentility of the eastern establishment. Impressed by the man's character and principle, a year later Dreiser wrote a long free-lance piece on Davenport, "A Great American Caricaturist." "His caricatures of Hanna, McKinley, Reed and Croker," Dreiser commented, "are perhaps better known by now than the circulated photos of these men." More important, Dreiser learned that a cartoonist such as Davenport was not merely a political medium; "I have convictions," Davenport told Dreiser, "and I wouldn't deride a man, unless I felt that there was cause for it." [11]

If *Ev'ry Month* had been sensitive only to the social and political climate of the decade, it would not have been a significant record of the future novelist. But Dreiser obviously persuaded Howley and Haviland to make *Ev'ry Month* as much a literary and intellectual journal as possible. With a limited budget, however, the magazine could not hire established writers; thus much of the literary content, at least in the beginning, came from Dreiser's own pen. Interestingly enough, he assumed various pen names that appeared in the same issue. "The Prophet," the magazine's philosopher who commented on things social and cultural, started each issue with his "Review of the Month." "Edward Al," [12] which was also one of Dreiser's pseudonyms in free-lance writing, was the magazine's resident critic who reviewed books and contributed his commentary in a column entitled "The Literary Shower." "S.J. White"—deriving from his future wife Sara Osborne White—wrote a sentimental column called "We Others" and informed the readers on forthcoming literary events in the city. "Th. D." was the drama critic; the initial was significant because though Dreiser was a newspaperman in St. Louis, he seriously thought about becoming a playwright. Finally, "Theodore Dreiser" appeared at least twice during his editorship, with a short story and a poem of his own.

The survival of a poorly funded monthly must be the result of Dreiser's abilities to solicit material without costing the magazine a great deal of money. One who helped out an old friend by contributing short stories and poems with his own illustrations was Dreiser's fellow journalist in St. Louis—Peter McCord. As Dreiser recalls in *A Book About Myself*, McCord was his first intellectual mentor who not only provided him with knowledge in ancient history and culture but also introduced him to the works of Huxley, Darwin, and Taine. Richard Wood, another close friend of Dreiser's in St. Louis, was, like McCord, a staff artist for the *Globe-Democrat*. Wood was known then as a self-styled aesthete and a bohemian, and he now sent Dreiser romantic tales and verse. One of the best-known journalists in St. Louis at that time was William Marion Reedy. Dreiser may have been acquainted with Reedy in St. Louis since he was a friend of Joseph McCullagh, Dreiser's editor on the *Globe-Democrat*, but it was years later when they came to know each other as writers. As editor of *Ev'ry Month*, Dreiser somehow obtained permission to reprint Reedy's writings, among them an obituary of McCullagh in the *Sunday Mirror* and a poem on Eugene Field in the *Globe-Democrat*.[13]

Once Dreiser's efforts became known, some noted journalists in New York began to respond to his call for contributions. With new revenue coming in from the early issues of the magazine, he was now able to pay for more prestigious contents. George C. Jenks, a free-lance journalist and critic, wrote book reviews for *Ev'ry Month*. Richard Duffy, editor of a major popular journal, *Ainslee's*, contributed a story for the May 1896 issue. After Dreiser left *Ev'ry Month*, he was hired as a consultant on *Ainslee's* and, between 1898 and 1902, he wrote nearly thirty essays, short stories, and poems for that magazine. There was also Gilson Willets, who was in Pittsburgh when Dreiser was on the staff of the *Dispatch*. Dreiser and Willets may not have known each other then but both moved to New York at about the same time. Willets provided Dreiser with his fiction and, as a resident writer on *Ev'ry Month*, Willets wrote an article, "The Havemeyers at Home."

In September 1896, just a year after the magazine's birth, Stephen Crane's "A Mystery of Heroism" (later included in *The Little Regiment*) was first published in *Ev'ry Month*. By that time Crane had become one of the most famous and indeed controversial journalists-turned-novelist in America with his *Maggie* (1893) and *The Red Badge of Courage* (1895). Crane's story was followed by Madeline S. Bridges' "An Irish Love Story," Grant Allen's "Love's Old Dream," Robert Barr's "An Errand of Mercy," Gilbert Parker's "Mathurin," Bret Harte's "A Night in the Divide," and Morgan Robertson's "Where Greek Met Greek." Using such stories, Dreiser was obviously following the public taste for sentimentalism that was prevalent during America's *fin de siècle*.

Ev'ry Month, unlike Dreiser's newspaper experience, was an apprenticeship uniquely tied to his literary career. As a newspaperman a few years earlier, he learned the essential lessons of how to observe; as an editor he learned how to express himself not only to his own satisfaction but to the satisfaction of others eager for information as well as for entertainment. *Ev'ry Month* was primarily a music magazine; in fact, Dreiser efficiently included in each issue new songs that were handed down by Howley, Haviland, and his brother Paul. Among these songs,

"On the Banks of the Wabash, Far Away" with part of the lyrics written by Dreiser became the official state song of Indiana, as mentioned earlier.

Above anything else, editing *Ev'ry Month* turned out to be an indispensable experience for developing his latent philosophy of life. For that reason, an examination of his column called "Reflections," which appeared in almost every issue of the magazine during his editorship, sheds important light on Dreiser's fiction. When Dreiser first read Herbert Spencer, as he related later, Spencer's ideas on man's relationship to nature "quite blew [him], intellectually, to bits" (*Book*, p. 457). This was a lasting impression that remained deep in Dreiser's mind during the subsequent years preceding his creative writing. And it is safe to suppose that this impression provided the philosophy of determinism that would influence Dreiser's novels throughout almost his entire career.

Three years after the original impact from Spencer, Dreiser often showed this influence. Thus, he wrote in praise of Spencer:

> . . .He is a great father of knowledge, and his word is to be spread before all; but at present many are too young to understand him, and many more too idle to heed. But the young and the truants will all gather about his teachings after a while, and then the world will be vastly better.

. . . .

> His is generalship of the mind—the great captaincy of learning and literature, the field-marshalship of the forces of reason. . . . He learned where the sands are, and where the stars, and where the types and tribes and races. By long and patient study he learned of the nations, their lives and deeds, and of the men of nations, and of the deeds and accomplishments of men. Through the long ages he traced the progress of this circular earth of ours, and found where it came from and to where it is going, and all that which sunlight has done and is doing for it. . . . Everything submitted to him; each province of knowledge took its subordinate place in his empire of the mind; everything fell into his order and scheme, and he has now proceeded to rule in peace.

. . . .

> . . .Spencer has pointed the history of the past—it is he who has defined our puny place in the world and the universe; it is he who has bound our minds together into one empire, and pointed the path along which progress is easiest and best. All life has been comprehended

best by him. He has explained the value of the things that are, and the
purposes for which they are intended. Rain, sunlight, the seasons;
charity, generosity, virtue,—all these are set down in their true order,
and having established the empire of mind, he invites you, as subjects, to acquaint yourselves with its laws. They are unalterable laws,
these of the empire . . . . (*Ev'ry Month* 3, No. 5 [1 February 1897]:
3–4)

Spencer could be compared to Napoleon, according to Dreiser, in the
sense that, as Napoleon studied the military map of Europe, so Spencer
examined the intellectual map of the world. As Cyrus united Persia, so
Spencer united the world. When Cyrus united Persia, it was years
before the union was known by all. In the same way, Dreiser maintained, Spencer united the world of knowledge, and his pupils were
going forth into far-reaching regions for the proclamation of Spencer's
laws and his fame. Time must pass before Spencer's doctrine would
completely be known and all mankind would conform to the universal
laws.

Dreiser's mission as a faithful disciple of Spencer can be seen in his
free-lance article in the *Metropolitan Magazine* in 1898. In this article
Dreiser noted that the uninformed generally believed that the United
States was taking but moderate interest in scientific discoveries. But
pointing out the expeditions conducted under the auspices of New
York's American Museum of Natural History, Dreiser stated his confidence that America was one of the foremost among the nations interested in the advancement of science. In a quarry located in Wyom-
ing the expeditions made an unexpected discovery of two reptile skeletons. Dreiser expressed the hope that, when the collections were completed, one could learn a great deal about the physical species of man
as well as man's relation to nature. Dreiser wrote:

The object of the Museum is to make plain the evolutionary idea, so
that every one may see the order in which animals have developed . . . . From these cases [containing skeletons] the student may
learn of the endless ages that have already gone by, the enormous
monsters that appeared and disappeared with succeeding cycles.
Beginning with the perissodactyls, the order of evolution is shown,
step by step, by skeletons of animals with immense scientific
names, until at some distance in the chain the early rhinoceros is
shown, and still later in the chain the early form of the horse.[14]

As late as June 1900, Dreiser was interested in the evolutionary theory as evidenced by another article of his entitled "The Descent of the Horse." [15]

From the reference to the change in animals through time and environment, Dreiser called his readers' attention to the condition of man. To Darwin and his spokesmen, Spencer and Huxley, man was as susceptible as animals to forces in the environment. Dreiser, moreover, believed that man was essentially a solitary animal struggling to survive in a world controlled by cold impersonality. What made Dreiser wonder, first of all, was those impersonal and indifferent forces in nature. He thought about Tyndall, who, after being for many years in awe of the Alps, upon which time seemed to have no effect, observed how torn and deprived the Matterhorn was and came to realize how strong the influence of natural forces was, even on inanimate objects. "At St. Louis," said Dreiser, "the wind rises, rain and hail sweep onward, and a few hundred are lacerated beneath the ruins of their habitations, whereon the sun rises on the morrow and shines, and in life there is no difference." In conclusion, Dreiser was convinced that man is the sport of nature and a necessary yet worthless dust in the scheme of nature. At any moment man may be completely obliterated so that "some element or force may complete its mission unimpeded" (*Ev'ry Month* 2, No. 6 [1 September 1896]: 5).

On the basis of such deterministic views, there was absolutely no room left for orthodox religious feelings. Dreiser thus pointed out that, because of presumptuous power and unjustifiable pride, men have protected themselves against the fact that they were not particularly considered in the great scheme of nature and have believed that their power must be guaranteed and specifically guarded by a higher power. In reality, Dreiser asserted, men could be swept to nothingness by simple wind or water, and could be destroyed by the fall of a stone or annihilated by contagious diseases. These phenomena, he believed, have ever proved repugnant to these men, and "they have built up a faith that takes account of them and their deeds, and makes of them agents instead of mere clods in the scheme of the universe" (ibid., 6).

Conscious of the natural conditioning of man, Dreiser became inevitably aware of the social conditioning of individuals and ultimately of the historical complexities that make understandable the uniqueness of each individual experience in American society. It is quite possible that

Dreiser at this time, despite his predilection for natural law, became more interested in a world of social and historical individuals. Indeed, the America described by Dreiser in *Sister Carrie* and *Jennie Gerhardt* may be primarily this world of social and historical individuals. Thus, Dreiser at this time expressed his feeling that "man seems not only the sport of nature, but of his fellowmen" (ibid., 5). Dreiser asked:

> Do you not know that human beings are innately greedy—avaricious? Do you not know that they dream of fine clothes and fine houses and of rolling about luxuriously in carriages while others beg along their pathway? Will you not realize that some will stoop to anything for this, will lie, will steal, yes murder, to make this dream come true? Are you unaware that the strongest are sore tempted by money and offers of place and name, and will you then let the affairs of your country fall into the hands of those who will not stop at aught to gain their shameless ends? (ibid., 2)

Dreiser would hasten to point out that our society has the influential charitable organizations distributing aid to the needy, the police courts consigning the oppressed to the workhouse and the weak to the hospital, and the general public helping others without any pharisaical discrimination. And yet the unfit were bound to be the castaways, whereas the fit survived the most severe conditions. The fit creature was either fit to make money, or to beg it, or to steal. Whatever his methods, the fit person was fit to gain what he needed and to keep himself intact. "It is the fit creature," wrote Dreiser,

> who manipulates bank, mining, or general market stock, and puts the acquired wealth between himself and possible destitution, and equally is it the fit creature who steals when hunger threatens, and who employs weapons and becomes a noiseless footpad when anything is to be gained and the discomfort of poverty is to be set aside. Both classes are not "fit" in the same degree, but in the theory of their fitness to survive there is no flaw. (*Ev'ry Month* 3, No. 5 [1 February 1897]: 4)

The fit somehow operated in keeping body and soul together; they would not hesitate and retreat, because hesitancy and retreating caused bodily injury. They would complete their action, whether it was good or evil, and by doing good or evil they survived, the result that proved their fitness.

As a prime example of the unfit, Dreiser chose a news article that disclosed the shocking arrest of a native of West Indies named William Wilson. The story concerns a weak, short man, four feet, three inches tall, who was arrested by the police one night and brought into a court, charged with vagrancy. Neighborhood citizens had noticed that the arrested man spent his night rummaging in garbage cans and devouring parts of discarded food. When a policeman approached him, the man slunk away like a hunted animal, staggered and fell against a post and hurt his head. Wilson's hair was found to be eighteen inches long, and his beard had not been shaved for so long that his face could hardly be seen. He wore no shirt and was wrapped in a torn coat and a pair of ragged trousers. A pair of soles that had once been attached to shoes were now tied to his feet. At the police station Wilson complained that, because he was unable to get work or aid, he was compelled to go to the garbage cans in attempting to stave off starvation. Wilson was later thrown into the workhouse (*Ev'ry Month* 3, No. 1 [1 October 1896]: 7).

A spectacle projecting "the survival of the fittest" was also found in the economic world. Accusing the trust combine of being selfish and heartless and harmful to individuals, Dreiser saw it as a sign of economic struggle for money and power. It was, however, admitted that the trust operated according to the very law and nature of commerce. Dreiser's explanation was that, if two or more men combined their faculties and capital in one business, incorporating two or more businesses in one trust would naturally prove more effective. The purpose in each case was exactly the same. All desired money; all desired power; all desired superiority over others. Here again Dreiser cited the principle of life, in which the higher form should live by the death of the lower (*Ev'ry Month* 3, No. 6 [1 March 1897]: 3).

☆ ☆ ☆ ☆

Although Dreiser accepted the law that the strong prosper at the expense of the weak, he was not so completely satisfied with the universality and morality of the law for man as might be expected. Indeed, the reason why Dreiser's outlook on man's life in society was not so pessimistic as many critics maintain can be found in many of the statements he made during this period. In the case of forming the trust, Dreiser readily subscribed to the principle that the higher form of life outlives the lower, and he observed that "the trust is laying claim to be the higher.'' But if ''it is not,'' Dreiser reasoned, ''there are the oppressed free to defend themselves; and if they do not, they merely admit their degradation. If they do, the trust, and those who stand sponsor for it, must be crushed in the struggle. Such a culmination will prove how wrong is the trust, and how right are the many in advocating kindness, generosity, love and mercy'' (ibid., 3).

Such human qualities as love and friendship, according to Dreiser, must be considered separately from the law of the survival of the fittest. Dreiser, as editor of a national magazine, called his readers' attention to the evil bred by the competitive life in American society. ''No one denies,'' said Dreiser, ''that it was the speculative craze—the restless desire to 'turn a dollar' rapidly,'' a statement reminiscent of Mark Twain's satire on Colonel Sellers in *The Gilded Age* some twenty years earlier. Dreiser cited as an example the case of a man in New York who tried to make money through insurance by burning the homes of others. This criminal was totally unaware that what he did could be done to his own home, his wife, and his children. He only sought money—a better home, fine clothes and food, and a higher station in society. The desire for money was his sole purpose in life, and ''he expected money to bring him friends, and comfort, and peace, as so many others vainly expect it.'' The major trouble in American society, Dreiser thought, stemmed from the fact that almost everybody believed that man's happiness is purchasable. The financier might have mansions, carriages, servants, and numerous visitors, but he had no friends. ''They are higher up,'' Dreiser wrote, ''and are allured by the heart alone. He who has given that to his fortune has none for his fellows, and that is often the cost of riches.'' Dreiser discovered, as any sensible observer would, that America's commercial success was a paradoxical comment on its moral failure (*Ev'ry Month* 3, No. 5 [1 February 1897]: 2).

In bringing up such an instance Dreiser showed his intention of being a critic of American society. The writer, he believed, ought to study national defects, and it is especially his duty to detect the failings in society that were inconspicuous at present but sure to become paramount issues later. ''Rather,'' Dreiser maintained, ''it is a time when all the evils that have sprung up in the last half century of American life should be clearly in view so that each one, realizing that a score of great, distinct questions are awaiting their turn at the ballot, might be all the more determined to despatch whatever problem now confronts him, in order that all others may come up as soon as possible for examination and solution'' (*Ev'ry Month* 3, No. 2 [1 November 1896]: 2).

One of the most persistent evils Dreiser saw in his newspaper days and later as editor and free-lance writer was the centralization of wealth and its result—the arrogance of the rich and the misery of the poor. He observed that in New York, for example, the wealth of a few people was far greater than that of all the rest of the people combined. He often wondered whether "life forms really trend upward and onward, or downward toward mystic annihilation, or merely around and around in a vast, unsatisfactory circle as some of our philosophers see it." This question could never be answered, Dreiser thought, unless education was freely extended to the children of the poor. Those who would refuse to aid education were those who were neglecting to satisfy the instinctive cry for help coming from millions of people now living, as well as from the endless billions of men and women who were yet to be born in America. Those who opposed aid for education, either from ignorance or greed, or what was worse, by connivance, were, in Dreiser's eyes, "criminals of the deepest dye, defying both man and nature and plundering God by taking from man a portion of that eternal right to rise with which his God has so graciously endowed him." And, to Dreiser, these men shall eventually fail. This concentration of wealth was the curse of every civilization. He reminded his readers of the building of huge temples to Baal and Venus, where every right was denied except for the sword and the lash to the savage. Vast palaces had been built for kings and queens, while shelter and bread had been denied to the serfs. "To-day," declared Dreiser, "it shows itself in million dollar state capitols, in billion dollar coast defences, in million dollar forts and armories, palaces and libraries, while to the poor are denied a few pitiful schools" (ibid., 4).

Dreiser's unfailing sympathy for the underprivileged and oppressed can invariably be recognized in the articles he wrote during this period. One night he watched a luxurious function called the Bradley-Martin Ball. Those who were not lucky enough to attend the ball appeared to Dreiser like the swarm of insects crawling in the shadow of the pavements while other insects, unaccountably fluttering in the magnificent glow, were flying around the electric lamps. The unlucky ones might have wondered why their wings were not as active as those of the lucky and why they were excluded from the circle of light, and why they were thus made to crawl and were trampled on. Dreiser's compassion was naturally for those who, watching the throng of gay carriages and hearing the swish of expensive garments and the sound of music, felt the pangs of hunger inside. The poor and the unlucky would wonder by what peculiar arrangement they were thus placed in the world—without and sad instead of within and happy (*Ev'ry Month* 3, No. 6 [1 March 1897]: 2).

The inequality existing in court trials also became a topic of concern for Dreiser, and indeed disgusted him. As far as penal servitude was concerned, there was no difference between a man who had stolen a pocketbook or a watch and a man who had embezzled from the state a sum of $100,000 or $1,000,000. In this connection Dreiser cited as evidence the case of the eight "boodlers" who had defalcated with several million dollars from the treasury of Cook County, Illinois, served only two years in prison, and later opened a gilded resort of vice on Chicago's Clark Street (*Ev'ry Month* 3, No. 2 [1 November 1896]: 2–3). In many of the court proceedings Dreiser noticed that the accused were confident of the prevalence of right only when they possessed money with which to defend it, whereas their submission to evident wrong was aggravated by the lack of money.

For these evils in society, however, Dreiser never failed to seek means of amelioration. And his constant suggestions for improvement were based on his optimistic attitude concerning the forces in nature and society that would often depress man. As editor of *Ev'ry Month*, Dreiser thus looked for stories in which the theme would reflect "a sunset glow" which enlightened "the bleakness of the dreary moorland." (*Ev'ry Month* 2, No. 6 [1 September 1896]: 3). He furthermore solicited from his friend Arthur Henry essays titled "The Philosophy of Hope" and "The Good Laugh" in order to reinforce his own optimistic view. Later this optimism could also be detected in his own writing as a novelist. Dreiser would have wanted his readers to realize that Sister Carrie is saved because she is hopeful. Indeed, it now seems easier for us to understand his implication in the novel that, whereas Hurstwood falls because of disintegration in the mind, Carrie rises because of hope as a basis for her actions.

In his own editorials, too, Dreiser expressed man's hope for progress:

> In conclusion, let it be accepted that man should be hopeful, and at the same time be ready and willing to do battle for his hopes. For that future which pictures itself to his mind as one of peace after sorrow, and justice after retribution and restitution, let him be ever ready to labor . . . . Through affairs of to-day, he would look as through a field of battle to the fort beyond. Through the mass of arguments and

re-statements of conditions, he should look to the principals [sic] and conditions that never change, and by them arrange his conduct. (ibid., 7)

Granted, men always toiled and progressed toward nothing and thus became wearisome with their worries. But he reasoned that, as it is, "we are happy in having something which we cannot know, joyous in being subject to greater laws" (*Ev'ry Month* 3, No. 2: 7). He reminded his readers of the unity in nature—the wide and blue sky, the fair and green fields, the gentle and restful hillsides, the silvery and soothing streams. Should we ask "why" of every piece of evidence of supervision in the universe? Should we depress ourselves by being dissatisfied because our insight into all was impossible, let alone our control over it?

That would be unreasonable to Dreiser, because we would deprive ourselves of "the one sustainer in all trials, faith." Faith has given us all that is necessary to unfold the mysteries, but—he would hasten to point out—not the greatest of all the mysteries. Instead he urged that we should "unravel the tangled affairs of men first, and make them smooth. . . . We will be concerned with making things good, and with living so that things shall be better. . . . there will be naught but hope, unfaltering trust and peace" (ibid., 7). One of the ways in which things could be made good was through the advancement of science and technology. Through science, he thought, man could control some of the natural forces, and "as an earnest part of [them] man is safe" (*Ev'ry Month* 2, No. 6: 7). As an example, he considered electricity, which would help decipher the mystery of the universe by exploring "the outer darkness and [traversing] the spaces which now seem so immeasurable" (ibid., 7).[16] In a later article, giving a detailed account of a gun factory, Dreiser concluded that nature seemed to mock this destructive design for which the factory existed. But on second thought, Dreiser said, "it is the enemy of war, in that the motive is to make implements wherewith to compel peace." In this view the endless production of guns did not bode ill; to Dreiser, it was even satisfying in that "war by them is made so swift and decisive, that after a while there may be no longer need of war."[17] "The world," Dreiser quoted a western journal as saying, " is not going downward to ruin, as the writer would have us believe. Everything in this splendid country has an upward trend, despite the wail of the cynics." Instead Dreiser found "a firm and undisturbed faith in nature, and in men true to nature, despite the decay of a few of the species, or schools, or tribes, of which there are so many" (*Ev'ry Month* 3, No. 4 [1 January 1897]: 7). That man should always keep faith in the grand design of nature rather than be disheartened by its occasional signs of cruelty was Dreiser's answer to the pessimist.

☆ ☆ ☆ ☆

The optimistic attitude toward life that Dreiser took during his editorial period lasted for some time, as shown by an essay he wrote at the close of the decade. In a vein similar to that of Stephen Crane's "The Open Boat" (1898) Dreiser described the dreadful forces of the sea but with a deliberate hint of optimism:

> We sat with subdued spirits at the prow, discussing the dangers of the sea. McLaughlin, who had been five years in the service, told of accidents and disappearances in the past. Out of the night once had rushed a steamer, cutting such a boat as ours in two. One pilot boat that had gone out two years ago had never returned. Not a stick or scrap was found to indicate what had become of her fifteen men. He told how the sounding of the fog-horns had chilled his heart the first year of his service, and how the mournful lapping of the waters had filled him with dread. And, as we looked and saw nothing but blackness, and listened and heard nothing but the sipping of the still waters, it seemed as though the relentless sea merely waited its time. Some day it would have them all, sailor and cook, and where now were rooms and lockers would be green water and strange fishes.
>
> That night we slept soundly. A fine wind sprang up, and when morning came, we were scurrying home over a threshing sea. We raced past Sandy Hook and put up the bay. By eight o'clock we were at the Narrows, with the Battery in sight. The harbor looked like a city of masts. After the lonely sea, it was alive with a multitude of people. Tugs went puffing by. Scows and steamers mingled. Amid so much life, the sea seemed safe.[18]

Dreiser could believe that what the sea does not maim or destroy, it returns safely to port where a scene of vibrant and unceasing life reasserts man's ability to survive and to hope. Some of the poems Dreiser wrote at this time also dealt with the effect of evil and disaster in man's life but always left the impression that somehow the rightness of man's good cause will triumph in the end.[19] In a poem entitled "Resignation"[20] Dreiser called himself a child of Nature, and this concept of man as under the protective wing of Nature perhaps is implicit in all of his writings not only in his editorial period but as late as the turn of the century. Thus, man is not so helpless as Dreiser's reading of Spencer had at first convinced him.

But, in order to be a significant part of Nature, Dreiser believed, man must first understand accurately where he stands in the scheme of Nature. Man ought to recognize that he is mortal and necessarily has limitations. If man realizes his helplessness, then he can progress. In this sense, Spencer's deterministic view was important for man's clear vision of himself. Spencer showed Dreiser how certain beautiful laws existed and how, by these laws, all animate as well as inanimate things had developed and functioned. Dreiser's understanding of Spencer was thus tinged with optimism; as Dreiser wrote, Spencer showed "how life has gradually become more and more complicated, more and more beautiful, and how architecture, sculpture, painting and music have gradualy [sic] developed, along with a thousand other features of our life of to-day" (*Ev'ry Month* 2, No. 6: 4).

At the same time, Dreiser began to think seriously about the duty of an artist. Many of the sketches about people and places he drew in his editorial writing contained a strong element of human interest. The downtrodden man, William Wilson, for instance, could thus involve a young writer emotionally. But Dreiser was also able to look at Wilson in a larger perspective; the latter was now visualized among the numerous shades of human suffering, as many as "the countless tints of a roseate sky," and the numerous grades of poverty as "the hues of a changeful sea" (*Ev'ry Month* 3, No. 1 [1 October 1896]: 7). Literature as Dreiser saw it, as he maintained years later, was "this other realm, that of the painter, the artist, the one who saw and reported the non-transitory, and yet transitory too, nature of all our interests and dreams."[21]

Though he looked at life in his early youth and wrote about it in much the same way as in his editorial days, Dreiser could now theorize in the light of Spencer's concept that man's existence is a balance between opposing forces and interests. Dreiser's interpretation of this idea was that without contrast there is no life: as he said, the sketches included in *The Color of a Great City* "are the very antithesis . . . of all that glitter and glister that made the social life of that day so superior"

(*Color*, p. vi). And Dreiser readily applied the theory by asserting that men complaining about the snowstorm, for example, were "a bit of dramatic color in the city's life, whatever their sufferings" (*Color*, p. 233). It was this quality of detachment that permeated Dreiser's vision of the heightened contrasts of life. He could see life whole, yet now without the personal involvement of his previous years. The new sense of detachment unified and strengthened his grasp upon the materials of his work and would be reflected later in his fiction.

6 Free-lance Writing

The published criticism of Dreiser's work has dealt almost exclusively with his novels. His nonfictional writings are seldom commented on, partly because his novels are artistically far more important than his other writing, and partly because his nonfictional work is not readily available in modern editions. But scholars have long known that between his resignation from the editorship of *Ev'ry Month* in September 1897 and the publication of his first novel *Sister Carrie* in November 1900 Dreiser wrote more than 120 pieces that appeared in various magazines. We also know that a few of his articles were reprinted in the early decades of this century. In recent decades only a very few of these articles have been republished, and they have never been collected and published as a unit.

It is time to read this massive body of writing that casts considerable light not only upon Dreiser the novelist, but more importantly, upon the 1890s, an exciting era in the development of American civilization. As a cultural historian of sorts, and more significantly as a young man who was to become a major American writer of the new century, Dreiser made thoughtful judgments on the status of the arts in America—painting, sculpture, architecture, music, and literature. Moreover, his interest was diverse, his vision wide, and he could not fail to encompass the entire spectrum in viewing what was happening in the United States in the 1890s. The late nineties, in which Dreiser's free-lance writing was concentrated, was an important turning point in American history. Witness the booming economy—shortly after the worst depression the nation had experienced—the advancement of technology and industry, and the dissemination of new ideas in science and philosophy. In response to these changes in the lives of the American people, Dreiser wrote most of his magazine articles on the spectacle of contemporary society. He became sometimes a dispassionate chronicler of technology and agriculture; at other times he dramatized the delights and tribulations of people individually as well as collectively. All in all, the result is a rare remarkably coherent piece of Americana seen through the eyes of one man.

The first three of these free-lance articles—other than those pub-

lished in the newspapers and *Ev'ry Month* in 1892–97—appeared in
the November 1897 issues of the magazines. A great majority of his
articles were published during the period of 1898–1900, when he often
wrote at a rate of an article a week. According to Dorothy Dudley
Harvey, Dreiser's first biographer, who interviewed Dreiser, "One
day it occurred to him that he was wasting his time 'fixing up other
fellows' articles.' Why not market his own? He could see that
magazine readers were asking for lively stories about real people and
things. They would take him nearer to his heart's desire—to write
about life as he saw it. Or at least it seemed to him that such articles
would in a literal sense be true, while the fiction of the day must be
false in every sense."[1]

Most critics who have commented on Dreiser's magazine work in
the nineties agree that he was a hack writer.[2] He wrote a great number
of pieces, mostly articles, in a short period of time. But this experience
is important in Dreiser's development as a writer. The range of his
subject matter was diverse: he wrote poems, essays, sketches, and
short stories. Dreiser recorded interviews with famous writers, painters, musicians, financiers, inventors, and educators; he wrote about
the poor and the wretched; he discussed agriculture and mechanics.
The dream of success was one of his dominant themes in these essays,
but at the same time the problems and fears stemming from America's
urban life at the end of the nineteenth century often occupied his mind.
Dreiser's optimism can be detected in his oft-repeated affirmations of
progress, but hesitancy and doubt are also reflected in many of his
writings. Comparing his free-lance work with his newspaper and editorial writings, one cannot help noticing a great change in his mode of
expression. His syntax became more effective; his diction less repetitious. His prose at the end of this period showed none of the broody style
that was characteristic of his editorials a few years earlier. In short,
Dreiser's experience as a magazine writer greatly assisted the future
novelist; the scope and depth of his thinking during these years formed
an indispensable part of his work as an American realist.

If Dreiser had tried to publish these articles a decade earlier, he
would have experienced some difficulty. At the beginning of the 1890s
the most prestigious magazines were few: *The Century, Harper's,
Scribner's,* and *The Atlantic.* Most of the magazines cost thirty-five
cents a copy or more, and they catered to the elite. Toward the end of
the nineteenth century, however, all kinds of changes were taking

place in American life, which resulted in an increased demand among general readers for new knowledge in art, music, science, technology, and life in general. To respond to this popular cry for reading, a score of new magazines were introduced, including *McClure's, Munsey's, The Ladies' Home Journal,* and *The Saturday Evening Post.* The new magazines were sold at lower prices (in July 1895, *The Cosmopolitan* and *Munsey's* were ten cents a copy) and attracted a wider audience. At the turn of the century, the ten-cent magazines accounted for 85 percent of the total magazine circulation in the United States. In the first decade of the twentieth century twenty such magazines were published and their total circulation was over five and a half million.[3] Most of Dreiser's free-lance contributions appeared in such popular and low-priced monthlies.

This upsurge of periodical writing was a significant phenomenon of American culture. The rise of realism after the Civil War had been intimately related to the popularity of the elite magazines. Once these magazines were undercut by the lower-cost competition, the editors of the elite magazines began to direct their efforts toward reaching the general reading public. Prior to the nineties, magazines such as *The Century* and *Harper's* were out of touch with the world of real human interest. In 1895, Hamlin Garland recognized the importance of the New York-based magazines:

New York to-day claims to be, and is, the literary centre of America. Boston artists one by one go to New York. Literary men find their market growing there, and dying out in Boston. They find quicker and warmer appreciation in New York, and the critical atmosphere more hospitable. The present receives a larger share of attention than in Boston. Henceforward New York, and not Boston, is to be the greatest dictator of American literature. New York already assumes to be able to make or break a novelist or playwright. Certainly it is the centre of magazine production; and the magazine is, on the whole, the greatest outlet for distinctive American art.[4]

Garland's point about the magazine's having been the vehicle for "distinctive American art" implies that before this time the taste of American readers had been greatly influenced by the widely circulated British magazines. The distinctive American qualities in literature were what the readers looked for and what the writers were eager to supply. Walter Besant, writing in the London *Author*, noted the "great success" of the American periodicals, which he observed were more popular in London than their English rivals.[5] William Archer, a Scottish critic and playwright, also remarked on this literary phenomenon. Praising the American magazines' "extraordinarily vital and stimulating quality," Archer wrote: "There is nothing quite like them in the literature of the world—no periodicals which combine such width of popular appeal with such seriousness of aim and thoroughness of workmanship."[6]

What made the magazines so vital and thus attractive to their readers? The answer cannot be found in the copious and lively illustrations the magazines included or the fresh cosmopolitan outlook they provided. The elite magazines in the previous decades had also offered variety in subject matter and kept up with major world events. But these older magazines failed to come down to the level of the readers and share the excitements and tribulations of their daily living. Comparing such a magazine as *The Century* with the newcomers, George Horace Lorimer, who took over *The Saturday Evening Post* in 1899, realized that the magazine must respond to the public's interest in business and romanticize it. Lorimer argued that the common men in the streets would buy these magazines and that the women would soon follow. A magazine such as *The Century*, Lorimer thought, failed to keep in mind that those who read it worked.[7]

Dreiser appeared on the scene at an opportune time and, as a reporter or an author of fiction, would never fail to keep Lorimer's advice in mind. Although he recognized in his later career how helpless and meaningless man's struggle for existence was, Dreiser did not lose his sensitivity to the dream and power that accompanied that struggle. Dreiser's capacity for compassion, so often discussed in connection with his novels, is equally obvious in his early periodical writings. Recalling the material in the magazines and newspapers in the nineties, Dreiser wrote: "The saccharine strength of the sentiment and mush which we could gulp down at that time, and still can and do to this day, is to me beyond belief. And I was one of those who did the gulping; indeed I was one of the worst."[8] Dreiser was deliberately attempting to conform to the journalistic style of the time. Even though he later looked back on his magazine writing with some contempt, that writing clearly reflected the decade's ideas and sentiments—the significance of which Dreiser himself then scarcely noticed. Moreover, his pedestrian prose style was an indication of his lifelong commitment to deal with common problems in the most common way possible.

☆ ☆ ☆ ☆

Among Dreiser's magazine articles, by far the largest part, about thirty items, dealt with art and artists. His interest in the visual arts was demonstrated in his own works—*The Financier* (1912), *A Traveler at Forty* (1913), *The "Genius"* (1915), *A Hoosier Holiday* (1916), *Twelve Men* (1918), *The Color of a Great City* (1923), and *A Gallery of Women* (1929). In these works one is struck by Dreiser's intimate and often professional knowledge of the subject. Small wonder that his acquaintance with art was first made while he was a free-lance writer in the late nineties. In the early nineties, however, Dreiser's interest in drama was greater than it was in art. As a struggling newspaper reporter, his ambition was to become a playwright. In those days, drama criticism occupied a prominent place in the newspaper, and Dreiser's interest was naturally developed in that direction. Once he had established himself as a magazine editor and contributor, he could not help noticing the readers' attraction to the colorful illustrations that were included in the popular magazines. Also the art of engraving was making a change in the conduct of monthly magazines. The contents of many periodicals, too, reflected a growing sentiment for the aesthetic in general. After the industrial development of the new nation, its citizens looked for their spiritual satisfaction in art. Such men as William Vanderbilt and John Pierpont Morgan were celebrated not only as successful financiers but also as passionate art lovers with huge collections of paintings.

Despite his enthusiasm for the visual arts, Dreiser was by no means an expert in the field. In the beginning, his writings about painting and sculpture betrayed superficiality and showed at best a layman's unabashed wonder at the vague notion of the beautiful. As he cultivated his taste and accumulated experience by visiting studios and making the acquaintance of artists, Dreiser became more confident in his commentary. Late in 1897 he was already a member of the Salmagundi, the most prestigious artists' club in New York. Through such affiliations, he was requested by the painter J. Scott Hartley to compile an album of the work of George Inness, Hartley's father-in-law.[9]

In his dealing with artists, Dreiser was always trying to elicit a theory of art to which he was congenial. Initially, he was anxious to resolve the artist's dilemma of reconciling poetry with that newly born child of the times—realism. In "Art Work of Irving R. Wiles," he made a sweeping indictment of realism: "A painter who must needs take a striking situation from every-day life and paint in all details as they would probably be found in real life, is, in a way, photographic and not artistic." [10] Dreiser agreed with Wiles' "art for art's sake" doctrines; realizing that each of the painter's works was based on "a prosaic enough reality" (*Metropolitan* 7: 359), Dreiser concluded that the artist's sense of beauty came not from reality itself but from the artist's imagination. This concept was also expressed in another article published at the same time. After venturing an analogy with the "idealist" school of Watts and Rossetti, Dreiser wondered how both the ideal and the real could coexist in the work of Benjamin Eggleston, a portrait painter from Minnesota well known around the turn of the century. "Perhaps it would be better to say," Dreiser wrote, "that he has the gift of imparting to subjects realistically treated the poetry of his own nature, thus lifting them far above the level of 'faithful transcripts' of nature and life." [11]

Many of his articles about artists during this period were also concerned with what was to become a major theme in his own work: the relationship of man to nature. Dreiser was convinced earlier in his career that the artist's obligation was to portray man in his natural state. This duty, of course, often clashed with convention as his novels show. In commenting on artists, Dreiser praised and respected those who shunned convention. Homer C. Davenport, a well-known caricaturist of the time, was like Dreiser a product of the West. Davenport succeeded, in Dreiser's opinion, in satirizing the pretense, dishonesty, and unnaturalness of a refined society. "One would suspect," Dreiser observed, "that he would draw roughly, for like all Westerners he has no taste for luxury, and rather pities those creatures who are so refined and re-refined that they lack vitality enough to digest a plain meal." [12] Later, in a survey of various artists, Dreiser was appalled by their blatant hypocrisy: they often formed an exclusive community for themselves by severing themselves from nature as well as from society itself. [13]

In criticizing such "anemic" and fragile artists, Dreiser pleaded for the artist's liberation from the indoor life as Whitman did in his poetry. Dreiser's fondness for the strength and roughness of nature underlay many of his remarks on painting and sculpture. After tracing the inspirations of C. C. Curran, an Ohio painter, to those of the French painter Dagnan-Bouveret, Dreiser compared Curran's painting to Robert

Louis Stevenson's poetry. Curran's picture with glimpses of children digging in the earth, sailing boats, and playing on the greensward awakened such a responsive mood in Dreiser that he quoted lines from Stevenson's "Child's Garden of Verse":

> I called the little pool a sea;
> The little hills were big to me,
> For I am very small.
> I made a boat, I made a town,
> I searched the caverns up and down
> And named them one and all.[14]

Even as late as 1899, when he first attempted to write fiction, Dreiser was intensely curious about nature's effects on man. Lawrence E. Earle's work, Dreiser noted, abounded with aged, weather-beaten figures that suggested "the wear and nature of the various callings from which they are selected." Every time Dreiser looked at one of Earle's paintings, he was reminded of Thoreau's description of "the old, quiet fisherman in his worn brown coat, who was so regularly to be found in a shady nook at a certain bend in the Concord River." Earle's figure, like Thoreau's, became part of the soil and landscape like the stumps and bushes. Those garments the man in the picture wears, in Dreiser's words, "are queer baked products of sun and rain; quaint, pleasant old creatures, selected by a feeling mind. In a way, they seem to illustrate how subtle are the ways of nature; how well she coats her aged lovers with her own autumnal hue." [15]

A more direct study of man in the natural state, Dreiser wrote, could be accomplished artistically in the nude as a genre. Discussing the works of Fernando Miranda, a Spanish-born sculptor, Dreiser quoted Miranda's defense of the human form in its natural beauty as "God's greatest work." Dreiser despised those who disliked nudes; with approval he repeated Miranda's comment that they were "misled by narrow conceptions of what is noble and good in the universe." [16] In such remarks, Dreiser hastened to point out the misguided concept of the viewer who was tempted to seek only the prurient from the nude. According to Dreiser, clothes distorted and concealed the beauty of form. The success of Frederick W. MacMonnies' masterpiece, *Bacchante and Child*, was, therefore, the result of the sculptor's momentary capture of the pose upon one foot. The sculptor's motive, Dreiser suggested, "has plainly been to represent the beauty of a sudden and

spontaneous movement, and not to glorify either inebriety or wanton-
ness."[17]

These magazine contributions seldom gave a sign of the pessimism
that, from time to time, marked his own fictional writings. This might
well have been the result of the "success story" pattern that Dreiser
was asked to follow by the magazines. In this connection one must
recall Dreiser's disposition of mind during his editorial days. The
columns he wrote in *Ev'ry Month* show that he was a disciple of
Herbert Spencer and most notably that he interpreted the Spencerian
cycle of existence as progress for man. Nothing since then seemed to
have altered his view, and he readily applied the theory to the artist's
mission in life. Dreiser's faith in man's worth remained unshaken for a
long time, as evidenced by the statement he made in 1909 as editor of
The Delineator. Dreiser's policy then was to accept only those contributions that were tinged with idealism and optimism and, in the case
of a story, with a "truly uplifting character."[18] In a brief sketch of
Bruce Crane, who was then recognized as a leading successor to the
famous landscape artist George Inness, Dreiser praised Crane's work
not because it adhered to nature but because it displayed a joyous and
hopeful atmosphere.[19] In "E. Percy Moran and His Work," Dreiser
cited Moran's view of an artist's function as "to make it [life] better,
handsomer, more pleasing."[20] In surveying the gifted young portrait
painters of the day, he came to this conclusion: "Intellectually, they
are men of broad minds, and look upon art with clean, wholesome
spirits."[21]

Only one short year before his actual writing of *Sister Carrie*, what
he learned from these artists was not merely the attitude or personality
of a true artist. It was the technique of delineating how man delighted in
a modern city and yet, when luck turned against him, was baffled by
the complexity, impersonality, and loneliness that the city presented.
Alfred Stieglitz, a contemporary artist-photographer, became one of
the individuals who provided Dreiser with this technique and vision. In
an essay on Stieglitz, Dreiser explained with detail how such well-
known photographs as *A Rainy Day in Fifth Avenue* and *The L in a
Storm* had been produced. Stieglitz was the first photographer to perfect the techniques of night pictures.[22] He would stand for hours at
night in order to capture the photographic impressions of some of the
glittering night scenes in New York. Although Dreiser says that the
famous *Winter on Fifth Avenue* was called "a lucky hit," he adds:

"The driving sleet and the uncomfortable atmosphere issued out of the picture with uncomfortable persuasion. It had the tone of reality. But *lucky hit* followed *lucky hit*, until finally the accusation would explain no more, and then *talent* was substituted."[23]

By far the most influential artist for Dreiser in these years was William Louis Sonntag, Jr. The inspiration that Dreiser received from Sonntag was so personal that Dreiser wrote a poem about him—and published it as an obituary in *Collier's Weekly* in 1898—when Sonntag, like Stephen Crane and Frank Norris, died an early death. Years later, Dreiser's short biography of Sonntag, "The Color of To-Day," became one of the chapters in *Twelve Men* under the anonymous title "W. L. S."[24] The sense of insecurity and loneliness that Carrie and Hurstwood experience in Chicago and New York, Dreiser tells us, was born in his newspaper experiences. But his actual portrayal of the scenes in the novel could not have been accomplished without the ideas of Sonntag.

Dreiser's first acquaintance with this artist goes back to Dreiser's editorial days with *Ev'ry Month* in the winter of 1895, as has been noted. What struck Dreiser's eyes in the works of Sonntag was the artist's use of color. Good coloring, as Dreiser often maintained, was above all the first element of a successful painting after idea, form, or purpose.[25] What was to become Dreiser's own use of color in describing the urban scenes—streetlights, carriages, department stores, restaurants, luxurious garments—was acquired through his apprenticeship under Sonntag. One drizzly autumn night Sonntag took Dreiser to this scene on their way to the theater while, Dreiser recalled, they were in the midst of a serious discussion of art and life:

> He took me to a point where, by the intersection of the lines of the converging streets, one could not only see Greeley Square, but a large part of Herald Square, with its huge theatrical sign of fire and its measure of store lights and lamps of vehicles. It was, of course, an inspiring scene. The broad, converging walks were alive with people. A perfect jam of vehicles marked the spot where the horse and cable cars intersected. Overhead was the elevated station, its lights augmented every few minutes by long trains of brightly lighted cars filled with truly metropolitan crowds.
> "Do you see the quality of that? Look at the blend of the lights and shadows in there under the L."
> I looked and gazed in silent admiration.
> "See, right here before us—that pool of water there—do you get

that? Now, that isn't silver-colored, as it's usually represented. It's
a prism. Don't you see the hundred points of light?''
    I acknowledged the variety of color, which I had scarcely ob-
served before.
    ''You may think one would skip that in viewing a great scene, but
the artist mustn't. He must get that all, whether you notice or not. It
gives feeling, even when you don't see it.'' (*Harper's Weekly* 45:
1273)

This is evidence that Dreiser was indebted to a practicing artist of the
day and, more importantly, indicates how strongly Dreiser committed
himself to capture an incisive vision of the contemporary scene. Furthermore, what fascinated Dreiser at this time was the artist's amazing
versatility. Not only was Sonntag well versed in fiction, drama, music,
history, and politics, but he surprised Dreiser by revealing the fact that
he was an engineer (competent to handle marine, railroad, and other
machinery), architect, mathematician, and philosopher. Dreiser was
intimately drawn to Sonntag's unique talents and experiences; Dreiser
himself was thus conscientiously pursuing his apprenticeship not only
as a critic in art and literature but also during this period as a journalist
who addressed himself to facts and ideas in science, technology, agriculture, commerce, politics, and many other fields of human interest.
The intensity and width of vision that Dreiser achieved as a commentator on art and artists was to have a pervasive effect on his own writing
as a novelist.

Although Dreiser vigorously pursued art criticism in these years, at
times with immature haste, he did not deal with literary criticism with
equal enthusiasm. It is common knowledge that Dreiser was inciden-
tally a literary critic during his entire career. Interestingly, however, he
was always conscious of his fellow writers and quite sensitive to their
remarks on his own writing. As his numerous letters clearly indicate,
Dreiser took his critics seriously. Many of his periodical writings in the
nineties thus contained his views on men of letters in the past as well as
in the present. In his interviews with successful men in various walks
of life, Dreiser was, of course, curious as to how one would achieve
eminence in the literary profession. Sometimes he violently disagreed
with a theory of literature he came across. Later in his career Dreiser

often confessed his aversion to many of his contemporaries because he felt that their works did not square with life as he himself experienced it. Such a distaste for much American writing may have been part of the reason for Dreiser's relative silence about his fellow writers during his free-lance period. But, whenever he found an attitude or personality he felt an affinity with, he never failed to applaud it. Despite the fewer number of articles he wrote on this subject, Dreiser seems to have been testing his hand as critic in these years for a long literary career he was to make for himself later.

Dreiser's first attempt came with a nostalgic description of Tarrytown with its world-renowned Sleepy Hollow where rose Washington Irving's tombstone. Dreiser's interest was not so much in the famous storyteller and the legend that surrounded him as in the modern history of the region, particularly the Dutch settlement, and the feeling and color of this locale. In spite of his usual excitement over modern technology, Dreiser was vocal in his criticism of such an "incongruous trick" as the arc lights with their unseemly glare that had invaded the Hollow road.[26] Dreiser's homage to the American past came to a climax with a long article on Hawthorne, which was published in two separate issues.[27] As in his article on the Sleepy Hollow, this biographical sketch of the haunting romancer opens with reference to the undesirable effects of the modern era on the town of Salem—the railroad, electric light, and trolley that "glared upon and outraged its ancient ways" (*Truth* 17 [21 September 1898]: 7). Similar in kind to this sketch is a well-detailed account of William Cullen Bryant, which appeared in *Munsey's* in the following year.[28] The thrust of Dreiser's commentary was given to Bryant's courageous activities as journalist and poet during his last thirty-five years in the Long Island town of Roslyn. Dreiser astutely observed that although it was an old settlement with high "hopes and pretensions" years earlier, the town had "faltered and lagged in the race of modern progress" (*Munsey's* 21: 240). Dreiser's fondness of the poet is clearly shown by his frequent quotations of Bryant's poetry in this article and elsewhere. Dreiser admired Bryant for "a deep seated, rugged Americanism, wholly unconventionalized by his success in the world" (ibid., 245). Dreiser could have felt that Bryant's often quoted lines from "To a Waterfowl"—"Lone wandering, but not lost"—could be applied to his own disappointments and hopes as journalist and future writer. To Dreiser, Bryant was "intrepid, persistent, full of the love of justice, and rich in human

sympathies," a simple statement of what were to become his own
qualities as a novelist (ibid., 244).

All of these literary essays contained the two leading and inseparable
themes of Dreiser's free-lance work: disillusionment with city life and
longing for the beauty of nature. When he turned to the contemporary
authors, Dreiser searched for some transcendental reality beyond material appearances. He was thus surprised and at the same time gratified
to discover that the commercial environment of Wall Street made no
mark in Edmund Clarence Stedman's creative work.[29] The work and
career of the poet Bayard Taylor, who is largely forgotten today,
provided Dreiser with quiet reflections and warm sentiments.[30] Unlike
Stedman, Taylor was born on a farm and struggled for existence in his
early years. Much like Dreiser himself, Taylor was a self-made man,
having left his native place in his youth and built up a literary career in
the city. Taylor, Dreiser learned, was not a financially successful man,
and in his old age Taylor achieved happiness and peace of mind by
retiring to Cedarcroft, his birthplace. The most significant point of a
tribute to Taylor written by Dreiser comes toward the end where
Dreiser, foreshadowing his own characteristic turn of thought, portrays
the old poet, who "drew out his rocking chair in the evening, and
swayed to and fro as the light faded and sights and sounds gave place to
the breath of night and the stars." Dreiser infuses the scene with an
Emersonian, mystic quality that one frequently finds later in his
novels: "The pale moonlight flooded all the ground, the leaves gained
voices from the wind, and over them all brooded the poetic mind,
wondering, awed, and yearning" (*Munsey's* 18: 601).

Dreiser was more impressed by a mystic poet of an older generation
such as Taylor than by a contemporary analytical critic who, Dreiser
felt, often smacked of egotism. This is why when he encountered an
influential British critic, Israel Zangwill, Dreiser became most indignant in his attack on the man and his philosophy.[31] Zangwill's critical
tenets, Dreiser believed, were not entirely original, and Dreiser was
readily prepared to make such a pronouncement for his American
audience. Zangwill's rule was not to criticize a book for not being
some other book, and yet his first criterion was that a book must be
worth criticizing. What irritated Dreiser was a dogmatism that underlay Zangwill's standard of judgment. "All that remains," Zangwill
said, "is to classify it. It is of such and such period, such and such a
school, such and such merit." Dreiser realized that, in Zangwill's

criticism, judgment necessarily preceded classification and analysis. In any event, Dreiser argued that what was lacking in such criticism was the heart of a critic:

> It is the great analytical spirit, useful no doubt, but the world loves an enthusiast better, who criticizes not at all, but seizes upon the first thing to his hands and toils kindly, if blindly, in the thought that his is the great and necessary labor. Certainly such a life bespeaks a greater soul, if keen sympathies make soul, then [sic] does that of the man who can sit off and eternally pass judgment, unmoved forever to ally himself heart and hand with any one great effort for the uplifting of humanity. (*Ainslee's* 2: 355–56)

Another eminent critic whom Dreiser met was William Dean Howells, "the Dean of American Letters," as he called him.[32] Before the interview Dreiser had read *My Literary Passions* and now found his image of the great novelist readily confirmed. He found Howells "one of the noblemen of literature"—honest, sincere, and generous. Such laudatory remarks sound incongruous today since it has become legend that the two men never liked each other. We know from what Dreiser said later that Howells' novels failed to give him a sense of American life. Dreiser thus confided to one critic: "Yes, I know his books are pewky and damn-fool enough, but he did one fine piece of work, *Their Wedding Journey*, not a sentimental passage in it, quarrels from beginning to end, just the way it would be, don't you know, really beautiful and true" (*Dreiser and the Land of the Free*, p. 143). On numerous occasions Dreiser revealed to his friends that *Their Wedding Journey* was the only work of Howells that he liked,[33] but he did admire Howells for championing young talents. In *Ev'ry Month*, and again in *Ainslee's*, Dreiser called Howells a "literary Columbus" for discovering Stephen Crane and Abraham Cahan. Howells' support for Hamlin Garland and Frank Norris is well known, but Howells was blind to *Sister Carrie* and he never tried to appreciate Dreiser the rest of his life.

In order to understand Dreiser's "change of heart" as regards Howells, we must look into a transformation that took place in Howells' later years. The Howells whom Dreiser met in New York was not an aloof, genteel novelist, the product of New England culture. A decade earlier Howells had witnessed the suppression of justice in the wake of the Haymarket massacre. With a vehemence that was reminiscent of Zola, Howells protested against the incident, which he felt destroyed

forever "the smiling aspect" of American life. With this social and
political upheaval that shook his conscience, Howells was also under
an important literary influence that subsequently was to change him.
Dreiser's "The Real Howells" thus concluded with a personal tribute
that Howells had made to Tolstoy:

> Tolstoi's influence had led him back, as he puts it, "to the only true
> ideal, away from that false standard of the gentleman to the Man
> who sought not to be distinguished from other men, but identified
> with them, to that *Presence* in which the finest gentleman shows his
> alloy of vanity, and the greatest genius shrinks to the measure of his
> miserable egotism." (*Ainslee's* 5: 140)

For the sixty-three-year old novelist, such a revelation came rather
belatedly, but for Dreiser, the unpublished novelist, it served to
strengthen the already hardening literary foundation that he had been
building all these years.

In the period immediately preceding the publication of *Sister Carrie*,
the lives of various artists and writers strongly captured Dreiser's interest, and at times he envied them. He was always fascinated by their
unique concept of beauty and their sympathetic treatment of life itself.
Dreiser was convinced more than ever of the inseparable ties between
art and human life. One of the dominant subjects in his magazine
writing was, therefore, American life as he saw it. And one common
theme that Dreiser was consciously developing was American progress.

This theme scarcely sounded humanistic at that time, nor does it
today; it was a journalist's attempt at providing the public with information on technology as it affected the urban scene. Disillusionment
with new science and distrust of progress were not uncommon reactions in many quarters of American intellectual life. But Dreiser in the
late nineties was undoubtedly an optimist; he had earlier interpreted the
Spencerian law of existence as inevitable progress for mankind.
Dreiser discussed, for example, the impact that the recent development
of "motor carriages" had made on transportation in the city. Using
specific details and designs in the manner of an engineering journal,
Dreiser demonstrated how electricity had been converted to motor

power. He even projected the invention of "motor cars," as he called them, which would be operated by gasoline engines in the near future. After spelling out the enormous economic gains such development would generate for the country, he concluded the article with what must seem to many modern readers a false prediction: "The saving of time, the added comfort and the improved health which would result from the system can hardly be overestimated." [34]

The introduction of motorcars in American life must have given such a compassionate man as Dreiser a sense of relief because watching clattering horses in the streets was "itself too often an object of real and piteous interest" (*Demorest's* 35: 154). As a naturalist in the vein of John Burroughs, Dreiser could hardly promote the cause of man's happiness on earth without due consideration for the welfare of other creatures. This is perhaps why Dreiser was curious about the intelligence and efficiency of pigeons as they were utilized for secret communications. But at the same time he expressed his idiosyncratic concern for pigeons as he concluded his essay with a quotation from Bryant's "To a Waterfowl." [35] His expression of sympathy was extended not only to animals but also to plants. Discussing the importance of studying plant roots scientifically, Dreiser illustrated how a microscope could trace down their "infinitesimal . . . threads as light as gossamer, almost—they did not naturally end." "In that unseen part," he interjected, "there was a friendly union between the life of the plant and the life of the earth, and the latter had given some of itself to course up the hair-like root and become a part of the plant." [36] On the basis of new research on the relationship of weeds to the soil, Dreiser even pleaded for the preservation of some weeds: "There are weeds that are soil renewers, weeds that are food for man and beast, and weeds without which thousands of acres of our most fertile lands would be wastes to-day." [37]

Such sensitive treatments of plant and animal life in the light of human progress were characteristic of Dreiser the philosopher. But as a historian Dreiser paid far more attention to the various technological innovations being made in the American 1890s. Thus, the development of transportation in the urban and rural areas became a focal point of his argument for progress. In "The Railroad and the People: A New Educational Policy Now Operating in the West," Dreiser's purpose was to correct the term "soulless corporation" that was often used to describe the nature of the largest commercial organization then existing in the United States.[38] The railroads were usually described as "dark, sinister, dishonest associations which robbed the people 'right and left,' . . . and gave nothing in return" (*Harper's Monthly* 100: 479). But like Shelgrim, the railroad president in Norris' *The Octopus*, Dreiser put forward an argument in favor of the railroads' "cordial and sympathetic relationship with their public" and, with meticulous detail, illustrated how both would benefit under such an enterprise. Dreiser's view of capitalism in this instance is evenhanded. "For if the public has had nothing save greed and rapacity to expect of its railroads," he went on, "the sight of the latter adopting a reasonable business policy, whereby they seek to educate and make prosperous the public in order that they in turn may be prosperous, is one which, if not inspiring, is at least optimistic" (ibid., 479).[39] A sense of optimism could even be detected in Dreiser's account of manufacturing small arms. The evil connected with weapons moved him to despair, but his explanation of this sinister enterprise became a curious rationalization, as mentioned earlier: the ultimate purpose of weapon production is to build peace.[40]

The jubilant mood in which Dreiser dealt with the events of the day seemed to have touched almost all his writings in this period. In explaining how battleships were built, he even failed to reflect on the baleful purposes for which technology might be used; instead he dramatized the majesty of the ships and the ingenuity involved in constructing them. As for road construction, Dreiser contrasted the enterprise to that of Imperial Rome, which thrived on slavery. American roads came into being, Dreiser emphasized, "with awakening reason and sympathy in all the hearts of men"; true greatness lay in the fact that the roads were built by the people and for the people. "Unlike the magnificent public structure of the empires long since departed," he asserted, "they will neither conceal squalor nor want, nor yet a race of whip-driven Helots, but rather bespeak a nation of freemen and beauty lovers—men strong in the devotion and enjoyment of good."[41] Whether Dreiser was describing how the Chicago drainage canal was completed, how trains were manufactured in the Midwest, how pilot boats were operated in New York harbor, how trolleys ran between New York and Boston, or how the subway was laid in New York City—in these spectacles, Dreiser's vision of progress always dramatized the excitement of the people involved.[42]

In reporting America's industrial development, Dreiser suspected that some people had built their personal fortunes in the name of progress for all men. Earlier, when he was a newspaperman, Dreiser observed successful men such as Andrew Carnegie and Joseph Pulitzer, but he was somehow compelled to be reticent about their private conduct, which he could not admire. Now as a free-lance writer Dreiser was able to write about these wealthy men as he pleased. Consequently, through his magazine work, Dreiser became acquainted with Dr. Orison Swett Marden, the founder and editor of *Success*, the first issue of which appeared in December 1897. Trusting Dreiser's abilities to brighten up the contemporary scene, Marden engaged his services to interview successful men in business, industry, science, art, and literature. Although Marden's format for these articles does not seem to have restricted Dreiser's ideas on the subject, Dreiser's writing nevertheless lacked the sensitive approach that marked his best essays. Indeed, the traditional success stories that dramatized the rags-to-riches ideal were still popular. It was easy for Dreiser to follow the well-established pattern of a Horatio Alger story; one could hardly expect any originality in treatment of this theme.

The rapidity with which Dreiser composed these stories was indicated by the fact that an interview by him appeared almost every month in the first two years of *Success*.[43] The monotonous similarity of these articles stemmed from several identical questions he put to the men he wrote about: "What quality in you was most essential to your success?" "Were you rich or poor before starting a career?" "Were reading and school work necessary for your success?" "What is your concept of happiness?" To these stock questions there were stock answers. All the men interviewed, of course, said that hard work led to their success. To this they added such traits as "perseverance" and "consistency" in their work; they all emphasized "honesty" and "integrity" as the moral scruples rewarded by success. Except for Thomas Edison, however, they did not believe in "overwork." All were convinced that the fewer advantages one had in his youth, the greater chances for success one could hope for. Even a man coming from a relatively distinguished family such as Joseph H. Choate, a leading lawyer and later an ambassador, retorted: "I never met a great man who was born rich" (*Success* 1 [January 1898]: 41). To accumulate wealth, they all advocated thrift, saving, and investment. They also replied that so-called education and book learning had little effect on their successful careers, a point with which Dreiser could certainly agree.

Finally, despite the prestige and glory accorded to successful men,

Dreiser learned that only constant labor, not luxury and wealth, constituted their happiness. "... when it is all done and is a success," Edison, for instance, confessed, "I can't bear the sight of it. I haven't used a telephone in ten years, and I would go out of my way any day to miss an incandescent light" (*Success* 1 [February 1898]: 9). Once these men achieved their eminence, most of them looked for satisfaction in their humanitarian causes, but to them labor itself preceded such happiness. Thus, Philip D. Armour, a businessman and philanthropist, explained: "If you give the world better material, better measure, better opportunities for living respectably, there is happiness in that. You cannot give the world anything without labor, and there is no satisfaction in anything but labor that looks toward doing this, and does it" (*Success* 1 [October 1898]: 4). Whether Dreiser trusted Carnegie's words on humanitarianism here is questionable in view of the various reservations Dreiser had previously expressed about the industrialist. In *Success* magazine, Dreiser somewhat inflated Carnegie's motive for a large-hearted liberality.

Among Dreiser's thirty *Success* articles, exactly half were later reprinted in three separate volumes edited by Marden without reference to Dreiser's authorship: *How They Succeeded* (1901), *Talks with Great Workers* (1901), and *Little Visits with Great Americans* (1903). One could easily speculate why the other articles were not selected by Marden, but there were some obvious reasons. In each case, Marden certainly wanted to dramatize the life story of a single figure; seven of the articles that were not selected by Marden, such as "American Women as Successful Playwrights" and "America's Greatest Portrait Painters," dealt with more than one individual and so did not suit Marden's purpose. The rest of the articles were left out for some other reasons. Whether or not Marden disagreed with Dreiser's point of view on the subject of the unselected articles is unknown, but it is interesting to note that most of the eliminated articles from the volumes of reprints lacked a sense of glamour that is often associated with the American Dream of Success. Marden's intention in this project was to inspire young men and women who wanted to be somebody but felt that they had no chance in life. However, the list of Dreiser's *Success* stories that were omitted—for instance, interviews with Alice B. Stephens (a well-known woman painter), H. Barrington Cox (inventor), Clara S. Foltz (a leading woman lawyer), Edward Atkinson (a food scientist), and Thomas B. Reed (onetime Speaker of the House)—demonstrated, contrary to common belief, that success was necessarily derived from one's advantages over others at the start of life including a solid educational background.[44]

Perhaps the most significant point to be drawn from Marden's selection is that he did not approve of Dreiser's interest in humanistically oriented portrayals of successful men. Two articles of this nature were carefully omitted from Marden's reprints: "A Cripple Whose Energy Gives Inspiration" and "A Touch of Human Brotherhood." In the first piece, Dreiser, as if writing a story, describes how bleak a small fishing town on the coast of Connecticut had become through a decline in the whaling business and shipbuilding industry. "A friend of mine and myself," Dreiser begins the tale, "were sitting on the lawn surrounding the local Baptist church, one morning, discussing the possibilities of life and development in so small and silent a place, when a trivial incident turned the arguments to the necessity of doing something to promote the organization and intelligence of the world." The author's ensuing narration reveals an idea that would later clarify the meaning of struggle in his novels: while other young boys, complaining about their unfortunate social and economic conditions, cursed the world and idled away their energy and ambition, a physically handicapped youth, persisting in his labor and winning public trust and love, achieved happiness and success in life.[45]

The second story was concerned with the concept of success and happiness according to a less glamorous and totally strange figure whom Dreiser had found on Broadway and Fifth Avenue in New York City. This man's story was so striking that Dreiser used it toward the end of *Sister Carrie*, where a lone, poverty-stricken man known only by his title of Captain created a job for himself.[46] In both versions, Captain solicits passersby to contribute money to shelter bums during nights when the cold was like that pictured in Stieglitz's photograph. In the eyes of this self-styled philanthropist, people think that life is beautiful outside rather than inside. They would regard as happiness the "hotels and theaters, the carriages and fine homes—they're all in the eye .... it's only for a season" (*Success* 5 [March 1902]: 176). The same scene had earlier appeared in another magazine article entitled "Curious Shifts of the Poor."[47] To Dreiser's surprise, many of the poor in the streets, though they appeared helpless and isolated, were not complaining as common people were. These seemingly victimized men, Dreiser discovered, were merely indifferent, if not cheerful, toward their conditions; in fact, they were far more mentally stable than the rich.

Another *Success* article that failed to be reprinted by Marden was "The Tenement Toilers," one of several reports on the seamy side of city life that Dreiser wrote shortly after *Sister Carrie*. In it, in contrast to his other *Success* stories, Dreiser dispassionately told how city workers for cheap labor lived in inhumanly crowded tenements and taught their children that money was all they must aim at in life.[48] "Christmas in the Tenements" also discussed a contrast between the rich and the poor, but here Dreiser joyfully observed that despite their wretched living conditions in the tenements, Christmas brought the poor a temporary relief.[49] And curiously he proposed a *carpe diem* theme for them: "Eat, drink, and be merry, for to-morrow you must die" (*Harper's Weekly* 46 [6 December 1902]: 53). A little earlier his essay on "The Transmigration of the Sweat Shop" (*Puritan* 8 [July 1900]: 498–502), which was to serve him for Carrie Meeber's sweat-shop in the novel, disclosed that such conditions did indeed exist in the factories he had visited in New Jersey. Dreiser's argument here was interesting because he presented himself as a reformer, not merely a compassionate and philanthropic observer, but one who believed that these conditions could be eliminated by men of good will, honesty, and justice—employees as well as employers. Society was full of in-adequacies and inequalities, but now he could suggest positive rem-edies for society to use in coping with the problem. Man, Dreiser began to see, was not necessarily a victim of his conditions; it would be possible for man himself to ameliorate them. Likewise, "Little Club-men of the Tenements" served Dreiser for a counterargument to Crane's "An Experiment in Misery."[50] The subtitle of Dreiser's piece reads "A remarkable boys' club established in Fall River, Mas-sachusetts, for the children of the slums who find there the resources of a city and the pleasures of a home" (*Puritan* 7: 665). His experiment showed that no matter how poorly such children were brought up in the tenements, they could still acquire good manners and attitudes once they were placed in the club. In the past some of the boys had lived with alcoholic parents; others had been orphans, motherless, father-less, or had been turned out to roam the streets at night. Scars of environment on the children were deep enough, yet Dreiser learned that these scars could be healed.

What emerged from such social criticism was that Dreiser was not easily swayed by the appearances of reality. Although the dreams of contemporary Americans were dramatized in his accounts, it was still possible for Dreiser to delve into their miseries and fears as well. He could now look at social phenomena from the vantage points of a worker and a capitalist. As a social critic, Dreiser was not superficial; his analyses and details were balanced by his arguments and points of view. "Man's ingenuity," he opened a report on the cartridge factory, "finds many contradictory channels for its expression. The labor to perfect those sciences which tend to save human life goes on side by side with the labor to create new and more potent methods for its destruction."[51] From a commercial point of view, the Chicago River provided him with a symbol of progress. The river not only gave the corporations the most efficient services but also offered the city its beauty: "At night, when the heavy traffic ceases and the bridges lose their throngs of vehicles and pedestrians, it glows beneath the lamps and sky like a stream of silver."[52] But, from a citizen's point of view, it was already the most polluted river in the country despite the federal laws that were intended to protect this navigable stream. Dreiser also had his second thoughts on the sacred Mississippi River, still fresh with its echoes from Mark Twain. Though aware of its scenic charms and literary memories, Dreiser thought its traditions to be an anachronism in the light of later and more civilized conditions:

> The overseers howl terribly without taking breath, brandish sticks, wave their arms, stamp their feet, and make startling lunges in all directions. They threaten the idle, curse the active, bluff the bystanders, and add prodigously [sic] to the tumult of the scene without otherwise affecting it. Regardless of these busy-bodies that buzz about like gnats, the darkies shuffle here and there, rolling with rhythmic motions and with more rests than efforts the cotton bales. The character of the negro in the situation is no doubt picturesque, but the fact that business is more or less dependent upon such labor, and the impossibility of securing active, systematic, skilled service forms one of the serious problems in the commerce of the river.[53]

In his discussion of successful public figures Dreiser was also critical, often undercutting their image and reputation. In "The Real Choate," the celebrated lawyer-diplomat was assailed, for Dreiser believed that Choate was unworthy of his reputation. In another article on Choate, published a few months earlier in *Success*, Dreiser was unable to criticize him freely because of Marden'a theory of success.

In the later article Choate's assiduity and skill as a lawyer were generously praised, but Dreiser could not help pointing out his inadequacies
as a human being.[54] Choate was known for his brilliant quotations
from Shakespeare; his name and background in the New England stock
shone brightly in people's minds. But Dreiser hastened to add: "There
is not enough of that radiant humanity in him which the common
people understand and make fellowship with" (*Ainslee's* 3: 324). The
problem with Choate's personality, Dreiser argued, derived not so much
from his intellect and air of superiority as from his profession itself, in
which his mind was preoccupied with the cold corporations, his time
spent "with entanglements never seen of the people" (ibid., 326).
Englishmen, to whom Choate represented Americans, would admire
"his brilliancy, his unfailing humor, his persuasive powers, and his fine
show of courage and chivalry"; but for American purposes, Dreiser
insisted, Choate needed other qualities, the chief of which should have
been "a craving for distinction at the hands of the people" (ibid., 326).
What was worse, Choate was attacked on moral grounds. "It is curious," Dreiser wondered, "that this powerful analytical sense is seldom
joined with any tenderness of heart, or with any defined leanings to right
or wrong" (ibid., 328). That man must be judged not by what he says
but by what he does was Dreiser's reminder to his readers. Dreiser's
conclusion was simple: "he has done for himself nobly, not for others"
(ibid., 333). For Dreiser, then, Choate's talents—"arrayed in all their
subtlety in defense of some execrable Tammany scapegoat, some or-
ganized industry seeking to avoid the fulfillment of its just obligations,
some corporation caught in act of the [sic] false dealing with the
State"—served to symbolize the evil forces that were to dominate the
American political system for generations to come. And the portrayal of
the underdog in the rising civilization that Dreiser later wove into his
fiction was to be a faithful reflection of reality in America.

Dreiser's understanding and feeling for American life were reflected
in full force in his novels. That picture of American life, some critics
argued, was distorted, but Dreiser spoke the truth as he saw it. In
"True Art Speaks Plainly" published in 1903, shortly after the turmoil
over the publication of *Sister Carrie*, Dreiser stated: "The extent of all
reality is the realm of the author's pen, and a true picture of life,

honestly and reverentially set down, is both moral and artistic whether it offends the conventions or not.''[55] It is now easy to see that Dreiser's magazine writings in the 1890s show his characteristic reverence for his material. Whether he was commenting on artists, writers, or society in general, this attitude resulted from Dreiser's lifelong conviction that "the surest art guide is a true and responsive heart."[56]

Qualities of sympathy and compassion undisputably characterize his fiction, but what his magazine work indicates is the fact that Dreiser was not a simple "commiserator" as Edward D. McDonald portrayed him in a picture attached to an article in the *Bookman*: Dreiser, in tears, devouring a tragic story in the newspaper.[57] Dreiser's compassionate appreciation of any stories of human interest cannot be doubted, but more importantly Dreiser before *Sister Carrie* also acquired a capacity for detachment and objectivity; rarely did his magazine essays display passionate outbursts. In effect, Dreiser was a literary realist in the best sense of the word. These magazine contributions suggest that although he was eager to learn from literary and philosophical sources, he trusted his own vision and portrayed life firsthand.

H. Alan Wycherley has maintained that Dreiser's nonfiction after 1900 fluctuated between "mechanism" and "vitalism."[58] If one agrees with Wycherley's assessment, Dreiser was clearly a vitalist in his free-lance work of the 1890s. This vitalist philosophy was so deeply rooted in the most important period of his development that it likely remained in him the rest of his career. In his novels, Dreiser often writes of the apparently indifferent and uncontrollable forces that sweep over man's life, but in reality he does not seem to have abandoned man's capacity to determine his own destiny. Although Dreiser has often been labeled as a literary naturalist in the manner of Zola and the other French naturalists, his magazine writing suggests that he was perhaps, at least in his early years, more a naturalist in the vein of Thoreau and John Burroughs than a literary naturalist. Many of his early writings reveal that Dreiser was genuinely an American patriot; he was unabashedly an advocate of the American values and an exponent of national character. Thus, his writing in this period constantly stressed the value of contentment in one's daily living; Dreiser was not a religionist or mystic as he was characterized toward the end of his life. Whatever assessment a modern reader may make of Dreiser's magazine writing, the fact remains that it was indeed comprehensive. And what we have is a substantial portion of the vital impressions a major American writer received from his environment at the dawn of the twentieth-century in America, which are rapidly fading from our memories.

7 Early Short Stories

In the summer of 1899, shortly before the writing of *Sister Carrie*, Dreiser tried his hand at the short story, his first concentrated effort to write fiction. Whatever technical devices he might have conceived, or whatever technical difficulties he might have encountered in producing his first short stories, the disposition of mind that lay behind and shaped these stories must have grown out of the disposition of the previous years. It must be remembered that as a newspaperman in the early nineties Dreiser felt severely restricted. He often detested the city editor's control over his selection of news material and his interpretation of it before the draft of an article was sent to press.

There is a great deal of information in *A Book About Myself* concerning the restrictions imposed on Dreiser by the press. But an article Dreiser wrote as late as 1938 still poses a question of the difference between literature and journalism. In this article Dreiser recalls a routine assignment given him while he was a young reporter in St. Louis. He was to interview an old millionaire about the city's new terminal project, and naturally he expected to meet a forceful experienced businessman. Unexpectedly, Dreiser met a pathetically aged and feeble man who thought of his success and power as useless. During the interview the old man could only say to Dreiser: "My interest in all these things is now so slight that it is scarcely worthwhile." Dreiser thought that this old man was "a spectacle for God and Men . . . ." Upon his return to the city desk, Dreiser asked the editor whether he should write about the old man's age. "No, no, no!" the editor almost shouted. "Can that stuff! Write only his answers. Never mind how old he is. That's just what I *don't* want. Do you want to queer this? Stick to the terminal dope and what he thought. We're not interested in his age." "No doubt," Dreiser reflects, "the vast majority of the people thought of him even then as young, active, his old self. But all this while this other picture was holding in my mind, and continued so to do for years after. I could scarcely think of the city even without thinking of him, his house, his dog, his age, his bony fingers, his fame." Dreiser then concludes:

> Those particular matters about which the city editor had asked to know concerned, as I now saw, only such things as were temporary

and purely constructive in their interest, nothing beyond the day—the hour—in which they appeared.

Literature as I now saw, and art in all its forms, was this other realm . . . which observed life as a whole and drew it without a flaw, a fact, missing. There, if anywhere, were to be reported or painted such conditions and scenes as this about which I had meditated and which could find no place in the rush and hurry of our daily press.

Then it was, and not until then, that the real difference between journalism and literature became plain.[1]

Compared with such an experience, Dreiser's editorial and free-lance work was less inhibited in the expression of ideas. As editor and "arranger" of *Ev'ry Month* Dreiser was not always in command of its material; he complained of the limitation imposed by the publisher and of the necessity to cater to the predilection of the magazine's readers. In his free-lance articles, Dreiser's freedom in selecting topics, of course, became much greater, as pointed out earlier. By the time he became involved in magazine work, particularly his free-lance writing, the kind of restriction that Dreiser suffered in his newspaper experience had clearly become less severe.

During this period Dreiser managed to express himself on the concepts that had been latent in his mind for a long time. When he first read Herbert Spencer's work, Dreiser absorbed the technical theories of Spencerian determinism as he confessed in *Ev'ry Month*. Seeing the proof of determinism in his own experience, Dreiser ignored Spencer's inherent theory of unending progress and chose to believe that man was a victim of natural forces. Dreiser's conclusion then was that "man was a mechanism, undevised and uncreated, and a badly and carelessly driven one at that." More significantly, he declared with an implication of pessimism:

I felt as low and hopeless at times as a beggar of the streets. There was of course this other matter of necessity, internal chemical compulsion, to which I had to respond whether I would or no. I was daily facing a round of duties which now more than ever verified all that I had suspected and that these books proved. With a gloomy eye I began to watch how the chemical—and their children, the mechanical—forces operated through man and outside him, and this under my very eyes.[2]

Whatever else he might have been in these years, Dreiser was a thoroughgoing determinist. He observed human behavior in terms of natural laws: the complexities of individual life were to be explained by physical and chemical reactions.

Despite the pessimistic conclusion at which Dreiser arrived in his interpretation of deterministic theory, it is still possible to find optimism in his belief that there is an inward, driving force, which is pushing mankind upward and onward. It is important here to consider the three related statements, separately quoted earlier. First, as Dreiser wrote with a sign of optimism, Spencer showed "how life has gradually become more and more complicated, more and more beautiful, and how architecture, sculpture, painting and music have gradualy [sic] developed, along with a thousand other features of our life of to-day."[3] Secondly, he expressed his latent hope: "We will be concerned with making things good, and with living so that things shall be better . . . . there will be naught but hope, unfaltering trust and peace" (*Ev'ry Month* 3, No. 2 [1 November 1896]: 7). Finally, Dreiser quoted a western journal as saying: "The world is not going downward to ruin, as the writer would have us believe. Everything in this splendid country has an upward trend, despite the wail of the cynics" (*Ev'ry Month* 3, No. 4 [1 January 1897]: 7).

The apparent discrepancy in Dreiser's thoughts in the period preceding the writing of his early fiction may account for the disharmony in his mind that is reflected in his novels. His critics, of course, have noticed this disharmony in discussing his fiction. R. L. Duffus, an early critic of Dreiser, believed that Dreiser's mind was not all of a piece, and regarded him as romantic, realistic, and mystic all at once.[4] As many critics have already pointed out, Dreiser's reasoning was not reliable. He leaped to conclusions, generalized too easily, and failed to examine narrowly enough. James T. Farrell remarked:

He accepted as science generalizations based on the ideas of nineteenth-century materialism. From these he adduced a deterministic idea, and this, in turn, was represented as biologic determinism. In *The Financier* and *The Titan* this biologic determinism is usually explained by the word "chemisms." Paradoxically enough, Dreiser's appeal to "chemisms" is made quite frequently in specific contexts concerning motivations of characters, where we can now see that the real rationale of these motivations can be most satisfactorily explained by Freudianism. Often his "chemisms" are overall generalizations of impulses of which the character is not aware. In this respect Dreiser asserted a biologic determinism, which, in terms of our present state of knowledge about man, is crude.[5]

This observation not only holds true of *The Financier* and *The Titan* but also is significant in revealing the loose formulas that Dreiser understood as laws, Dreiser himself admitted to the existence of discrepancies in his fiction. In reply to a question as to what motives were important in writing his fiction, Dreiser said, as quoted earlier: "From time to time I have had all the motives you list and many variations of the same. In connection with a work of any length, such as a novel, I don't see how a person could have a single motivation; at least I never had." [6]

In Dreiser's first stories, therefore, Dreiser might have had discrepant, or even contradictory thoughts. Significantly enough, "The Shining Slave Makers," [7] Dreiser's first effort at fiction, submitted to *The Century* late in 1899 and subsequently rejected by its editor, is an allegory embodying a deterministic world view. What Dreiser tells by way of this allegory is reiterated in his short story "Free," with which "The Shining Slave Makers" and the other early stories were later collected in a volume. Speaking for the plight of Rufus Haymaker, the protagonist of "Free," Dreiser makes this statement:

> One of the disturbing things about all this was the iron truth which it had driven home, namely, that Nature, unless it were expressed or represented by some fierce determination within, which drove one to do, be, cared no whit for him or any other man or woman. Unless one acted for oneself, upon some stern conclusion nurtured within, one might rot and die spiritually. Nature did not care . . . . All along he had seen what was happening to him; and yet held by convention he had refused to act always, because somehow he was not hard enough to act. He was not strong enough, that was the real truth—had not been. (*Free*, pp. 25–26)

In another of his short stories, "Butcher Rogaum's Door," [8] Drieser dramatizes a conflict between parent and child in much the same way as Crane deals with this conflict in *Maggie*. Unlike the first two stories, the other of Dreiser's stories in this group seem to mirror a considerable optimism and hope for man's condition. In "Nigger Jeff" [9] the protagonist recognizes how a helpless man, a victim of natural forces within him and a prisoner of hostile forces in soceity, encounters his tragedy—his death. But this story by no means paints a hopeless predicament for man; man is also destined to ameliorate. "Nigger Jeff" ends with the hero's proclamation of his new ambition and hope not only for himself as an artist but for all men. And somewhat blatantly, in "When the Old Century Was New," a fourth story,[10] there is more social optimism than Darwinism, so that Dreiser looks upon life as an easy struggle for Utopia rather than as a bitter struggle for survival.[11]

Arthur Henry, who later urged Dreiser to work on *Sister Carrie*, also influenced him to write these stories. The philosophical influences that Henry may have exercised on Dreiser during their friendship, especially before Dreiser wrote these stories, are hard to define clearly. Henry's letters show that he warned Dreiser against the dangers that were inherent in the contemplative disposition that Dreiser as editor revealed in the "Reflections" of *Ev'ry Month*. At that time Henry contributed essays entitled "The Philosophy of Hope" and "The Good Laugh" to Dreiser's magazine. Criticizing his despairing mood with a suggestion of optimism, Henry argued that Dreiser should turn to creative writing rather than pursue further his editorial work. And Henry, in the summer of 1897, invited Dreiser to visit the house at Maumee, Ohio, which Henry and his wife had bought, and suggested that he and Dreiser work together on various projects.[12] Because of further involvement in his work on *Ev'ry Month* and of his later venture into free-lance writing, Dreiser's visit to Maumee was postponed until the summer of 1899.

In the meantime, Dreiser and Jug (Sara Osborne White) were married in December 1898 in Washington. Henry, calling upon the newly wedded couple in their New York apartment, again insisted that Dreiser write fiction. However, as late as 1898, Dreiser was not at all enthusiastic about becoming a novelist. As he told Mencken later, he had a desire to write drama in these years. But Henry, seeing short stories in him, finally forced Dreiser to work on a story:

> I wrote one finally, sitting in the same room with him in a house on the Maumee River, at Maumee, Ohio, outside Toledo. This was in the summer of 1898 [1899]. And after every paragraph I blushed for my folly—it seemed so asinine[.] He insisted on my going on—that it was good—and I thought he was kidding me, that it was rotten, but that he wanted to let me down easy. Finally HE took [it], had it typewritten and sent it . . . Thus I began[.][13]

The theme of "The Shining Slave Makers," as might be expected from Dreiser's current preoccupation with deterministic philosophy, is the survival of the fittest. The setting of the story moves quickly from the human world to the world of ants. As Dreiser describes the environment and the action of the inhabitant, the ants' world is bizarre and fantastic yet turns out to be the same world with which he was familiar. That world is characterized by self-interest, greed, and the struggle for power.

"It was a hot day in August," Dreiser begins his tale. "The parching rays of a summer sun had faded the once sappy, green leaves of the trees to a dull and dusty hue" (*Ainslee's* 7: 445). The observer of this spectacle is a man named Robert McEwen, a sensitive and sympathetic student of life much like Dreiser himself. McEwen, taking leave of the drudgery of the busy city life, comes out to take a seat under a soothing old beech tree. And for a while he sinks into his usual contemplative mood. Suddenly McEwen's meditation is interrupted by an ant crawling on his trousers. Shaking it off and then stamping on another ant running along the walk in front of him, McEwen now finds a swarm of other black ants hurrying about. At last, when one ant more active than the others catches his eye, McEwen follows its zigzag course while it stops here and there, examining something and considering the object's interest value. Suddenly, with a drowsy spell, McEwen discovers himself in an imaginary world in which, during a famine, the black ants are at war with the red ants.

Some critics have noticed a similarity between the setting of this tale and one of the interpolations Balzac makes toward the end of *The Wild Ass's Skin*.[14] Balzac's passage reads:

> Who has not, at some time or other in his life, watched the comings and goings of an ant, slipped straws into a yellow slug's one breathing-hole, studied the vagaries of a slender dragon-fly, pondered admiringly over the countless veins in an oak-leaf . . .? Who has not looked long in delight at the effects of sun and rain on a roof of brown tiles, at the dewdrops, or at the variously shaped petals of the flower-cups? Who has not sunk into these idle, absorbing meditations . . .?[15]

In Balzac's story, however, the principal character, Valentin, is weary of his life and yet feels desperate at the thought of his approaching death. In order to divert his thoughts, Valentin tries to observe nature, thereby consoling himself with the equation of man and natural beings. "The leading idea of this human comedy," Balzac writes, "came to me first as a dream . . . . The idea came from the study of human life in comparison with the life of animals.'' [16] Balzac's vision, in his writing of *The Wild Ass's Skin*, is that of a human biologist. In writing ''The Shining Slave Makers'' Dreiser is not viewing man's life in terms of animal life. Rather, as in Thoreau's ant war in *Walden*, Dreiser is looking at ants in terms of man.

In its outline the first feature story that Dreiser wrote for the Pittsburgh *Dispatch*—''The Fly''—had the same intention as ''The Shining Slave Makers,'' though it is less developed in its treatment than the short story. In ''The Shining Slave Makers,'' the first ant that encounters McEwen in the dream interrogates him:

> ''Anything to eat hereabout?'' questioned the newcomer, in a friendly and yet self-interested tone.
> McEwen drew back.
> ''I do not know,'' he said, ''I have just—''
> ''Awful,'' said the stranger, not waiting to hear his answer. ''It looks like famine. You know the Sanguineæ have gone to war.''
> ''No,'' answered McEwen, mechanically.
> ''Yes,'' said the other, ''they raided the Fuscæ yesterday. They'll be down on us next.'' (*Ainslee's* 7: 445)

McEwen, upon seeing another ant carrying a crumb as large as the ant's body, eagerly asks the ant where it has found the crumb. The ant answers McEwen at once:

> ''Here,'' said Ermi.
> ''Will you give me a little?''
> ''I will not,'' said the other, and a light came in his eye that was almost evil. (ibid., 445–46)

With vivid dramatic force this situation projects a junglelike world. And, more interestingly, McEwen, who is now a member of the same tribe—the black ants—cannot secure help from the ants of his own family. The persistent, reciprocal warfare among members of the family is more evocative of life in the animal kingdom than it is of the world of civilized man. Ironically, Dreiser intended to project an image of the survival of the fittest, not in the world of men but in the world of ants.

Dreiser's major motif here is man's selfishness as it is illustrated by the ants' behavior toward their fellow beings at the time of strife:

"All right," said McEwen, made bold by hunger and yet cautious by danger, "which way would you advise me to look?"

"Why, any way," said Ermi, and strode off.

. . . .

He eagerly hailed the newcomer, who was yet a long way off.

"What is it?" asked the other, coming up rapidly.

"Do you know where I can get something to eat?"

"Is that why you called me?" he answered, eyeing him angrily. "Certainly not. If I had anything for myself, I would not be out here. Go and hunt for it like the rest of us."

"I have been hunting," cried McEwen, his anger rising. "I have searched here until I am almost starved."

"No worse that I or any of us, are you?" said the other. "Look at me. Do you suppose I am feasting?" (ibid., 446)

This is, to be sure, an allegory of life, but more importantly it is an allegory of Dreiser's own struggle in the past. In the newspaper experience of the early nineties, Dreiser viewed "life as a fierce, grim struggle in which no quarter was either given or taken, and in which all men laid traps, lied, squandered, erred through illusion" (*Book*, p. 70). One ant's angry reply to McEwen, the newcomer, "Is that why you called me? . . . . Go and hunt for it like the rest of us," is reminiscent of the scene of the survival of the fittest that Dreiser witnessed in the office of Pulitzer's *World* when he was on the staff of that great paper in the cold winter months of 1894–95. In that newspaper office, as Dreiser later remembered, the men working under Pulitzer appeared to Dreiser to be like tortured animals. This motif in "The Shining Slave Makers" is not contrived to fit the doctrine of survival but is based on an actual experience.

Later in the story, when another ant is facing death, the compassionate McEwen attempts to offer him aid, but the ant, now overwhelmed by his own despair and resignation, declines. McEwen now realizes how helpless a creature can be under these circumstances. He cannot but simply look silently on the ant. "The sufferer," Dreiser remarks, "closed his eyes in evident pain, and trembled convulsively. Then he fell back and died. McEwen gazed upon the bleeding body, now fast stiffening in death, and wondered" (*Ainslee's* 7: 446). Dreiser's inference from the scene is clear: man, just like an insect, is powerless against those incidental forces that always surround him. This scene also resembles the aftermath of a train accident Dreiser reported a few years earlier in St. Louis. He then asked viewing the dead bodies that were twisted and burned beyond recognition, "Who were they? I asked myself. What had they been, done? The nothingness of man! They looked so commonplace, so unimportant, so like dead flies or beetles" (*Book*, p. 163).

When a war breaks out between the black slave makers and the red Sanguineæ (in Thoreau's ant war, between the black imperialists and the red republicans), McEwen, of course, sides with the black ants, but finally meets his own death. Dreiser seems to be telling himself: join the crowd, fight for the crowd, die for the crowd. The struggle for survival continues without purpose or a goal in sight. Only the fittest will survive; death alone is safe. After McEwen finally returns to reality, he is now possessed by a "mad enthusiasm." He tries to figure out the advantage of having met his recent comrades—the Shining Slave Makers—but, Dreiser writes, "finding it not he stood gazing. Then came reason, and with it sorrow—a vague, sad something out of far-off things" (*Ainslee's* 7: 450).

By projecting a serious and significant human dilemma onto minute subhuman life, Dreiser achieves detachment. But, in the allegory, though detached from the violent scene in which the struggle for survival is carried on, he can look at McEwen somewhat in the same way that McEwen looks at these ants in the insect kingdom. In this way Dreiser does not reduce his life experience to a mere objective show but dramatizes it from a clumsy but instinctively derived point of view. By the solid material behind the theme and plot, the story became a powerful expression of his preoccupation at the time.

What Dreiser had to say in his first significant piece of fiction was exactly what brought about its rejection by the editor who first read the manuscript and returned it to its author with a letter protesting its "despicable philosophy."[17] If this were the way the young author thought about man's life, the less he wrote about it the better. The editor thought that Dreiser was saying that men are cruel and deceptive just as nature is. The editor's reasoning was that Dreiser enjoyed these qualities of man—the brutal, the deceptive, and the violent—and that Dreiser was, therefore, dangerous to human society. However, Dreiser, who was blazing in those years with a strong passion for society and his fellow men, was still lined up against them.

Despite this slap from the timid and conventional editor-ambassador,[18] Dreiser was soon to discover an ally. "The Shining

Slave Makers'' was accepted by *Ainslee's* for publication, and Dreiser probably took this acceptance as an encouragement for his continuing adherence to his own philosophy. He also wrote ''Butcher Rogaum's Door,'' ''The World and the Bubble,'' ''Nigger Jeff,'' and ''When the Old Century Was New,'' and, except for ''The World and the Bubble,'' which has eluded identification, these short stories subsequently appeared in print. In ''Butcher Rogaum's Door,'' Dreiser again justifies the value of Spencerian determinism. The events of the story happen with the mechanical consistency of the so-called chemisms. The story is a study of an incident that Dreiser sees as inevitable, granted the incipient milieu in which the character was placed.

The plot of ''Butcher Rogaum's Door'' first develops with the tension between an old father and his teenage daughter, Theresa, who has begun to be allured to the streetlights and the boys loitering outdoors on summer evenings. As the title suggests, the door to Rogaum's apartment above his butcher shop on Bleecker Street in New York City becomes significant. Old Rogaum tries to exhort against his daughter's going out after dark. But adolescent Theresa, awakening to a burgeoning sexual feeling, now wants ''to walk up and down in the as yet bright street, where were voices and laughter, and occasionally moonlight streaming down'' (*Mirror* 9 [12 December 1901]: 15); thus, she cannot help disregarding her father's discipline. The stubborn German father's last resort is to threaten to lock her out, and indeed one night the determined old Rogaum does lock his daughter out when she fails to return by nine from dallying with her young friend. At the door, Theresa overhears her father talking savagely to Mrs. Rogaum, ''Let her go, now. I vill her a lesson teach.'' Rattling the door again and getting no answer, she grows defiant. ''Now, strangely,'' Dreiser observes, ''a new element, not heretofore apparent in her nature, but, nevertheless wholly there, was called into life, springing in action as Diana, full formed. The cold chill left her and she wavered angrily'' (ibid., 16). And she walks back to her friend George Almerting. The night deepens; there is no sound of Theresa, and Rogaum starts searching for her. Returning in fear and without success, he sees at the door a young woman writhing in unmitigated pain as a result of her having drunk acid in a suicide attempt. Rogaum at first mistakes the woman for his daughter Theresa. However clumsy the coincidence that Dreiser devises to suggest Theresa's possible fate, this story in the simple truth of its setting and characters mirrors the world Dreiser had grown to accept.

The suicide, like Theresa, was once locked out, but Theresa, unlike the suicide, is never to become a prostitute or suicide, or both, like Crane's Maggie. Theresa obviously was written about as though she were one of Dreiser's own sisters. He was portraying the life of the people he knew by heart and what they could have become.

Fortunately, Theresa comes back safely, unlike the girl at the door who comes to a tragic end. But this was exactly his own family, since the religious old father, strict with the wanton daughter, locked her out one night and then worried, so that when he regained her unharmed, he refrained from beating her as he had intended. In the story, Dreiser, as elsewhere—*Dawn, Jennie Gerhardt, The "Genius", An American Tragedy*—treats the father with a sympathetic tone. A too Calvinistic German butcher, Rogaum emerges as a strangely appealing and rather pathetic figure. As in another of Dreiser's short stories, "Typhoon," the father is a German immigrant with a heavy accent and has a moderately prosperous small business. The children in the Dreiser family, and indeed those in the Gerhardts' and Griffiths' families, attempted to run away from their oppressive poverty-stricken households. The chief difference between the Rogaum family and the other families is that it is not poverty-stricken. But here Dreiser's emphasis is upon the inability of parents to understand not only the social desires—in this case, money—but the natural desires and inclinations of their children.

Mrs. Rogaum, "a particularly fat, old German lady, completely dominated by her liege and portly lord" (ibid., 15), is warmhearted but is in no position to advise her daughter. Dreiser's image of the mother is a significant departure from that of a modern American mother. What Dreiser depicts as a family situation in his fiction cannot be compared to that of today's America but to that of many an immigrant in the late nineteenth century. And this is exactly the scene of the family he knew in his youth. Thus Dreiser delineates not so much the social conditioning of his individuals, as critics maintain, but the historical complexities that make understandable the uniqueness of each individual's experience.

The city life to which Theresa is attracted is also important historically. Dreiser is here interested in the family in America in the 1880s and 90s, as in *Sister Carrie* and *Jennie Gerhardt*, which was changed and perverted by artificial lures. Theresa, like the children of the Dreiser family, is discontented with family ties and enchanted by the outside forces that separate her from her family. This is the same situation in which Dreiser describes Carrie's approaching the city in the summer of 1889 with the same "wonder and desire" he himself had felt in approaching Chicago two summers earlier. The role of the parent in the American family structure was diminishing; the truth of this becomes obvious when the family of Dreiser's fiction is compared with that of the present day. And this change, although important in the values of the children, was devastating in its effects on the parents.

In "Butcher Rogaum's Door," the concepts of individual morality are bound to the larger, overall concept of man in a society where the artificial restraints of social position are removed and where the chemical urges of the blood are observed and respected. If Theresa could become enthralled with the lures of the city and meet a fine young man with "a shrewd way of winking one eye" (ibid., 15) within the boundary of her household, she would not have gone out to the streets at night. Dreiser's point is that evil in man results not so much from an inherent tendency for evil in the individual as from the unreasonable and often unjust demands in society—in Theresa's case, the father, his customers, the police, and the townsmen on Bleecker Street. She is, first of all, the result of a home environment that has alienated her from life, so that when she faces its risks and might possibly be betrayed, it is the society that has provided such a milieu which is to blame. Likewise, whoever might exploit Theresa is not so much the result of a limitation of character as the result of society's failure to develop necessary virtues in the would-be exploiter. And these are represented less as the natural virtue of the passively innocent than as the qualities of aggression, selfishness, deceptiveness, and competition, which Dreiser perceives as the law of nature. In this sense "Butcher Rogaum's Door" is analogous to Dreiser's first story, "The Shining Slave Makers."

In both of these stories, the image of life that Dreiser presents is necessarily colored by a rather pessimistic frame of mind in accord with the philosophy of the gloomy determinism that accounts for human conditions. This is, perhaps, most obviously shown at the end of "The Shining Slave Makers," where McEwen's vision of life as he is awakening from his recent dream is tinged with sorrow. This is also shown in the story of Rogaum and Theresa, but in this story the sense of sorrow is somewhat lightened by the hopeful tone that Dreiser gives to the outcome of the incident. The story, of course, does not say that one should lock out his daughter at night lest a dire fate befall her. Nor does it say that Theresa has learned a lesson so that she will not wander off at night again. For the author does not believe that man's life is only at the mercy of fate. Old Rogaum has learned that he must not be too harsh toward his daughter because he now recognizes the necessary demands of a young woman.

In his second story, then, Dreiser was to tell the reader that such a conflict between father and daughter could be adjusted. Since man's unreasonable environment was being ameliorated, man could learn. Dreiser was to weave this sign of hope into the third story, "Nigger Jeff," in which he created patterns of action with architectonic skill. As a result, he achieved in the texture of the story a cumulative effect of no little significance. Because his two earlier stories derive from his own experiences (the characters in those stories are like himself, his family, and the people he knew, and the incidents are those he saw) his expression is spontaneous and markedly consonant with the feelings that were deeply rooted in his heart. Also in "Nigger Jeff" Dreiser was to express such congenial feelings as he remembered from an incident that occurred in his newspaper experience in St. Louis.

The story develops around a report of an apparently nefarious rape; it is not simply an illustration of man's conduct observed in terms of the deterministic philosophy but rather the process of revelation a newspaper reporter goes through. One day the reporter is sent out by the city editor to cover the lynching of a Negro rapist. The reporter, Eugene Davies, much like the young Dreiser in St. Louis, is portrayed as a naive youth. On that day, a bright spring afternoon, Davies "was feeling exceedingly well and good-natured. The world seemed worth singing about" (*Ainslee's* 8: 366). But, after learning the circumstances of the rape, the Negro Jeff's behavior, his family's grief, and above all the transcending beauty and serenity of nature in contrast with the human abjection and agonies, Davies realizes that his sympathies have shifted. This reporter, then, is not simply the obtuse observer, a mystery story character who watches the plot unfold. He is the perceiving center; he recognizes that the world is not neatly dichotomized as black and white. The action of the story takes place in the hero's reaction to the dreadful violence and in his understanding of American society and himself as artist.

One of the most salient technical devices displayed in this story is the contrast in the images of man and nature. Although in the beginning the reporter is convinced that Jeff is guilty, he grows increasingly less certain. Even before he reaches the site of the lynching, Davies takes note of "the whiteness of the little houses, the shimmering beauty of the little creek you had to cross in going from the depot. At the one main corner a few men [a part of the mob] were gathered about a typical village barroom" (ibid., 366). As the mob hurries on with the horror impending, the "night was exceedingly beautiful. Stars were already beginning to shine . . . . The air was fresh and tender. Some pea fowls were crying afar off and the east promised a golden moon" (ibid., 369). Again, a contrast of the light and the dark is maintained in a later scene:

> The gloomy company seemed a terrible thing . . . .
> . . .He was breathing heavily and groaning. His eyes were fixed and staring, his face and hands bleeding as if they had been scratched or trampled on. He was bundled up like limp wheat . . . .
> . . .Still, the company moved on and he followed, past fields lit white by the moon, under dark, silent groups of trees, through which the moonlight fell in patches, up hilltops and down into valleys, until at last the little stream came into view, sparkling like a molten flood of silver in the night. (ibid., 373)

As Davies watches the limp body plunging down and pulling up with the sound of a creaking rope, in

> the weak moonlight it seemed as if the body were struggling, but he could not tell . . . . Only the black mass swaying in the pale light, over the shiny water of the stream seemed wonderful.
> . . .The light of morning began to show as tender lavender and gray in the east. Still he sat. Then came the roseate hue of day, to which the waters of the stream responded, the white pebbles shining beautifully at the bottom. Still the body hung black and limp, and now a light breeze sprang up and stirred it visibly. (ibid., 374)

On the one hand, the hero clearly recognizes the signs of evil indicated by "the struggling body," "the black mass," and "the body hanging black and limp." On the other, the images of the dark are intermingled in Davies' mind with those of the light that suggest hope: "the weak moonlight," "the pale light," "the shiny water of the stream," "the light of morning," "tender lavender and gray in the east," "the roseate hue of day," "the white pebbles shining beautifully at the bottom." As the story progresses toward its end, the images of good increasingly dominate those of evil, a pattern already revealed in this scene.

Later, visiting the room where the body is laid and seeing the rapist's sister sobbing over it, Davies becomes aware that all "the corners of the room were quite dark, and only in the middle were shining splotches of moonlight." For Davies, the climactic scene of his experience takes place when he dares to lift the sheet covering the body. He can now see exactly where the rope tightened around the neck. The delineation of the light against the dark is, once more, focused on the dead body as Dreiser describes it: "A bar of cool moonlight lay across the face and breast" (ibid., 375). Such deliberate contrasts between the light and the dark, hope and despair, suggest that man has failed to appreciate "transcending beauty" and "unity of nature," which are really illusions to him, and that he has only imitated the cruel and the indifferent that nature appears to symbolize.

At the end of the story, Davies is overwhelmed not only by the remorse he feels for the victim but also by his compassion for the victim's bereft mother he finds in the dark corner of the room. "Davies," Dreiser writes, "began to understand . . . . Out in the moonlight, he struck a pace, but soon stopped and looked back. The whole dreary cabin, with its one golden door, where the light was, seemed a pitiful thing. He swelled with feeling and pathos as he looked. The night, the tragedy, the grief, he saw it all" (ibid., 375). The emphasis of the story is not, therefore, upon the process of the young man's becoming an artist; it is upon the sense of urgency in which the protagonist is compelled to act as a reformer. With his final proclamation, "I'll get it all in," the hero's revelation culminates in a feeling of triumph. Although, to Dreiser, man appears necessarily limited by his environment and natural feeling, Dreiser asserts that man can learn.

"Nigger Jeff," in disclosing true social conditions, can be construed as a powerful expression of Dreiser's hope for the better in American society. And it is quite reasonable to suppose that all this time there was in Dreiser as much optimism in viewing life as a struggle for Utopia as there was pessimism. For among his earliest short stories the last, "When the Old Century Was New"—though generally considered inferior—is clearly more a wistful Utopian picture than the others. In this story, Dreiser reconstructs one day in the spring of 1801 in New

York City after the turn of the century. In such a world there is no misery, no struggle; the gulf dividing the rich from the poor is unimportant, and the friction between social classes is totally unknown. William Walton, a dreamer, taking a day off from his business engagements, strolls down the social center of New York. There he notices the celebrities of the city, even Thomas Jefferson and "the newly-elected President" Adams.[19]

Walton is also Dreiser himself; Walton, too, like Dreiser with Jug in New York, is accompanied by his fiancée:

> Elatedly they made their way to the old homestead again, and then being compelled to leave her, while she dressed for the theatre, he made his way toward the broad and tree-shaded Bowery, where was the true and idyllic walk for a lover. . . . Here young Walton, as so many others before him, strolled and hummed, thinking of all that life and the young city held for him. Here he planned to build that mansion of his own—far out, indeed, above Broome Street. (*Pearson's* 9: 140)

Unlike Walton, however, Dreiser cannot help noticing "the aristocracy, gentry, and common rabble forming in separate groups" (ibid., 133). Although Walton at heart feels optimistic toward the new century, Dreiser at his side could not escape the prospect of misery and oppression. Dreiser observes with a touch of irony that Walton "had no inkling, as he pondered, of what a century might bring forth. The crush and stress and wretchedness fast treading upon this path of loveliness he could not see" (ibid., 140). F. O. Matthiessen can legitimately call "When the Old Century Was New" only a sketch "with nothing to distinguish it from other paper-thin period pieces."[20] But it is worth noting that even in this slight piece of fiction we find Dreiser's dramatization of the American success story with his world of changing cities, where new careers and new fortunes are made daily. Despite the gloom hovering under the deterministic theory of life at his disposal, there was in Dreiser's mind during this period as much joy and optimism that influenced his writing.

Robert E. Spiller in the *Literary History of the United States* maintains that Dreiser's short stories "in theme and treatment add little to an

analysis of the novels and may be compared to a painter's sketches."[21]
But these short stories written before his novels are, nonetheless, closely
related to his early novels. In subject matter these stories are various
studies on the conditions of men and women in society, sometimes as
individuals and at other times as groups. Man tends to be a victim of
forces not only within him but about him. Dreiser, moreover, views men
not only as social individuals but also, as in "Butcher Rogaum's Door,"
as historical individuals. Much can be learned from the pages of *Sister
Carrie* and *Jennie Gerhardt* about the nature and structure of American
society and the American family in the years before the turn of the
century. But, delineating the growth of cities, exhibiting the forceful
lures of city life, and emphasizing the conflict between convention and
individual demands, Dreiser shows one of the basic motifs of his early
novels in such stories as "Butcher Rogaum's Door" and "When the Old
Century Was New."

His early stories, like the ant tragedy developed in "The Shining
Slave Makers," give Dreiser a congenial means of expression, primarily because they contain characters, whether in an allegory or a historical romance, like Dreiser himself, personages he knew or events he
remembered from his personal experience. It is arguable that Dreiser's
early short fiction would have been more significant had he not been
influenced by many of the specific technical concepts of the Spencerian world. More important for the argument here is that, as an artist,
Dreiser transcends these technicalities and writes fiction with living
individuals, whose personalities express their historical milieu and do
not reflect merely the abstract motivations of "chemisms." This is,
perhaps, why Eliseo Vivas has observed: "Fortunately the sincere
artist magnificently contradicted the self-taught materialist and found a
purpose that, had he been consistent, he could not have found . . . .
And if life's meaning is something sad or tragic, in Dreiser's own life,
in his enormous capacity for pity, we find an example of a man who,
through his work, gave the lie to his own theories."[22] What prompted
Dreiser to write fiction was his overwhelming desire to understand
human beings. Unlike other literary naturalists, Dreiser attempted to
discover an ideal order in man's life as he does in these stories. In this
sense, Dreiser is more an idealist than a pessimist. And his understanding of humanity often goes beyond the deterministic philosophy he
learned from Spencer.

This ambivalence in Dreiser's thoughts in the making of the early stories gave rise to his practice of applying the theory of determinism as well as designing his stories with a historical, and often personal, significance. This is why consistency in these stories is nearly impossible. Even though Dreiser's characters tend to be controlled by circumstances, the focus of his stories is upon the individual and the moral consequences of his actions, as shown by Eugene Davies in "Nigger Jeff." Dreiserian characters are sometimes larger than the author's occasional philosophy, and they are able to speak for themselves. Dreiser the philosopher only gets in their way; Dreiser the artist remains true to them. In the end the interest of the story lies not in Dreiser's mind, but in his heart. Hence, his frequent tone of optimism, mingled, as it frequently is, with his pessimism, can be reasonably accounted for.

My Dear Mr. Doubleday:—

I return herewith my novel partly revised according to your wishes. The names of Francis Wilson Charles, F. Whitman Schluncker and Mayer, the Waldorf, the Morton House the Broadway and so on have been removed. Also I have found occasion to agree with you in most of the passages indicated and too strike out those lines which seem to you too suggestive.

On this and the following pages appears the draft of a letter Dreiser wrote around September 1900 to Frank N. Doubleday to criticize the publisher's censorship. Doubleday had earlier attempted to nullify the contract for the publication of *Sister Carrie. Courtesy of the University of Pennsylvania Library.*

two have been question marks
opposite names which are wholly
fictitious. These of course need
not be disturbed.

As for the name of Sherry I have
substituted Delmonico throughout
the book. Your question mark
is opposite that also as something
to be removed but I cannot agree
with you. Like Daly and Wallack,
it is already too common in literature,
Richard Harding Davis and Paul
Leicester Ford have used these so
frequently that I cannot be
accused of going beyond the pale
of literary usage in this matter.

Daly, Wallacks and Delmonicos must claim.

In one place you mark my mention of E.P.P. Roe & "The Opening of a Chestnut Burr" as something to be changed. In another place you have Balzac "Père Goriot" unquestioned. Why is this? Mr. Roe is dead. His novel was well known. May a writer not mention a standard piece of American fiction or a well known American author. Is the preference given to foreigners? As a publisher of Mr. Kipling's works you should have execrated his mention of Besant and Stevenson, both contemporaries and living at

the two he mentioned them, ~~———~~ Mr.
Foote and Mr. Dawes err in the
same seemingly to you objectionable
manner and their novels are
scarcely to reckoned as failures.

I have noted your statement.
"We have taken out profanity which
we regarded as imperative". If you
mean you have already stricken
it from the pages, I do not see
where. If you mean that all
you have questioned must be
changed I will have to disagree
with you. Since when has the
expression "Lord Lord", become
profane. Wherein is "Damn", "By
the Lord" and "By God".

8 *Sister Carrie*

With the completion of his first short stories in the summer of 1899 Dreiser began to take Arthur Henry's flattery seriously. When Dreiser had some of these stories eventually accepted for publication by popular literary magazines of the day, he felt that his dream was being realized. Conceiving Dreiser's possible success as a novelist, Henry had earlier urged him to make specific plans to write a novel. In September 1899, Dreiser came back to New York, and Henry followed him there. They lived together in Dreiser's apartment and collaborated on several magazine articles, enjoying their friendship and even more their exchange of ideas. More than anyone else, Henry knew this unknown writer who was to produce that phenomenal American novel—*Sister Carrie*.

Henry was later to write about their relationship:

> Dreiser's chronicle of our association is correct. He is generous toward me but I who know him better than anyone know that he is the most generous—the least self interested of men. You are right as to his impelling desire of analysis and corresponding lack of egotism . . . . Unlike the scientist, however, his vision is obscured or rather colored by a profound tenderness which unfortunately he has learned to mistrust—by a compassion that torments him with a magnified idea of the misfortunes of others. He gives his coat to a beggar in rags, just as he seeks to clothe in virtue all the tattered characters of the world. I know no one more sensitive to beauty or . . . luxury and convenience, but he is at the same time more conscious than anyone I know, of the multitude who are deprived of these. He seems to feel responsible for all the misery of the world and for every unqualified wretch of abortive scoundrel born into it . . . .
>
> For many years I fished and hunted and played with Dreiser in a World of Thought and found him always a true sportsman. The ideas I caught seemed to him larger than his own . . . . If I inspired him it was because I insisted on his looking at and appreciating *His Own*. Dreiser will not have fulfilled his mission in the world until he sits down to a novel in the mood in which he composes a poem— and sustains that mood with all his people, rich and powerful and poor and weak, until he finishes it.[1]

Because Henry wanted to proceed with the writing of his own novel, *A Princess of Arcady*, he told Dreiser to begin work on a novel at once so that they could work simultaneously and encourage each other. Dreiser agreed and immediately searched for possible subjects. It is quite probable that Dreiser thought of the career of his brother Paul, for, as he says in *Dawn*, he always wanted to develop a novel based on Paul but failed to "find the time to write." [2] As his autobiographies and "My Brother Paul" (included in *Twelve Men*) well indicate, Dreiser, always fascinated by this brother's character since his early youth, admired and respected his brother. And Paul was, to be sure, one of the personages whom Dreiser knew best and to whom he was closest in his early career. But because he considered Paul a success, Dreiser knew that Paul would not serve as the prototype of a major character in his novel. What Dreiser needed was a tragic figure who would provide the implications of life tinged with the misery of the world and its pathos. Then one of his sisters came to his mind, and her wandering in the cities of Chicago and New York suggested to Dreiser a vague picture of the human conditions that he had long brooded upon and still did when Henry implored him to begin a novel.

"Finally—September 1899," Dreiser says, "I took a piece of yellow paper and to please him wrote down a title at random—*Sister Carrie*—and began." [3] He later said: "My mind was a blank except for the name. I had no idea who or what she was to be. I have often thought there was something mystic about it, as if I were being used, like a medium." [4] Dreiser seems to have felt at great ease in writing the first part of *Sister Carrie*. Once in a while he would drop in at Maria's restaurant on West Twelfth Street to see his bohemian friends, including Richard Duffy, the editor of *Ainslee's*. "The fecundity of the man was amazing," Duffy later wrote in retrospect. "Every few days he could make the breezy announcement that since he last came into view he had written as many as ten or twenty thousand words." [5] Dreiser wrote continuously until the middle of October and got as far as the point where Carrie is introduced to Hurstwood.

"Then," Dreiser says, "I quit, disgusted[.] I thought it was rotten." [6] Nowhere does he explain exactly why he felt this way. We may suppose, perhaps, that Dreiser was simply suffering from first novel "jitters." This feeling may have been exacerbated by his knowledge that he was attempting something in a relatively new vein and was himself unsure of its potentialities. He tried to continue but, as he says, he could not. Feeling that the novel was a total failure and neglecting it for two months, Dreiser went back to writing short stories and also thought that he should resume writing magazine articles. He started again on *Sister Carrie* and managed to reach the point just before Hurstwood steals the money. Then he had to stop again, "because I couldn't think how to have him do it. Two months more of idleness. I was through with the book apparently[.] Actually I never expected to finish it[.]"[7] Before the beginning of March 1900, Henry returned from an affair with the black-haired Anna Malone, directress of a typing agency in New York, whom Dreiser had earlier introduced to him. Henry at once read the manuscript and, thinking "there was nothing wrong with it, told me I must go on."[8] Solving the problem of Hurstwood's stealing the money from the safe, Dreiser encountered no more difficulties until Hurstwood's deterioration somehow reminded Dreiser of his bitter days when he was working for Pulitzer's *World* and later resigned from it. "Then," he says, "I had to stop again. Somehow I felt unworthy to write all that. It seemed too big, too baffling, don't you know?"[9] Moreover, at this time, Dreiser tells us, his own financial situation harassed his mental energy, and slowed down his writing. However, because of the persistent pressure from Henry, he arrived at an end of the novel.

Yet he was dissatisfied with the ending he made. He originally wanted to leave the impression that Carrie's story would be continuous. He felt the ending should be focused upon the unending wonder of Carrie— rocking her chair endlessly. But this exact impression, Dreiser later wrote in the New York *Herald*, evaded him. Failing to hit the right note he sought, Dreiser left his apartment and went to the Palisades overlooking the Hudson River. There for two hours he let his thoughts wander freely. "Then suddenly," he tells us, "came the inspiration of its own accord."[10] Quickly he wrote down:

> Oh, Carrie, Carrie! Oh, blind strivings of the human heart! Onward, onward, it saith, and where beauty leads, there it follows. Whether it be the tinkle of a lone sheep bell o'er some quiet landscape, or the glimmer of beauty in sylvan places, or the show of soul in some passing eye, the heart knows and makes answer, following. It is when the feet weary and hope seems vain that the heartaches and the longings arise. Know, then, that for you is neither surfeit nor content. In your rocking-chair, by your window dreaming, shall you long, alone. In your rocking-chair, by your window, shall you dream such happiness as you may never feel.[11]

Sister Carrie was completed in the spring of 1900. As he wrote to Mencken later, Dreiser "took an intense interest in the last few [chapters] much more so than in anything which had gone before."[12] Henry, reading the novel in its entirety, suggested that he should not change a word, but later they came to agree on a considerable cutting. As a result, Dreiser recalled, the manuscript was shortened by about forty-thousand words.[13] In May or June 1900, Dreiser sent the manuscript to Harper's because he knew one of the editors. Harper's rejected it, but suggested that he submit the manuscript to Doubleday, Page and Company.

Frank Norris was one of the influential readers for the Doubleday firm, and recommended the book for publication with great enthusiasm. The rest of the publishing history of the novel is well known[14] and is unnecessary to reiterate here. But in view of Frank Doubleday's conservatism and genteelness in taste, it is easy to understand that the firm was reluctant to publish such a novel. The same company had earlier published Norris' *McTeague*, but Doubleday justified the publication of Norris' book by asserting that it gave the reader an ideal moral lesson. All the characters in *McTeague* are punished for their "immoral" conduct; in the eyes of the publisher, Dreiser's heroine, far from being punished, does not regret her dealings with the two sinners and becomes a successful actress. Perhaps the influence of Doubleday's wife has been exaggerated; Doubleday himself could have been sufficiently influenced by a personal dislike for Dreiser's theme and treatment.

As Jack Salzman observes, "Not only have we misunderstood the order of events and various commitments involved in the publication of *Sister Carrie*, but we may have also exaggerated the role played by Frank Norris, while perhaps unjustifiably condemning Mrs. Doubleday" (ibid., 127). Norris' support of the novel may not have been as ardent as that of Arthur Henry, to whom Dreiser was most indebted throughout the history of the composition and publication of *Sister Carrie*. Evidently, Norris was at first enthusiastic about the novel, but in the light of his own career and, most specifically, his relationship with the publishers, Norris probably felt it best to remain subservient to Doubleday and Page. This observation can be further strengthened by Dreiser's contemptuous attitude toward Norris' role as an American writer: in Dreiser's words, as quoted earlier, "Norris wrote *McTeague* and *The Octopus*. Then he fell into the hands of the noble Doubleday who converted him completely to *The Pit*, a bastard bit of romance of the best seller variety'' (*Letters*, 1: 329). In short, we can still do little more than speculate, but it is now clear that Norris is also partially responsible for the suppression and subsequent unpopularity of *Sister Carrie*.

Dreiser's attempts to publish *Sister Carrie* and its seven-year suppression and subsequent reception, once published, have become legendary. One of the major reasons why this novel was frowned upon in 1900 was precisely Dreiser's obvious adherence to the deterministic view of human conditions. Many of his early critics considered Dreiser to be solely a victim of the so-called central truth about man as he saw it. They felt that he knew no more or no less than this crudely generalized mechanism of man—the theory that man is an animal subject to no human law but only the law of his own instinct, behaving as he desires, controlled only by natural forces. According to this theory, the male of the species is characterized by his greed for material gains and his desire for the opposite sex. The female is, then, a weaker, vain, pleasure-seeking creature who cannot resist the flattery of the male. The place where these creatures live is much like a jungle where, in the conflict of interests, the victory goes to the beast that is physically fittest in the environment and mentally most ruthless to his fellow creatures.

These critics saw in *Sister Carrie* the dominant influence of literary naturalism. Philip Rahv, though implying that ideological consistency and fictional practice should not be equated, nonetheless made the following assertion in 1942 in his controversial essay, ''On the Decline of Naturalism'':

I know of no hard and fast rules that can be used to distinguish the naturalist method from the methods of realism generally. It is certainly incorrect to say that the difference is marked by the relative density of detail. Henry James observes in his essay *The Art of Fiction* that it is above all ''solidity of specification'' that makes for the illusion of life—the air of reality—in a novel; and the truth of this dictum is borne out by the practice of the foremost modern innovators in this medium, such as Proust, Joyce, and Kafka. It is not, then, primarily the means employed to establish verisimilitude that fix the naturalist imprint upon a work of fiction. A more conclusive test, to my mind, is its treatment of the relation of character to background. I would classify as naturalistic that type of realism in which the individual is portrayed not merely as subordinate to his background but as wholly determined by it—that type of realism, in other words, in which the environment displaces its inhabitants in the role of the hero. Theodore Dreiser, for example, comes as close as any American writer to plotting the careers of his characters strictly within a determinative process.[15]

Dreiser's critics tend to take either one of two basic positions: first there are those who, though recognizing the influence of naturalistic theory on Dreiser, do not necessarily find it detrimental to the effectiveness of a novel and may, in fact, find naturalistic theory well used; second, there are those who find naturalism a decided liability to the novel. Lars Åhnebrink, representing the first view, writes in *The Beginnings of Naturalism in American Fiction*: "Scholars generally agree that naturalism in the United States came of age in the writings of Theodore Dreiser, whose first novel, *Sister Carrie* (1900), is a fairly typical work of the movement."[16] The second group of critics thought that Dreiser made no contribution to the theory and technique of the novel in American literature. The fallacy of these critics is nowhere more clearly stated than by Stuart P. Sherman. Distinguishing between realism and naturalism, Sherman wrote: "But a realistic novel is a representation based upon a theory of human conduct. If the theory of human conduct is adequate, the representation constitutes an addition to literature and to social history. A naturalistic novel is a representation based upon a theory of animal behavior. Since a theory of animal behavior can never be an adequate basis for a representation of the life of man in contemporary society, such a representation is an artistic blunder."[17] It is obvious that Sherman here has drawn an artificial distinction between realism and naturalism. This distinction, of course, is neither widely recognized by critics nor meaningfully applicable as a criterion for distinguishing among modern novels.

Even if we consider Sherman's distinction partially valid, we must disagree with his applying it to *Sister Carrie*, for Dreiser nowhere even theorized about the possibility of treating his characters as animals. And our reading of Dreiser's work convinces us of the human sensibilities of his characters. Recent critics of American naturalism tend to apply a less rigid definition of literary naturalism to Dreiser's early novels. Redefining *Sister Carrie* with Norris' *McTeague* and Crane's

The Red Badge of Courage from this modified point of view, Donald Pizer disagrees, for instance, with Lionel Trilling. "The naturalist," says Pizer, "often describes his characters as though they are conditioned and controlled by environment, heredity, instinct, or chance. But he also suggests a compensating humanistic value in his characters or their fates which affirm the significance of the individual and of his life." [18]

Such criticism as Sherman's was more common among the early critics of Dreiser. Since the criticism such as Philip Rahv's is still common, we are impelled to examine the characters in *Sister Carrie* in order to see how they portray the idiosyncrasies of man viewed in terms of the naturalistic philosophy. Indeed, we recognize as an outline of the novel that *Sister Carrie* depicts the characters caught in the forces of chance and circumstance. Interestingly enough, one of the characters is tossed upward to the eminence of success, and another is cast downward to an ignominious end of death. The heroine, called Carrie Meeber, in the beginning is described as "a waif amid forces" and rises successfully to prominence on the stage as Carrie Madenda; the well-groomed, successful restaurant manager George Hurstwood falls as George Wheeler to a penniless suicide in the slums.

☆ ☆ ☆ ☆

Even though it may seem repetitious simply to recount the well-known events of the novel, it is necessary that we establish the way Dreiser uses the setting and circumstances to introduce the tone of the novel and foreshadow the role of deterministic forces in his characters' lives. Thus, as Dreiser describes it, on one summer afternoon in 1889 an eighteen-year-old country girl goes to the biggest city in the Midwest, Chicago, aboard a train. She is "bright, timid, and full of the illusions of ignorance and youth" (p. 1). Her total possessions consist of a small suitcase, a cheap-looking imitation alligator-skin handbag, a yellow leather purse containing her train ticket, a lunch in a paper bag, and four dollars in cash. She looks out the window, and the green landscape passes in swift repetition, "until her swifter thoughts replaced its impression with vague conjectures of what Chicago might be" (p. 2). The story develops quickly to reveal what happens to this young girl. It seems inevitable from the outset that a girl of this type—innocent and unaware—will fall under the sway of forces working from within and without. Charles Drouet is a symbol of these forces; he is a moderately prosperous canvasser, or "drummer," in the more popular terms of the day. Carrie is a product of the conventional society in which she is supposed to reject familiarity with such a man. But it does not take long until "the daring and magnetism of the individual, born of past experiences and triumphs" (p. 3), prevail.

Dreiser's clinical analysis of the so-called chemisms is direct and markedly to the point. With Drouet's congenial cheeks, light moustache, grey "fedora" hat, new suit, and shiny brown shoes—an urban air of sophistication—and with his clean greenbacks, Carrie falls an easy prey to this salesman. "She now turned and looked upon him in full," says Dreiser, "the instincts of self-protection and coquetry mingling confusedly in her brain" (p. 3). Carrie's almost unconscious reaction to the magnetism displayed by Drouet is further intensified by her meeting with her sister on the station platform. Carrie now notices the change of atmosphere at once. "Amid all the maze, uproar, and novelty she felt cold reality taking her by the hand. No world of light and merriment. No round of amusement. Her sister carried with her most of the grimness of shift and toil" (p. 11). And the contrast of the atmospheres is most acutely portrayed when Carrie arrives at the dismal apartment where her sister and her silent, lifeless husband live. Carrie instantly feels "the drag of a lean and narrow life" (p. 13).

Carrie soon realizes that what is epitomized by the depressed atmosphere of the life of her sister's family is a fate she must avoid. Vigorously Carrie goes out hunting for a job. She fails, and accidentally Drouet's planned call on her does not occur. Although she finally secures a meager $4.50 a week job in a shoe factory, Carrie loses this job because of her unexpected illness. Carrie worries and feels gloomy, but by sheer coincidence she sees the radiant Drouet, who happens to be walking on his way to eat. He hurries Carrie to a high-class restaurant, impressing her with a $1.25 a plate sirloin steak. "As he cut the meat," Dreiser describes, "his rings almost spoke. His new suit creaked as he stretched to reach the plates . . . He helped Carrie to a rousing plateful and contributed the warmth of his spirit to her body until she was a new girl" (p. 67).

The image of the her sister's dreary flat and of herself walking in miserable weather from one "sweat shop" to another for employment chills Carrie's spirit and it becomes inevitable that this "little soldier of fortune took her good turn in an easy way" (p. 67), by accepting the twenty dollars Drouet insists on as a loan. When Drouet wants to buy Carrie a new jacket, the saleswoman helps her on with it, and "by accident" (p. 79), it fits her perfectly. In the account of Carrie's early "pilgrimage," Dreiser is primarily concerned with her natural instincts. She is passive rather than active, pushed rather than pushing. As these events indicate, her course of action is largely determined by the elements of chance and subconscious direction.

Carrie's rise, furthermore, signifies a neat pattern formulated by her perennial instincts craving for better things. It is apparent that the incidental forces controlling life command that man be, whatever achievement he makes, always dissatisfied. This is, then, true of Carrie. The boys who try to attract her attention at the factory appear to Carrie to be glaringly inferior to Drouet. When Drouet introduces Carrie to Hurstwood, she "instinctively felt that he was stronger and higher, and yet withal so simple" (p. 121). Drouet is as well dressed as Hurstwood, but Hurstwood is "more clever than Drouet in a hundred ways. He paid that peculiar deference to women which every member of the sex appreciates" (p. 106). Comparing the clothes the two men wear, Carrie makes a minute observation:

> He was in the best form for entertaining this evening. His clothes were particularly new and rich in appearance. The coat lapels stood out with that medium stiffness which excellent cloth possesses. The vest was of a rich Scotch plaid, set with a double row of round mother-of-pearl buttons. His cravat was a shiny combination of silken threads, not loud, not inconspicuous. What he wore did not strike the eye so forcibly as that which Drouet had on, but Carrie could see the elegance of the material. Hurstwood's shoes were of soft, black calf, polished only to a dull shine. Drouet wore patent leather, but Carrie could not help feeling that there was a distinction in favour of the soft leather, where all else was so rich. She noticed these things almost unconsciously. They were things which would naturally flow from the situation. She was used to Drouet's appearance. (pp. 107–8)

By the end of the third act of Joseph Jefferson's performance in *Rip Van Winkle*, to which Hurstwood invites Drouet and Carrie, she becomes convinced that "Drouet was only a kindly soul, but otherwise defective. He sank every moment in her estimation by the strong comparison" (pp. 121–22).

For Hurstwood, the difference between this young, pretty country girl and his petty, nagging, vain wife becomes equally obvious. Mrs. Hurstwood is a sophisticated woman; she is well informed in the social mores and well polished in her etiquette. Carrie is uneducated and rather limited in her speech. Why Carrie captivates such a titan as Hurstwood in the presence of his wife is not cogently explained. Dreiser, perhaps intentionally, omits the details of "chemisms" in this case, but his tone clearly implies that some kind of similar magnetism and chemical reactions have taken place in Hurstwood's brain.

If Dreiser has neglected to account for Hurstwood's infatuation with Carrie, he does not fail to elaborate Hurstwood's deterioration. Though love is involved in Hurstwood's running away with Carrie, *Sister Carrie* is not essentially a love story. Nor does even Drouet love Carrie; to him, she is only a lucky chance to satisfy his own vanity. He is merely using her to flatter his own sense of importance. Nobody in the course of the story shows genuine love toward Carrie. And Carrie, in turn, loves nobody but herself. Hurstwood, then, pursues Carrie for the thrill of making a conquest of a pretty, young girl; only later does he discover that her youth and prettiness are important to his ego. Carrie symbolizes for Hurstwood all that is lacking in his pitiful marriage, his selfish children, his routine existence, and his vanishing youth. Carrie, on the other hand, may feel affection and even tenderness and occasionally compassion, but her selfish desire for success preempts any feeling toward others. Whatever love and passion are contained in the novel are provided by Hurstwood, a man who finds himself a victim of his own emotions and circumstances.

When he meets Carrie, Hurstwood is enjoying the zenith of his career. His position is respected in his circle, and economically he belongs to the class just below that of the luxuriously wealthy. Dreiser was always keenly interested in the forces in society that influence man's position. Here in *Sister Carrie* as elsewhere Dreiser is concerned with the vulnerability of man's social position. As Dreiser delineates Hurstwood, one is intensely aware of the man inseparably tied to his position and rigidly molded by the city he inhabits. At the age of forty, Hurstwood's flight from such an environment is obviously doomed from the beginning. But, swayed by his blind infatuation for a young girl, he commits a blunder. And, when Hurstwood accompanies Carrie and Drouet, he carelessly tells his friends the lie that his wife is unable to attend a theatrical function because of illness.

One of Dreiser's most ingenious explanations of the deterministic philosophy appears when he has Hurstwood steal the money from the safe at Fitzgerald and Moy's. How successfully Dreiser manipulates this scene can be evidenced by the success of his similar treatment of the subject in Clyde's drowning of Roberta in *An American Tragedy*. In dramatizing man's utmost helplessness when strength of will is most needed, Dreiser creates a superb sense of irony on the fate of man. "After he had all the money in the hand bag," Dreiser describes,

> a revulsion of feeling seized him. He would not do it—no! Think of what a scandal it would make. The police! They would be after him . . . . Oh, the terror of being a fugitive from justice! He took out the two boxes and put all the money back. In his excitement he forgot what he was doing, and put the sums in the wrong boxes. As he pushed the door to, he thought he remembered doing it wrong and opened the door again . . . .
>
> . . . .
>
> While the money was in his hand the lock clicked. It had sprung! Did he do it? He grabbed at the knob and pulled vigorously. It had closed. (pp. 288–89)

There is no way for Hurstwood to explain the incident to his employer, and he has embezzled the money in spite of himself. His moral victory is thus ironically invalidated by sheer chance, and he has become a victim of cruel fate. Shortly before this scene Dreiser makes this interpolation:

> To those who have never wavered in conscience, the predicament of the individual whose mind is less strongly constituted and who trembles in the balance between duty and desire is scarcely appreciable, unless graphically portrayed. Those who have never heard that solemn voice of the ghostly clock which ticks with awful distinctness, "thou shalt," "thou shalt not," "thou shalt," "thou shalt not," are in no position to judge. Not alone in sensitive, highly organised natures is such a mental conflict possible. The dullest specimen of humanity, when drawn by desire toward evil, is recalled by a sense of right, which is proportionate in power and strength to his evil tendency. We must remember that it may not be a knowledge of right, for no knowledge of right is predicated of the animal's instinctive recoil at evil. Men are still led by instinct before they are regulated by knowledge. It is instinct which recalls the criminal—it is instinct (where highly organised reasoning is absent) which gives the criminal his feeling of danger, his fear of wrong. (pp. 286–87)

One can argue that if Hurstwood had not wanted to steal, he would not have touched the open safe and examined its contents. And, of course, a safe would not lock itself. But Dreiser is emphasizing the effect of a mysterious combination of subconscious direction and chance which often determines man's fate.

After this climactic event, the novel deals with Hurstwood's rapid deterioration as George Wheeler. Hurstwood, deprived of a position and of business influence in his home city, is much like a wheel which has lost its controlling mechanism. Dreiser's explanation is to the point and convincing:

> Whatever a man like Hurstwood could be in Chicago, it is very evident that he would be but an inconspicuous drop in an ocean like New York. In Chicago, whose population still ranged about 500,000, millionaires were not numerous. The rich had not become so conspicuously rich as to drown all moderate incomes in obscurity. The attention of the inhabitants was not so distracted by local celebrities in the dramatic, artistic, social, and religious fields as to shut the well-positioned man from view. In Chicago the two roads to distinction were politics and trade. In New York the roads were any one of a half-hundred, and each had been diligently pursued by hundreds, so that celebrities were numerous. The sea was already full of whales. A common fish must needs disappear wholly from view—remain unseen. In other words, Hurstwood was nothing. (p. 321)

This image of the survival of the fittest is very much like the one Dreiser later used at the beginning of *The Financier*—the scene of the life struggle between a squid and a lobster the young Cowperwood witnesses in a fish tank.

Luck now turns further against Hurstwood in his struggle for survival in New York. He invests his precious sum of money in a saloon, and loses it when the building in which the saloon is located is sold to erect a new building. As his reservoir of money dwindles, winter arrives and he cannot get employment. As a last resort Hurstwood goes gambling—a situation quite different from the time when he used to gamble for pleasure—and, indeed, loses.

Significantly, Hurstwood and Carrie move to a cheaper and shabbier apartment, and he loses his tidiness. He shaves once every other day, then every two days, and finally only once a week; his dress changes from a new suit to an old jacket and finally to rags. Eventually Carrie

leaves him and secures a better position on the stage, while Hurstwood
floats into beggary. Dreiser now theorizes:

> A fortune, like a man, is an organism which draws to itself other
> minds and other strength than that inherent in the founder. Beside
> the young minds drawn to it by salaries, it becomes allied with
> young forces, which make for its existence even when the strength
> and wisdom of the founder are fading. It may be conserved by the
> growth of a community or of a state. It may be involved in providing
> something for which there is a growing demand. This removes it at
> once beyond the special care of the founder. It needs not so much
> foresight now as direction. The man wanes, the need continues or
> grows, and the fortune, fallen into whose hands it may, continues.
> Hence, some men never recognise the turning in the tide of their
> abilities. It is only in chance cases, where a fortune or a state of
> success is wrested from them, that the lack of ability to do as they
> did formerly becomes apparent. (pp. 361–62)

For an analysis of Hurstwood's disintegration, Dreiser relied on the
experiments of one Elmer Gates, a physiological psychologist in
Washington, D.C.[19] Dreiser thus explains, borrowing Gates' terminology, that a constantly crushed frame of mind grows some kind of
poisons in the blood, called "katastates," in the same way that pleasant feelings at heart bring forth some kind of antidotes called "anastates." The poisons generated by distress attack the system, thereby
causing deterioration. "To these," Dreiser asserts, "Hurstwood was
subject" (p. 362). And when the poisons overwhelm the whole system, it is reasonably inferred from this formula that a man like
Hurstwood must die. The reverse action, of course, takes place by the
antidotes or "anastates" in the body. Dreiser apparently demonstrates
this principle when Hurstwood, now thinking of death as a solution, is
given a quarter by a gentleman passing by. "Hurstwood moved on,
wondering," Dreiser says in a simple passage. "The sight of the large,
bright coin pleased him a little. He remembered that he was hungry and
that he could get a bed for ten cents. With this, the idea of death
passed, for the time being, out of his mind" (p. 545).

Dreiser's treatment of characters in *Sister Carrie* thus seems to
demonstrate his rigid adherence to the deterministic philosophy, which

is the most important characteristic of French literary naturalism. Man, Zola believed, is totally the product of his heredity and environment, and the action and interactions of these forces control his life. Although man has a will, he does not have a *free* will, because his fate is governed by those internal forces within him and those external ones of his environment. The two chief characters of *Sister Carrie*—Carrie and Hurstwood—seem to be subject to these forces, and Dreiser seems to have treated these characters accordingly.

However, upon further examination of the characters and of Dreiser's treatment of them, we have every reason to suspect that Dreiser only superficially understood the mechanistic theory of determinism and that, at the time of writing his first novel, he was only halfheartedly a conscious literary naturalist. The naturalistic views contained in *Sister Carrie* may have been the result of Dreiser's personal and subjective interpretation of the concepts that he principally derived from his reading of Darwin and Spencer.

The first clear example of this subjective interpretation of deterministic philosophy can be found in the early part of the novel where Carrie is about to leave her sister's dreary household in order to live in the rooms rented by Drouet. "Among the forces," Dreiser comments, "which sweep and play throughout the universe, untutored man is but a wisp in the wind. Our civilisation is still in a middle stage, scarcely beast, in that it is no longer wholly guided by instinct; scarcely human, in that it is not yet wholly guided by reason" (p. 83). Man, he maintains, is an essentially different creature from an animal. The tiger possesses no responsibilities, because it is motivated only by natural forces. Without thought or reasoning it is protected by nature. Man, on the other hand, has emerged from the lairs of the jungles and has acquired free will; however, he has not quite sufficiently developed his capacity for free will to the point at which it can provide ideal guidance and replace his bestial instincts:

In this intermediate stage he wavers—neither drawn in harmony with nature by his instincts nor yet wisely putting himself into harmony by his own free-will. He is even as a wisp in the wind, moved by every breath of passion, acting now by his will and now by his instincts, erring with one, only to retrieve by the other, falling by one, only to rise by the other—a creature of incalculable variability. (p. 83)

At the outset of the novel, then, Dreiser does not follow a deterministic theory of man. And it is important to recognize that he does not seem to apply a systematic theory of behavior according to Zola's experimental novel. Clearly in *Sister Carrie*, man at the present stage of his development is not regarded as the master of forces, but he is not entirely the victim of forces as Zola would argue he is. Dreiser argues that this vacillation between instinct and will should finally yield to the sovereignty of will. In this way man, guided by reason, will eventually see truth and gain the good life and happiness.

How does this concept apply to the character of Carrie? Dreiser, of course, does not present an explicit explanation. But he tries to show that this instinct and reason, or desire and understanding, are constantly at war within Carrie. Dreiser can only say, "She followed whither her craving led. She was as yet more drawn than she drew" (p. 84). Carrie seeks happiness all her life. When we see her rocking her chair endlessly by the window and dreaming at the end of the novel, we become aware that she is not completely happy and satisfied with her material success. Interpreted in terms of Dreiser's theory, this scene clearly indicates that Carrie has failed to attain the triumph of reason and will, though her instinct may have been gratified. The fact remains that though Dreiser shows in the rest of the novel how Carrie is driven by her passions, he does not again use the deterministic view for an explanation of her character.

Later in the story, Dreiser does dismiss Spencerian philosophy in discussing the problem of morality. He states that the entire question of morality is as yet a mystery. Carrie's actions are judged only by an arbitrary conception—a conventional standard in society by which all things are measured. Dreiser now contends:

> For all the liberal analysis of Spencer and our modern naturalistic philosophers, we have but an infantile perception of morals. There is more in the subject than mere conformity to a law of evolution. It is yet deeper than conformity to things of earth alone. It is more involved than we, as yet, perceive. Answer, first, why the heart thrills; explain wherefore some plaintive note goes wandering about the world, undying; make clear the rose's subtle alchemy evolving its ruddy lamp in light and rain. In the essence of these facts lie the first principles of morals. (p. 101)

Dreiser further explains that Carrie has accepted help from Drouet because she does not like to be "beaten by every wind and gusty sheet of rain'' (p. 102). There is no alternative; her particular situation does not allow her to take a conventional solution. Carrie's action cannot be judged as right or wrong; society is wrong in judging her on the basis of its conventional morality. Carrie has not intended to become Drouet's mistress; in fact, only later does she yield her ''flesh'' to him. And Dreiser explicitly makes this known: ''She really was not enamoured of Drouet.'' ''Carrie accepted this,'' Dreiser concludes, ''as basis for hope—it was a sort of salve to her conscience, a pleasant way out. Under the circumstances, things would be righted. Her actions would be justified'' (p. 106). Ironically, Dreiser states, ''She was saved in that she was hopeful'' (p. 305).

Likewise, for an explanation of the character of Hurstwood, the mechanistic theory of Spencerian determinism cannot be substituted. As Dreiser describes it, Hurstwood's theft at Fitzgerald and Moy's seems, indeed, naturalistic. But Dreiser could also mean that Hurstwood's own inner failings have given rise to his weakness of character, an element that has little to do with environment. Since Hurstwood is morally weak, he does not have the character to meet his own problems. The automatic locking of the safe is certainly accidental, but one must argue that originally Hurstwood brings himself to be tempted, thereby allowing chance to work against his will. Hurstwood's weakness in this incident is his own making.

Although Dreiser obviously defines Hurstwood's deterioration in New York in terms of chemisms, it may be argued that his downfall was caused by his personality. Dreiser's discourse on the poisons in the blood causing man's deterioration must be thought of as being purely naturalistic. But, in the case of Hurstwood's disintegration, such an explanation does not satisfactorily seem to account for the cause-effect sequence. Hurstwood has not done his best to turn the tide; what paralyzes his drive in coping with life is the very pride that he has unduly clung to. When things get worse for Hurstwood in New York, his thoughts always go back to his good old days in Chicago. He remembers that he was once on the top, and thinks that he cannot possibly condescend to accept his present plight. This is one of the chief reasons for his suicide. Such elements as environment and heredity are not to blame for his downfall; he himself is to blame. As Camus argued, a person who ends his life by his own hand cannot be considered a victim. Hurstwood, then, is not a victim of circumstance in the true sense of the word applied in naturalism.

The mind—the psychological processes—is, Dreiser himself observes, the original element in Hurstwood's condition. As in the case of Carrie, the forces in society are responsible for Hurstwood's depression, but these social forces do not necessarily dominate the psychology of the man in question. In both Carrie and Hurstwood, Dreiser does not force his characters into arbitrary patterns of action merely for the sake of consistency.

These discrepancies in Dreiser's ideology in the treatment of the characters present a significant departure from Zola's treatment of characters, in which Zola substituted a systematic theory of behavior that was deduced from scientific observation. Dreiser's treatment of his characters and his essential attitude toward life can be explained by the statement he made later in his autobiography *Dawn*:

> In short, I have since thought that for all my modest repute as a realist, I seem, to my self-analyzing eyes, somewhat more of a romanticist than a realist.... How like all or nothing it seems, according to one's compound and experiences! Yet never would I say of any picture of it, realistic or otherwise, that so much as fragmentarily suggests its variety or force, that it is dull. The individual himself—the writer, I mean—might well be a fool, and therefore all that he attempts to convey would taste of his foolishness or lack of wisdom or drama, but life, true life, by whomsoever set forth or discussed, cannot want utterly of romance or drama, and realism in its most artistic and forceful form is the very substance of both.[20]

It is precisely Dreiser's own subjective feeling expressed through his characters and his consequent compassion for them, seen against "the mystery and wonder and terror of life,"[21] that makes one question whether he is really a literary naturalist.

One of the remarkable devices in Dreiser's early fiction that distinguishes it from naturalistic fiction is the omniscience[22] of Dreiser throughout the work. The author's omniscience in fiction is not, of course, an uncommon device. Every novelist makes his presence felt in the selection of fictional material, details, and tone, but Dreiser's presence is more obvious than that of other novelists. It has often been pointed out that Dreiser tends to identify his characters with himself.

William J. Handy observed: "Without the peculiar quality of meaning which results from viewing the American scene with a naive wonder at its magnificence and at the same time with a disappointment at its unconcerned indifference to the lot of a helpless individual—without that special quality of meaning, we would not have Dreiser." [23]

How this sensibility of Dreiser was derived ought to be carefully examined in the light of his experiences. First of all, the unique quality of Dreiser's sensibility is his deeply felt, rather than systematically formed or contrived, values that reflect his personal reactions to the pathos of life, the strong sympathy for his characters, and the naive wonder at the mystery of existence. His attitude toward Carrie at the beginning of the story, for example, clearly illustrates this sensibility. Dreiser concludes the first chapter:

> "Why, how are all the folks at home?" she began; "how is father, and mother?"
>
> Carrie answered, but was looking away. Down the aisle, toward the gate leading into the waiting-room and the street, stood Drouet. He was looking back. When he saw that she saw him and was safe with her sister he turned to go, sending back the shadow of a smile. Only Carrie saw it. She felt something lost to her when he moved away. When he disappeared she felt his absence thoroughly. (p. 11)

How Carrie feels at the loss of the sight of Drouet is simply portrayed, but Dreiser's next statement is concerned with the feeling of Carrie: "With her sister she was much alone, a lone figure in a tossing, thoughtless sea" (p. 11).

When Mrs. Hale invites Carrie to make an excursion of the city, how both feel is intermingled with how Dreiser himself feels:

> They rode first through Lincoln Park and on far out towards Evanston, turning back at four and arriving at the north end of the Shore Drive at about five o'clock. At this time of year the days are still comparatively short, and the shadows of the evening were beginning to settle down upon the great city. Lamps were beginning to burn with that mellow radiance which seems almost watery and translucent to the eye. There was a softness in the air which speaks with an infinite delicacy of feeling to the flesh as well as to the soul. Carrie felt that it was a lovely day . . . . As they drove along the smooth pavement an occasional carriage passed. She saw one stop and the footman dismount, opening the door for a gentleman . . . Across the broad lawns, now first freshening into green, she saw lamps faintly glowing upon rich interiors. Now it was but a chair,

now a table, now an ornate corner, which met her eye ... She imagined that across these richly carved entrance-ways, where the globed and crystalled lamps shone upon panelled doors set with stained and designed panes of glass, was neither care nor unsatisfied desire. She was perfectly certain that here was happiness. If she could but stroll up yon broad walk, cross that rich entrance-way, which to her was of the beauty of a jewel ... oh! how quickly would sadness flee; how, in an instant, would the heartache end. She gazed and gazed, wondering, delighting, longing, and all the while the siren voice of the unrestful was whispering in her ear. (pp. 127–28)

The sensations that Carrie feels in looking at the gay streets of the city, the lamps burning in the buildings, and the passing of luxurious carriages, were the exact sensations of Dreiser when he first came to Chicago by himself at almost sixteen and later returned there at the same age as Carrie. Dreiser wrote in *Dawn*:

Those were the days, though, in which the city was growing most fascinatingly. Certain streets, like Archer, Blue Island, and Cottage Grove Avenues, were already, to me, amazing thoroughfares, providing long vistas of vehicles and pedestrians ... On some of my walks I caught imposing views of enormous railroad yards, crossed by viaducts, or towering Catholic churches dominating regions of low, rain-sodden cottages, or amazing residence sections, like Grand, Michigan and Drexel Boulevards, where new and immense mansions were either present or in process of construction. In the downtown heart, to which I returned every evening at five, were immense skyscrapers, the earliest to be reared in America. New theatres and splendid hotels—the Auditorium, for one, with its solemn Florentine tower and heavy buttressed arches. The city, as I viewed it then, seemed like a lithe young giant, unkempt in the main and befogged with the unintelligence of youth, but smooth-limbed, erect, powerful, hopeful. (*Dawn*, p. 574)

In *A Book About Myself* Dreiser was preoccupied with the same sensation:

To me Chicago at this time seethed with a peculiarly human or realistic atmosphere. It is given to some cities, as to some lands, to suggest romance, and to me Chicago did that hourly. It sang, I thought, and in spite of what I deemed my various troubles—small enough as I now see them—I was singing with it. These seemingly drear neighborhoods through which I walked each day, doing collecting for an easy-payment furniture company, these ponderous

regions of large homes where new-wealthy packers and manufactur-
ers dwelt . . . that great downtown area, surrounded on two sides by
the river, on the east by the lake, and on the south by railroad yards
and stations, the whole set with these new tall buildings, the wonder
of the western world, fascinated me. Chicago was so young, so
blithe, so new, I thought.[24]

Dreiser's identification with Carrie extends to his having given her the
same age as his own—eighteen, in 1889, and though the small town
from which Carrie came is in Wisconsin, it is indistinguishable from the
towns in Indiana where Dreiser grew up. Carrie's attraction to the lures
of the city and her youthful hope for the future are unmistakably those of
Dreiser himself, and Carrie's search for jobs in Chicago and the sense of
bafflement mirror those of Dreiser in the same city. The step-by-step
promotion that Carrie achieves as a chorus girl and an actress in the
theatrical world, and the security and ambition that she feels as she
climbs her social ladder, closely parallel those of Dreiser in his newspaper work. Drouet is also a carefully drawn "type" of fresh, carefree,
flirtatious drummer of the day, but in his flashy clothes and compliant
demeanor toward women he reflects Dreiser. Hurstwood in his struggle
for survival is what Dreiser saw when he came to New York; and
Hurstwood in his maladjustment, decline, and ruin is a picture of what
Dreiser in New York feared he might experience. Dreiser's own ap-
prehensions under such circumstances are described in *A Book About
Myself*:

> The sea! The sea! And this great city! Never before was I so anxious
> to explore a city, and never before so much in awe of one either. It
> seemed so huge and powerful and terrible. There was something
> about it which make me seem useless and trivial. Whatever one might
> have been elsewhere, what could one be here? (*Book*, p. 437)

Dreiser recalls that he looked at the huge buildings surrounding him,
considering himself and the great offices in which he was looking for a
job. It was then, he tells us, "that the idea of *Hurstwood* was born"
(*Book*, p. 464). Certain events in his own life were foreshadowed by
this treatment of Hurstwood, for the suppression of *Sister Carrie* and
the failure of his first marriage caused Dreiser to fall into a depression
that led him to the brink of suicide.

Dreiser's growing identification with his characters as the novel
progresses is thus crucial in the formation of his vision. But his con-

stant observations of people around him in his youth also reinforced the pattern of this vision. Dreiser often tells in his autobiographies, as has been discussed in detail, that his sisters always craved for better things in life—clothes, furniture, apartments—and that, dreaming of the city where everything would turn out wonderfully, they were always lured on by its attractions. His oldest sister Mame accepted money for her intimacy with a prosperous colonel, and Emma, who was living in Chicago with an architect whom she did not love very much, met L.A. Hopkins, a trusted clerk of Chapin and Gore.[25] Hopkins, stealing money from his employer and deserting his wife and children, eloped with Emma to New York by way of Canada. Like Hurstwood, Hopkins was a successful clerk at a fashionable downtown restaurant in Chicago, but when he went to New York he was out of work. When Dreiser came to visit Hopkins and Emma in New York, Hopkins, "having fallen from his success, . . . was tractable" (*Book*, p. 439). Obviously, Dreiser used the architect as a model for Drouet and Hopkins as a model for Hurstwood. His sister Emma became Carrie, and like the heroine of Robert Hazard's unpublished novel, which Dreiser had read earlier,[26] Carrie climbs as an actress. Dreiser remembered a type of traveling salesman like Drouet who tried to coax one of his other sisters at home into eloping from such a place as a train station or a drugstore.

As for Hurstwood, Dreiser was familiar with many of the weaknesses betrayed by his father and by his brother Paul. The elder Dreiser was, in Dreiser's eyes, an unsuccessful man materially; Paul, though he became a successful songwriter, failed at midlife much like Hurstwood. Paul recalled his miserable days in New York, which resemble those of Hurstwood:

> I remember standing at the corner of Eighth Street and Broadway, New York, one evening, conscious of the fact that my sole worldly possessions amounted to sixty-five cents and the clothes I wore. I was an absolute stranger in New York, but everywhere I went I heard some one singing "The Letter That Never Came" [one of the songs Paul Dresser composed]. Another man was getting the money and I was getting the laugh. I did not know whether to invest my sixty-five cents in a bed and night's lodging or save it for breakfast; I finally decided that I would need the breakfast more than the bed, so I knocked around all night.[27]

In the novel, while Hurstwood is begging in the streets, Dreiser ironically has Lola, now Carrie's roommate in a comfortable chamber at the Waldorf, say, "But people never gave me anything when I was hard up" (*Sister Carrie*, p. 549).

One of the vivid images that Dreiser uses from his own observations in delineating Hurstwood's degradation is that of the poverty he saw in his newspaper work. In New York, particularly in the Bowery, Dreiser saw the defeated and the degraded swarming in the streets, in the parks, and in the cheaper shelters. During his free-lance period, as has been noted, Dreiser wrote an article for *Demorest's*[28] about the contrast between the poor and the rich, called "Curious Shifts of the Poor," the same title as a final chapter in *Sister Carrie*. The wide gulf dividing the rich and the poor is, in fact, one of Dreiser's favorite motifs in this novel as elsewhere.[29] As also mentioned earlier, Dreiser as a newspaperman reported on the downtrodden men—exactly like Hurstwood—who, eating very little and living in unsanitary lodging houses in the Bowery, were sent to Bellevue Hospital but discharged before their complete recovery and were again sent back to the streets.[30]

Dreiser is also acutely conscious of his characters' sensitivity to all the physical impressions that make for wonder, awe, fear, and envy. *Sister Carrie* is full of the details that Dreiser knew in his own experiences. One book reviewer who noticed the authenticity in Dreiser's observation observed, for example, that in the midst of his description of Carrie's excursion, Dreiser stops to comment: "It was a famous drug-store and contained one of the first private telephone booths ever erected."[31] Similarly, department stores, newspapers, saloons, and theaters never elude identification. In depicting the streetcar strike, Dreiser remembered vividly his own feeling and sympathy toward the exploited, which he experienced in watching these incidents in Brooklyn in 1896. And his thorough description of the life in the Bowery is deeply colored by his own emotions on the subject.

Dreiser's contemporary Stephen Crane, who once professed that the Bowery was the most fascinating place in New York, wrote in *Maggie: A Girl of the Streets* about the same contrast between poverty and wealth as Dreiser did. Crane's passage reads in part:

> The pavements became tossing seas of umbrellas. Men stepped forth to hail cabs or cars, raising their fingers in varied forms of polite request or imperative demand. An endless procession wended

toward elevated stations. An atmosphere of pleasure and prosperity seemed to hang over the throng, born, perhaps, of good clothes and of having just emerged from a place of forgetfulness.

In the mingled light and gloom of an adjacent park, a handful of wet wanderers, in attitudes of chronic dejection, was scattered among the benches.[32]

The reader would certainly be aware of Crane's impressionism in this novel. The flatness of this scene, however, is not the result of the weakness of Crane's technique but rather his lack of touch with the material. This problem would never occur in Dreiser's writing, particularly in describing Hurstwood's predicament. It seems as though Crane is a natural-born painter who, detached from the scene, stands aloof in front of the canvas; Dreiser is a natural-born writer who stands in tears in the midst of the scene, nonetheless hurrying his pen. In Crane's description there is little sense of humanity in the scene, neither of the people in question nor of the author who is showing his wonder and compassion.

Where Crane is an objective observer of surfaces, Dreiser subjectively penetrates the mental state of the outcast. Dreiser's efforts to record circumstances realistically are thus more complex than has often been recognized. In one respect, documentation in realistic fiction is a manner of presenting the facts as they could be viewed objectively by any observer; in the other respect, as in *Sister Carrie*, where there is often little distinction between the author and his characters, the view of life tends to be as subjective as that of a romanticist.

In *Sister Carrie* it may be impossible to minimize the significance of the deterministic philosophy that had been influential in Europe and America by the time Dreiser wrote the novel. But it would be an oversimplification to suggest that the influence of this philosophy on Dreiser was literary. Although Dreiser was impressed by Balzac in his casual reading, he had "never read a line of Zola,"[33] the literary champion of determinism. He had also not read Norris' *McTeague* until he had completed writing *Sister Carrie*. His reading of Herbert Spencer, obviously, made a permanent impression on Dreiser's concept of man and nature. But his studies of Spencerianism merely helped to confirm what he had already learned by experience. At the time he wrote his first novel, there is every reason to suspect that Dreiser had not gone so far as to accept the mechanistic concept of life completely.

Man's striving for the ideal is the keynote at the heart of *Sister Carrie*, and this call for the ideal is the essential motivation of each character of the novel. Even if Dreiser accepts the world as it is and things as they are, he could still assert in the end: "Not evil, but longing for that which is better, more often directs the steps of erring. Not evil, but goodness more often allures the feeling mind unused to reason" (*Sister Carrie*, p. 556). Dreiser, in this often quoted passage, tells his heroine: "Oh, Carrie, Carrie! Oh, blind strivings of the human heart! Onward, onward, it saith, and where beauty leads, there it follows. . . . In your rocking-chair, by your window, shall you dream such happiness as you may never feel" (p. 557). This is *not* so hopeless a situation a young girl like Carrie must face in life as some readers might think. In such a tone, it is difficult to substitute determinism as an explanation of man. Indeed, it is easy to understand Eliseo Vivas' previously discussed statement: "His characters are alive and real, moving and acting and brooding with all the urge and hesitation, passions and fears, doubts and contradictions, fully real human beings."[34]

It is this quality of life in *Sister Carrie*—moving, acting, hesitating, and contradicting—that captivates our attention, rather than the scenes of carefully and systematically analyzed forces operating under Zola's experimental conditions. Unlike literary naturalists, Dreiser does not even seem to control his conditions and discover truths about man's psychology and physiology. "It [*Sister Carrie*] is intended," Dreiser said, "not as a piece of literary craftsmanship, but as a picture of conditions done as simply and effectively as the English language will permit."[35] Thus, Ford Madox Ford is right in his remark:

> The writer of vast memory has an ease of production and in consequence a sureness that can never be aspired to by a writer who must document himself as he goes along. He can produce his instances without delay and, most important of all, he never has to force his subject around so as to bring in a second-rate instance. The difference between a supremely unreadable writer like Zola and a completely readable one like Dreiser is simply that if Zola had to write about a ride on a railway locomotive's tender or a night in a brothel Zola had to get it all out of a book. Dreiser has only to call on his

undimmed memories and the episode will be there in all freshness
and valour.[36]

The works of Dreiser's early phase, particularly *Sister Carrie*, are
not, then, in a true sense, naturalistic in their view of life. Whereas his
first novel is colored by the terms of the so-called Darwinian or
Spencerian philosophy, these terms do not shape the essential voice
that Dreiser the novelist is trying to convey. This voice is rather the
product of Dreiser's own experience and speaks meaningfully to those
who are capable of recognizing the direct, rather than the oblique,
apprehension of reality.

By the time Dreiser wrote *Sister Carrie*, he had become a writer
with a true and significant vision, a writer with a conscious literary
purpose. In writing his early works of fiction he availed himself freely
of the personal as well as impersonal material derived from his own
experience and observation. And this material, some general, some
detailed, came easily and strongly to Dreiser's hand and coalesced in
his imagination with his emerging artistic sensibility. Among the
unique experiences that shaped Dreiser's early fictional efforts, his
reading and studies of Darwin and Spencer made a strong impression
on his vision of life. But it is also important to recognize that their
concepts helped to confirm what Dreiser had already learned in his
own daily experiences. Without these experiences Dreiser would not
have been seriously interested in the technical theories of deterministic
philosophy. This doctrine, in turn, severed from him the remaining
trace of his religious thought and rid him of a lingering tendency
toward the romantic idealization of worldly happiness. It seems as
though Dreiser rejected any facile religious security and any jejune
belief in the inevitability of human progress. This dual loss, for instance, is reflected in the tone of *Sister Carrie*, which, in turn, derives
from Dreiser's philosophical commitment rather than from a strong
sense of artistic aptness.

As for literary influences, Dreiser became familiar with Balzac and
Zola indirectly during his journalistic career, and the newspaper work,
and later, magazine writing taught him the essential attitudes and
methods of a writer. According to Zola, a writer first establishes a

milieu taken from life and, into it, projects characters who then act in accordance with that milieu. The experimental novelist must record, without comment or interpretation, what actually happens. Dreiser is, perhaps, closest to this method in *The Financier* and, more saliently, in *An American Tragedy*. Dreiser is a conscious literary naturalist in recording Clyde's actions and mental processes, before and after the murder of Roberta, prior to his execution by the electric chair. Dreiser is almost like a scientist observing the process of a natural phenomenon, and he scarcely obtrudes as the omniscient author on the scenes he portrays, as he often does in the case of *Sister Carrie*. In his early writings Dreiser's subjective, and often personal, point of view tends to color his presentation of fictional material. In the light of his treatment, then, Dreiser's early works of fiction elude the classification in French naturalism. What change in his fictional theory and practice took place, if any, between his early works and his later ones must be further investigated.

While the young Dreiser was not brought in any distinct way under the influence of literary naturalism, he created his early works out of his own experiences and his ideas stemmed from these experiences. In his youth, Dreiser came to reject the conventional clear-cut dualism of good and evil, fact and fancy, reality and appearance. He realized that the writer must see life as a whole, the evil and ugly included, from a realistic point of view. And it was at this time that he began his never successful attempt to dismiss his romantic attitude toward life. During his journalistic career, Dreiser further learned to be a detached observer who accepted life as it is. Man, Dreiser felt, must recognize the stern fact that he is necessarily limited in his capacity to cope with the forces within and around him. Dreiser came to accept a contrast between wealth and poverty, power and weakness, delight and misery, which dramatized human conditions. He continued to insist that man should regard his conditions as wretched but not as inevitably so. Man can hope to ameliorate.

In the early short stories and in *Sister Carrie*, Dreiser delineated the changing complexity of American society in the latter days of its industrial expansion, showed the forceful attractions of city life, and emphasized the conflict between convention and individual demands. In so doing, he did not simply record the abstract motivational power of the "chemisms" in the individual. Dreiser transcended the technical concepts of the mechanistic theory of man; instead, he dealt with living individuals whose personalities reflect a historical, and often personal, significance. Even though his characters tend to be governed by circumstances, Dreiser's chief interest lay in the individuals and their endless aspirations. Unlike other literary naturalists, Dreiser attempted to discover an ideal order in man's life. Whatever struggle man encounters, this hopeful striving for the ideal remains at the heart of each of his early works. It is this voice that echoes his unique experience, and as such it reflects the artistic expressions of a man who emerged in a new civilization—America. It is the voice, not of a scientific observer, bent on uncovering the secrets of the universe, but of a sentient artist who understood that human beings, not theories, are the stuff of which novels are made.

Notes

CHAPTER 1: American Literary Naturalism

1. See Philip Rahv, "On the Decline of Naturalism," *Partisan Review* 9 (November-December 1942): 483–93.

2. Cf. Malcolm Cowley, "Sister Carrie's Brother," *New Republic* 116 (26 May 1947): 23–25; idem, "The Slow Triumph of *Sister Carrie,*" *New Republic* 116 (June 1947): 24–27; Lars Åhnebrink, "Dreiser's *Sister Carrie* and Balzac," *Symposium* 7 (November 1953): 306–22; Yoshinobu Hakutani, "*Sister Carrie* and the Problem of Literary Naturalism" *Twentieth Century Literature* 13 (April 1967): 3–17; Charles C.Walcutt, "*Sister Carrie*: Naturalism or Novel of Manners?" *Genre* 1 (January 1968): 76–85; idem, *American Literary Naturalism, A Divided Stream* (Minneapolis, 1956); Robert H. Elias, *Theodore Dreiser: Emended Edition* (Ithaca, N. Y., 1970), p. 395.

3. See F. W. J. Hemmings, "The Origin of the Terms *Naturalisme, Naturaliste*," *French Studies* 8 (April 1954): 109–21.

4. Gustave Flaubert in *Documents of Modern Literary Realism*, ed. George J. Becker (Princeton, N. J., 1963), p. 95.

5. Ibid., p. 118.

6. See, for instance, Donald Pizer, "Nineteenth-Century American Naturalism: An Essay in Definition," *Bucknell Review* 13 (December 1965): 1–18.

7. Edwin Cady, *The Light of Common Day: Realism in American Fiction* (Bloomington, Ind., 1971), p.51.

8. Cf. Walcutt, *American Literary Naturalism, A Divided Stream*; Dreiser, "Mark the Double Twain," *English Journal* 24 (October 1935): 615–27; Henry Adams, *The Education of Henry Adams* (New York, 1931), p. 9; Donald Pizer, *Realism and Naturalism in Nineteenth-Century American Literature* (Carbondale, Ill., 1966), pp. 12–13.

9. See Rod W. Horton and Herbert W. Edwards, *Backgrounds of American Literary Thought* (New York, 1952), pp. 251–52.

10. See Don Wolfe, *The Image of Man in America* (Dallas, 1957) and Richard Hofstadter, *Social Darwinism in American Thought* (Philadelphia, 1944).

11. Oliver Wendell Holmes, "Preface," *Elsie Venner—A Romance of Destiny* (New York, 1886), n. p. I am indebted here to Lewis Fried, who called my attention to *Elsie Venner* and Dugdale's *The Jukes*, which (to my knowledge) have never previously been brought into focus with the development of American literary naturalism.

12. Oliver Wendell Holmes, "Crime and Automatism," *Pages from an Old Volume of Life* (New York, 1883), p. 343.

13. Richard Dugdale, *The Jukes* (New York, 1877), p. 12.

14. Thomas Beer, *Stephen Crane: A Study in American Letters* (Garden City, N. Y., 1923), p. 148.

15. Dreiser, *A Book About Myself* (New York, 1922), p. 132. Hereafter cited as *Book*.

16. Frank Norris, *The Responsibilities of the Novelist* (Garden City, N. Y., 1928), pp. 167–68.

CHAPTER 2: French Naturalists

1. Alfred Kazin, *On Native Grounds: An Interpretation of Modern American Literature* (New York, 1942), p. 66.

2. *Letters of Theodore Dreiser*, ed. Robert H. Elias (Philadelphia, 1959), 2: 417–21. Hereafter cited in the text as *Letters*.

3. Frank Norris, *The Octopus* [1901] (Garden City, N. Y., 1956), p. 343.

4. David Brion Davis, "Dreiser and Naturalism Revisited," *The Stature of Theodore Dreiser*, ed. Alfred Kazin and Charles Shapiro (Bloomington, Ind., 1955), p. 230.

5. Dreiser, *A Book About Myself*, pp. 211–12.

6. Malcolm Cowley, "Naturalism in American Literature," *Evolutionary Thought in America*, ed. Stow Persons (New Haven, Conn., 1950), p. 306.

7. Émile Zola, *The Experimental Novel*, trans. Belle M. Sherman (New York, 1893), p. 53–54. Hereafter as *Experimental Novel*.

8. See Dreiser's correspondence with H. L. Mencken between 27 July 1916 and 26 November 1916 in *Letters*, 1: 220–37.

9. Dreiser, *The "Genius"* [1915] (Cleveland, 1946), p. 736.

10. See Dreiser's letter to Dorothy Payne Davis in *Letters*, 3: 886–90.

11. Ibid., 886–87.

12. See Dreiser's letter of 5 January 1927 to Sergei Dinamov, a Russian critic, who had asked Dreiser about Norris' influence and about Dreiser's views on capitalism, *Letters*, 2: 449.

13. See Dreiser's letter of 29 January 1919 to Howard Willard Cook, who, on behalf of the editorial department of Moffat, Yard and Company, had sent Dreiser a copy of this book with a supporting review by John Galsworthy in the hope that they might receive from Dreiser a favorable review, *Letters*, 1: 257–58.

14. Mrs. N. P. Dawson, "Books of the Week," the New York *Globe*, 30 October 1915; cf. *Letters*, 1: 200.

15. See Dreiser's letter to Mencken, 14 May 1916, in *Letters*, 1: 215.

CHAPTER 3: Youth

1. Lionel Trilling, "Reality in America," *The Stature of Theodore Dreiser*, p. 142.

2. Stuart P. Sherman, "The Barbaric Naturalism of Mr. Dreiser," ibid., p. 74.

3. H. L. Mencken, *A Book of Prefaces* (New York, 1917), pp. 92–93.

4. Robert L. Duffus, "Dreiser," *American Mercury* 7 (January 1926): 71.

5. Percy H. Boynton, *America in Contemporary Fiction* (Chicago, 1940), p. 136.

6. See Charles Shapiro, *Theodore Dreiser: Our Bitter Patriot* (Carbondale, Ill., 1962), p. 122.

7. Francis Hodgins, Jr., "The Dreiser Letters," *Journal of English and Germanic Philology* 59 (1960): 717.

8. Dreiser, *Dawn* (New York, 1931), p. 586. Hereafter referred to in the text.

9. See George Steinbrecher, Jr., "Inaccurate Accounts of *Sister Carrie*," *American Literature* 23 (January 1952): 490–93.

10. Dreiser, *An American Tragedy* [1925] (Cleveland, 1948), pp. 17–18.

11. Dreiser, *Sister Carrie* (New York, 1900), p. 17.

12. See F. O. Matthiessen, *Theodore Dreiser* (New York, 1951), p. 70.

13. See the three Dreiser articles published in *Tom Watson's Magazine*: "The Rivers of the Nameless Dead" 1 (March 1905): 112–13; "The Track Walker" 1 (June 1905): 502–3; "The Loneliness of the City" 2 (October 1905): 474–75. "The Track Walker" had appeared before the track walker's death took place as "The Story of a Human Nine-Pin," New York *Daily News*, 3 April 1904, p. 3 [unsigned].

14. See Dreiser, "My Brother Paul," *Twelve Men* (New York, 1919), pp. 76–109.

15. Dreiser, *Dawn*, p. 113. Cf. *Twelve Men*, pp. 76–78; idem, "Concerning the Author of These Songs," *The Songs of Paul Dresser* (New York, 1927), pp. v–x. Paul had Anglicized his family name.

16. Concerning Dreiser's participation in the composition of "On the Banks of the Wabash," his secretary wrote, in part: "Mr. Dreiser says that the song was not in its final form until many months after he and his brother had the conversation which led to the writing of the song." See letter to John H. Huth dated 2 February 1936 in the University of Pennsylvania Library Dreiser Collection.

17. See Dreiser, "Whence the Song," *Harper's Weekly* 44 (8 December 1900): 1165–66a; reprinted, with some minor stylistic alterations, in Dreiser's *The Color of a Great City* (New York, 1923), pp. 242–59.

18. Dreiser, *A Hoosier Holiday* (New York, 1916), p. 489. Hereafter cited in the text as *Holiday*.

19. Dreiser, *Dawn*, p. 193. Dreiser later corresponded with this teacher, who had become Mrs. May Calvert Baker. They reminisced about the fact that the famous author had had a great difficulty in learning school grammar. Dreiser's continuous affection for her was still reflected in a letter he wrote as late as 16 August 1919: "How are you, my good angel. Please don't think I've forgotten or am ungrateful. I'm not—." See Dreiser's seventeen letters to May Calvert Baker between 15 February 1917 and 13 February 1920 in the University of Pennsylvania Library Dreiser Collection.

20. See Joseph Katz, "Theodore Dreiser at Indiana University," *Notes and Queries*, n. s. 13 (March 1966): 100–101.

21. See Dreiser, *Dawn*, pp. 341–43, 358; cf. idem, *Dawn* ms. (The Lilly Library, Indiana University), ch. 60.

22. See Robert H. Elias, *Theodore Dreiser: Emended Edition*, p. 35; cf. Dreiser, *Dawn*, p. 397.

CHAPTER 4: Newspaper Days

1. Dreiser, *A Book About Myself*, p. 69. This volume is referred to hereafter as *Book*.

2. James L. Ford, *The Literary Shop* (New York, 1894), p. 154.

3. See Robert H. Elias, *Theodore Dreiser: Emended Edition*, p. 39; cf. Dreiser, *Book*, p. 75.

4. Dreiser, "Mathewson," *Esquire* 1 (May 1934): 20. Max Putzel writes on Dreiser in St. Louis in a study of Dreiser's contemporary William Marion Reedy entitled *The Man in the Mirror: William Marion Reedy and His Magazine* (Cambridge, Mass., 1963), p. 120: "Sixteen months may seem a brief stretch, but Dreiser magnified his days. For him the town [St. Louis] was radiant and golden with expectation. He saw intensely and stored up each impression . . . ." This impression by Dreiser as Putzel describes it seems to contradict Dreiser's.

5. Dreiser, *Twelve Men*, p. 7. Hereafter cited in the text.

6. Dreiser, "Theosophy and Spiritualism," St. Louis *Globe-Democrat*, 20 January 1893, p. 12.

7. Harry R. Burke, a writer who knew Dreiser in St. Louis, provides a great deal of information on Dreiser's experiences in St. Louis, including the latter's assignment of the train robbery, and his relationships to Peter McCord and other reporters, *From the Day's Journey* (St. Louis, 1924), pp. 165–71; cf. Dreiser, "His Own Story," St. Louis *Republic*, 4 June 1893, pp. 1–2. For Dreiser's description of the train wreck, see "Burned to Death," St. Louis *Globe-Democrat*, 22 January 1893, pp. 1–2.

8. Dreiser, *The "Genius"*, p. 104.

9. Dreiser, *A Book About Myself* ms. (University of Pennsylvania Library Dreiser Collection), ch. 12, pp. 11–12. Hereafter called *Book* ms.

10. Clarence E. Miller, "William Marion Reedy: A Patchwork Portrait," *Missouri Historical Society Bulletin* 17 (October 1960): 47.

11. Dreiser, *Book*, pp. 200–204; cf. ibid.

12. See St. Louis *Globe-Democrat*, 1 April 1893, p. 8.

13. William C. Lengel, "The 'Genius' Himself," *Esquire* 10 (September 1938): 120.

14. Dreiser, "Mathewson," *Esquire* 1 (May 1934): 21.

15. Dreiser, "The Trade of the Mississippi," *Ainslee's* 4 (January 1900): 742–43.

16. Dreiser, "Nigger Jeff," *Ainslee's* 8 (November 1901): 366–75. Cf. Dreiser's newspaper article, "A Negro Lynched," St. Louis *Republic*, 17 September 1893, p. 2.

17. See Dreiser, *A Hoosier Holiday*, p. 254.

18. Dreiser, "A Monarch of Metal Workers," *Success* 2 (3 June 1899): 453–54. Cf. idem, "Carnegie as a Metal Worker" in *How They Succeeded* (New York, 1901), pp. 253–75; idem, "A Poor Boy Who Once Borrowed Books Now Gives Away Libraries—Andrew Carnegie" in *Little Visits with Great Americans* (New York, 1903), pp. 51–70.

19. See Dreiser, "Thomas Brackett Reed: The Story of a Great Career," *Success* 3 (June 1900): 215–16. Cf. idem, *Book*, p. 407; Elias, *Theodore Dreiser: Emended Edition*, p. 72.

20. See Dreiser, "A Tale About Two Cats," Pittsburgh *Dispatch*, 20 May 1894, p. 2; idem, "Reapers in the Fields," 6 July 1894, p. 2; idem, "Odd Scraps of Melody," 7 July 1894, p. 3; idem, "Woes of Dog Catchers," 2 August 1894, p. 3.

21. Dreiser, "With the Nameless Dead," Pittsburgh *Dispatch*, 23 July 1894, p. 3.

22. Dreiser, "Hospital Violet Days," Pittsburgh *Dispatch*, 12 May 1894, p. 2.

23. Honoré de Balzac, *The Wild Ass's Skin* (London, 1895), pp. 83–86.

24. See Elias, *Theodore Dreiser: Emended Edition*, p. 76.

25. See Dreiser, "After the Rain Storm," Pittsburgh *Dispatch*, 19 May 1894, p. 2.

26. Jacob Riis, *How the Other Half Lives: Studies among the Tenements in New York* (New York, 1890), pp. 89–91.

27. See Dreiser, "Curious Shifts of the Poor. Strange Ways of Relieving Desperate Poverty. —Last Resources of New York's Most Pitiful Mendicants," *Demorest's* 36 (November 1899): 22–26; idem, "A Touch of Human Brotherhood," *Success* 5 (March 1902): 140–41, 176.

28. Joseph Katz, ed. *The Portable Stephen Crane* (New York, 1969), p. 154. Further quotations from Crane's work refer to this collection.

29. Thomas Beer, *Stephen Crane: A Study in American Letters*, pp. 140–41.

30. Frank Luther Mott, *American Journalism: A History of Newspapers* (New York, 1941), pp. 488, 582.

CHAPTER 5: Editorial Work

1. John F. Huth, Jr., "Theodore Dreiser: 'The Prophet,'" *American Literature* 9 (May 1937): 208. It is also interesting to note that some of Dreiser's letters indicate that he worked on the intended volume to a certain extent. In a letter of 8 October 1920 to Mencken, Dreiser said, "*Literary Experiences* is under way. I do a small bit—now & then. Ah, the opportunity that lies there, my good brother—the nobles of the nineties and nineteen tens! I once thought of a book about Paul. But he appears fairly well drawn in Vol. 1 [,] 2 & 3—youth, fame & death [.]" See *Letters of Theodore Dreiser*, 1: 289. On 10 March 1921 he again wrote a letter to Mencken saying,
> I have been intending to tell you for some time past that several years before I ever wrote *Newspaper Days* I wrote and laid aside for personal and family reasons volume one [*Dawn*] of what is to be, when completed, a four or five-volume *History of Myself*. Of this series *Newspaper Days* is, of course, volume two. Volume three, *Literary Aspirations*, was started by me some time ago, but I laid it aside for other work. (*Letters*, 1: 354)

Still later, on 25 March 1921, in a letter to Curtis Brown, a representative of an English publisher, Dreiser wrote,
> . . . I have another matter about which I wish to speak. It is this. Several years ago,—about four—I began, in my spare moments, upon a work which I have entitled *A History of Myself*. Perhaps I had better say *The History*. At any rate it is to be in four or five volumes and volumes one and two are now done and a third is under way. The titles are *Youth* [*Dawn*], *Newspaper Days* [*A Book About Myself*], *Literary Ambitions, Literary Experi-*

ences, and then one other volume, the character of which I have not, as yet, decided upon. (*Letters*, 1: 359)

2. Dreiser, *A Book About Myself*, p. 441. Dreiser was to write, before *Sister Carrie*, ten free-lance articles on music, two of which are about popular music: "Birth and Growth of a Popular Song," *Metropolitan* 8 (November 1898): 497–502; "Whence the Song," *Harper's Weekly* 44 (8 December 1900): 1165–66a.

3. *Ev'ry Month*, according to *The Union List of Serials*, exists in two copies, one at the Library of Congress and the other, in its incomplete volumes, at the Oberlin College Library. But the Library of Congress volumes have been missing since 1937, whereas the scattered issues at Oberlin were discarded many years ago. According to W. A. Swanberg, there are four scattered issues of *Ev'ry Month* at the Los Angeles Public Library. The University of Pennsylvania Library Dreiser Collection has many issues, but not a complete run, of the magazine. Robert Elias has informed me that, as far as he knows, no one knows about those lost Library of Congress volumes. Much of the present study, based on the microfilm copy of an incomplete run of *Ev'ry Month* available at the Yale University Library, appeared in my article "Theodore Dreiser's Editorial and Free-Lance Writing," *Library Chronicle* of the University of Pennsylvania 37 (Winter 1971): 70–85. Joseph Katz has since reported that he found all the issues of *Ev'ry Month* published during Dreiser's editorship except for the first two issues, October and November 1895. See Katz, "Theodore Dreiser's *Ev'ry Month*," *Library Chronicle* of the University of Pennsylvania 38 (Winter 1972): 46–66. Many of Dreiser's writings in *Ev'ry Month* have recently been collected in Donald Pizer, ed., *Theodore Dreiser: A Selection of Uncollected Prose* (Detroit, 1977).

4. Arthur Henry, *Lodgings in Town* (New York, 1905), p. 83.

5. Dreiser, *Twelve Men*, p. 101.

6. *Ev'ry Month* 3, No. 6 (March 1897): 4. All subsequent textual references to *Ev'ry Month* will appear in parentheses after the quotations.

7. Robert H. Elias, *Theodore Dreiser: Emended Edition*, p. 89.

8. Frank Luther Mott, *A History of American Magazines, 1885–1905* (Cambridge, Mass., 1957), p. 362.

9. Though Dreiser claims his close acquaintance with Sonntag, he does not seem to have obtained as much material as he wanted. The particular illustration he speaks of actually appeared in the Christmas 1896 issue.

10. Dreiser, "The Color of To-Day," *Harper's Weekly* 45 (14 December 1901): 1272.

11. See Dreiser, "A Great American Caricaturist," *Ainslee's* 1 (May 1898): 336–41.

12. Edward Al derived from two of his brothers, Edward and Alphonse.

13. For Dreiser's relationships with Reedy, see Max Putzel, "Dreiser, Reedy, and 'De Maupassant, Junior'," *American Literature* 33 (January 1962): 466–84.

14. Dreiser, "The Treasure House of Natural History," *Metropolitan* 8 (December 1898): 595–601.

15. Dreiser, "The Descent of the Horse," *Everybody's* 2 (June 1900): 543.

16. Cf. Dreiser, "Electricity in the Household,"*Demorest's* 35 (January 1899): 38–39.

17. Dreiser, "The Making of Small Arms," *Ainslee's* 1 (1898): 549. In this connection it is interesting to see another article by Dreiser concerning the dual purpose in the advancement of science and technology. In reference to the production of arms Dreiser commented:

> Man's ingenuity finds many contradictory channels for its expression. The labor to perfect those sciences which tend to save human life goes on side by side with the labor to create new and more potent methods for its destruction. This is significantly apparent in the dual operations of governments, which on the one hand expend vast sums in the development of plans more or less humanitarian in purpose, while at the same time even greater sums go toward the improving of those devices which shall be most effective when applied to the sinister processes of warfare. ("Scenes in a Cartridge Factory," *Cosmopolitan* 25 [July 1898]: 321)

18. Dreiser, "The Log of an Ocean Pilot," *Ainslee's* 3 (July 1899): 692. This article was later printed with numerous minor changes as a chapter in *The Color of a Great City* (New York, 1923), pp. 14–33, under the title "The Log of a Harbor Pilot." Hereafter, *The Color of a Great City* is cited as *Color*.

19. Dreiser, "With Whom Is Shadow of Turning," *Demorest's* 34 (June 1898): 189; idem, "Through All Adversity," ibid. 34 (November 1898): 334. The poems are as follows:

With Whom Is Shadow of Turning

Where the pleasure? Where the pain?
Where the bliss which men attain?
None, thou sayst. All a lure!
All a fancy, nothing more?
    O, my soul!

Where the reason for the right?
Where the nobleness of might?
But a dream born of despair,
But a passing dream, and fair,
    O, my soul!

Wrong triumphant, self the thought;
Peace alone with money sought,
Power sold and power bought?
    No, my soul!

Cry not "evil," everywhere.
'Tis the gospel of despair,
'Tis the knife to heart and brain.
Surely there is somewhere gain,
    O, my soul!

Through All Adversity

Serene, I wait, O Lord, I wait
What good abides within my fate,
Assured, however dark the way,
That good is all our destiny.
And when upon me falls the lash
With stinging pain, and blinding flash
Of human wrath makes keenly plain
Mine witless error, seen through pain,
O, humbled to the earth and wet
With mine own bitter tears, O yet,
Still doth abide, unchanged, the dream
That good prevails, howe'er it seem.

20. Dreiser, "Resignation," *Demorest's* 34 (April 1898): 137.
21. Dreiser, "Lessons I Learned from an Old Man," *Your Life* 2 (January 1938): 10.

CHAPTER 6: Free-lance Writing

1. Dorothy Dudley, *Dreiser and the Land of the Free* (New York, 1946), p. 142.

2. See, for instance, W. A. Swanberg, *Dreiser* (New York, 1965), p. 76. A notable exception is Ellen Moers; see Moers, *Two Dreisers* (New York, 1969), pp. 32–69.

3. Mott, *A History of American Magazines, 1885–1905*, pp. 6–8.

4. *Crumbling Idols*, ed. Jane Johnson (Cambridge, Mass., 1960), p. 116.

5. *Critic* o.s. 25 (11 August 1894): 97.

6. *Fortnightly Review* 93 (May 1910): 921–32.

7. See Isaac F. Marcosson, *Adventures in Interviewing* (New York, 1923), pp. 60–61.

8. Dreiser, *A Book About Myself*, p. 178.

9. See letters of J. Scott Hartley to Dreiser in the University of Pennsylvania Library Dreiser Collection.

10. Dreiser, "Art Work of Irving R. Wiles," *Metropolitan* 7 (April 1898): 359.

11. Dreiser, "Benjamin Eggleston, Painter," *Ainslee's* 1 (April 1898): 45.

12. Dreiser, "A Great American Caricaturist," *Ainslee's* 1 (May 1898): 340.

13. Dreiser, "A Notable Colony: Artistic and Literary People on the Picturesque Bronx," *Demorest's* 35 (August 1899): 240–41.

14. Dreiser, "C. C. Curran," *Truth* 18 (September 1899): 228.

15. Dreiser, "Lawrence E. Earle," *Truth* 20 (February 1901): 27–30.

16. Dreiser, "The Sculpture of Fernando Miranda," *Ainslee's* 2 (August 1898): 113–18.

17. Dreiser, "The Art of MacMonnies and Morgan," *Metropolitan* 7 (February 1898): 143–51.

18. See *Letters of Theodore Dreiser*, 1: 94.

19. Dreiser, "Concerning Bruce Crane," *Truth* 18 (June 1899): 143–47.

20. Dreiser, "E. Percy Moran and His Work," *Truth* 18 (February 1899): 35.

21. Dreiser, "America's Greatest Portrait Painters," *Success* 2 (11 February 1899): 184.

22. Dreiser, "A Master of Photography," *Success* 2 (10 June 1899): 471.

23. Dreiser, "The Camera Club of New York," *Ainslee's* 4 (October 1899): 329.

24. See Dreiser, "The Color of To-Day," *Harper's Weekly* 45 (14 December 1901): 1272–73; idem, *Twelve Men*, pp. 344–60.

25. See, for instance, Dreiser, "Benjamin Eggleston, Painter," *Ainslee's* 1 (April 1898): 41.

26. Dreiser, "Historic Tarrytown," *Ainslee's* 1 (March 1898): 25–31.

27. Dreiser, "Haunts of Nathaniel Hawthorne," *Truth* 17 (21 September 1898): 7–9; (28 September 1898): 11–13.

28. Dreiser, "The Home of William Cullen Bryant," *Munsey's* 21 (May 1899): 240–46.

29. Dreiser, "Edmund Clarence Stedman at Home," *Munsey's* 20 (March 1899): 931–38.

30. Dreiser, "The Haunts of Bayard Taylor," *Munsey's* 18 (January 1898): 594–601.

31. Dreiser, "The Real Zangwill," *Ainslee's* 2 (November 1898): 351–57.

32. Dreiser, "The Real Howells," *Ainslee's* 5 (March 1900): 137–42.

33. In a letter of 15 October 1911 to William C. Lengel, Dreiser wrote:

> You will not be surprised when I tell you that few American books if any interest me. I've enjoyed *Uncle Tom's Cabin* and *Huckleberry Finn* and *Roughing It* and *Ben-Hur* as a boy. More recently or rather somewhat later I liked *The Red Badge of Courage* (Crane) [,] *Main-Travelled Roads* (Hamlin Garland) [,] *With the Procession* (H. B. Fuller) [,] *McTeague* (Frank Norris) [,] *The 13th District* (Brand Whitlock) [,] *The Story of Eva* (Will Payne) [,] *Quicksand* (Henry White) & *Their Wedding Journey* (W. D. Howells). These are quite the sum total of my American literary admirations. (*Letters*, 1: 121)

As late as 1942 Dreiser told George Ade:

> In fact I entered it [the "gay nineties"] with your *Fables in Slang*, Finley Dunne's *Philosopher Dooley*, Frank Norris' *McTeague* and Hamlin Garland's *Main-Travelled*

Roads. And I stored it—or thought I had—along with these and a very few others of that time or earlier:—Howells' *Their Wedding Journey*, for example. These were the beginning of my private library of American Realism. (*Letters*, 3: 949)

Dreiser was possibly thinking about *A Modern Instance* when he kept referring to *Their Wedding Journey*, for his remark about the constant quarreling does not describe *Their Wedding Journey*.

34. Dreiser, "The Horseless Age," *Demorest's* 35 (May 1899): 155.

35. Dreiser, "Carrier Pigeons in War Time," *Demorest's* 34 (July 1898): 222–23.

36. Dreiser, "Plant Life Underground," *Pearson's* 11 (June 1901): 861–62.

37. Dreiser, "The New Knowledge of Weeds," *Ainslee's* 8 (January 1902): 533.

38. Dreiser, "The Railroad and the People: a New Educational Policy Now Operating in the West," *Harper's Monthly* 100 (February 1900): 479–84.

39. One example of the educational policy advanced by the railroads around the turn of the century was mapping and examining the soils for the benefit of farmers as well as for industry. See Dreiser, "The Problem of the Soil," *Era* 12 (September 1903): 249.

40. Dreiser, "The Making of Small Arms," *Ainslee's* 1 (July 1898): 549.

41. Dreiser, "The Harlem River Speedway," *Ainslee's* 2 (August 1898): 56.

42. See Dreiser, "Where Battleships Are Built," *Ainslee's* 1 (June 1898): 433–39; idem, "The Chicago Drainage Canal," *Ainslee's* 3 (February 1899): 53–61; idem, "The Town of Pullman," *Ainslee's* 3 (March 1899): 189–200; idem, "The Log of an Ocean Pilot," *Ainslee's* 3 (July 1899): 683–92; idem, "From New York to Boston by Trolley," *Ainslee's* 4 (August 1899): 74–84; idem, "New York's Underground Railroad," *Pearson's* 9 (April 1900): 375–84.

43. See Dreiser, "A Talk with America's Leading Lawyer [Choate]," *Success* 1 (January 1898): 40–41; idem, "A Photographic Talk with Edison," *Success* 1 (February 1898): 8–9; idem, "Life Stories of Successful Men—No. 10, Philip D. Armour," *Success* 1 (October 1898): 3–4; idem, "Life Stories of Successful Men—No. 11, Chauncey Mitchell Depew," *Success* 1 (November 1898): 3–4; idem, "Life Stories of Successful Men—No. 12, Marshall Field," *Success* 2 (8 December 1898): 7–8; idem, "A Leader of Young Mankind, Frank W. Gunsaulus," *Success* 2 (15 December 1898): 23–24; idem, "A Monarch of Metal Workers [Carnegie]," *Success* 2 (3 June 1899): 453–54.

44. See Dreiser, "A High Priestess of Art," *Success* 1 (January 1898): 55; idem, "A Vision of Fairy Lamps," *Success* 1 (March 1898): 23; idem, "The Career of a Modern Portia," *Success* 2 (18 February 1899): 205–6; idem, "Atkinson on National Food Reform," *Success* 3 (January 1900): 4; idem, "Thomas Brackett Reed: The Story of a Great Career," *Success* 3 (June 1900): 215–16.

45. Dreiser, "A Cripple Whose Energy Gives Inspiration," *Success* 5 (February 1902): 72–73.

46. Dreiser, "A Touch of Human Brotherhood," *Success* 5 (March 1902): 140–41, 176; cf. idem, *Sister Carrie*, pp. 517–25. Whether the article was written before *Sister Carrie* or possibly extracted from the novel is difficult to determine.

47. Dreiser, "Curious Shifts of the Poor. Strange Ways of Relieving Desperate Poverty. —Last Resources of New York's Most Pitiful Mendicants," *Demorest's* 36 (November 1899) 22–26. "Curious Shifts of the Poor" is also the title of Chapter 45 in *Sister Carrie*.

48. Dreiser, "The Tenement Toilers," *Success* 5 (April 1902): 213–14, 232. The same article appeared as "The Toilers of the Tenements" with some stylistic changes in *The Color of a Great City*, pp. 85–99.

49. Dreiser, "Christmas in the Tenements," *Harper's Weekly* 46 (6 December 1902): 52–53; reprinted in *Color*.

50. Dreiser, "Little Clubmen of the Tenements," *Puritan* 7 (February 1900): 665–72; cf. idem, "The Transmigration of the Sweat Shop," *Puritan* 8 (July 1900): 498–502.

51. Dreiser, "Scenes in a Cartridge Factory," *Cosmopolitan* 25 (July 1898): 321.

52. Dreiser, "The Smallest and Busiest River in the World," *Metropolitan* 8 (October 1898): 363.

53. Dreiser, "The Trade of the Mississippi," *Ainslee's* 4 (January 1900): 742–43.

54. Dreiser, "The Real Choate," *Ainslee's* 3 (April 1899): 324–33; cf. idem, "A Talk with America's Leading Lawyer," *Success* 1 (January 1898): 40–41.

55. Dreiser, "True Art Speaks Plainly," *Booklover's Magazine* 1 (February 1903): 129.

56. Dreiser, "Reflections," *Ev'ry Month* 2, No. 6 (1 September 1896): 3.

57. See Edward D. McDonald, "Dreiser Before 'Sister Carrie,'" *The Bookman* (U. S.) 67 (June 1928): facing p. 369.

58. H. Alan Wycherley, "Mechanism and Vitalism in Dreiser's Nonfiction," *Texas Studies in Literature and Language* 11 (1969): 1039–49.

CHAPTER 7: Early Short Stories

1. See Dreiser, "Lessons I Learned from an Old Man," *Your Life* 2 (January 1938): 6–10.

2. Dreiser, *A Book About Myself*, p. 458.

3. Dreiser, "Reflections," *Ev'ry Month* 2, No. 6 (1 September 1896): 4.

4. R. L. Duffus, "Dreiser," *American Mercury* 7 (January 1926): 71.

5. James T. Farrell, *The League of Frightened Philistines* (New York, 1945), pp. 13–14n. The essay from which this quotation is taken first appeared in the *New York Times Book Review* (4 July 1943) as "James T. Farrell Revalues Dreiser's *Sister Carrie.*"

6. *Letters of Theodore Dreiser*, 3:794.

7. After "The Shining Slave Makers" was rejected by *The Century*, it was sent to *Ainslee's*, a less sophisticated magazine at that time, and was accepted for publication, for which Dreiser received seventy-five dollars. The story was subsequently printed in the June 1901 issue (*Ainslee's* 7: 445–50). See *Letters*, 1: 212. "The Shining Slave Makers," when reprinted in *Free and Other Stories* (New York: Boni and Liveright, 1918), was entitled "McEwen of the Shining Slave Makers" with a number of stylistic changes in its content. In the collected volume, "McEwen of the Shining Slave Makers" is placed after "Free," which is, of course, the first story in the collection. Subsequent textual references are made to the *Ainslee's* edition and will be incorporated into the text.

8. "Butcher Rogaum's Door," first published in William Marion Reedy's *Mirror* 11 (12 December 1902), was titled "Old Rogaum and His Theresa" in *Free and Other Stories*. In the *Free* edition, as in "The Shining Slave Makers," Dreiser made stylistic revisions, mostly additions to flesh out particular scenes, but without change in theme or structure. Further textual quotations are taken from the *Mirror* edition.

9. "Nigger Jeff" first appeared in *Ainslee's* 8 (November 1901): 366–75, and was later collected in *Free and Other Stories*. According to Donald Pizer, the germ of the story is found in Dreiser's unpublished manuscript entitled "A Victim of Justice" at the University of Virginia Library. Like the other two stories, "Nigger Jeff" in the *Free* edition is revised from its first published version in a magazine. For a discussion of Dreiser's revisions in this story, see Pizer's "Theodore Dreiser's 'Nigger Jeff': The Development of an Aesthetic," *American Literature* 41 (November 1969): 331–41. Present textual references are to the *Ainslee's* edition.

10. "When the Old Century Was New" was first published in *Pearson's* 9 (January 1901): 131–40; it was republished with minor stylistic revisions in *Free and Other Stories*. Textual references for the discussion of this story are made to the *Pearson's* version.

11. According to Dreiser's letter of 13 May 1916 to Mencken, Dreiser wrote, in addition to the four short stories mentioned here, another entitled "The World and the Bubble." Robert Elias says that the latter story, originally intended for collection in *Chains*, has not been identified, and that it may exist only in manuscript form, if not published under a different title. See *Letters*, 1: 213.

12. See Dreiser's letter to Henry, 20 May 1897, in *Letters*, 1: 43–44.

13. See Dreiser's letter of 3 May 1916 to Mencken in *Letters*, 1: 212.

14. Cf. F. O. Matthiessen, *Theodore Dreiser*, p. 51.

15. Honoré de Balzac, *The Wild Ass's Skin*, pp. 272–73.

16. Quoted in *Père Goriot and Eugénie Grandet*, trans. and with an introduction, E. K. Brown (New York, 1946), p. ix.

17. Quoted in Dorothy Dudley, *Dreiser and the Land of the Free*, p. 157. In regard to the criticism, which also contributed to the rejection of Dreiser's story, he made the following observations in a letter to the editor:

> It seems to me that the calling in of an expert to say whether a fancy concerning an ant tragedy is scientific or not, borders a little upon the ridiculous. Your reader swallowed, without hesitation, the assertion that McEwen became an ant, but marveled quickly at the possibility of his becoming any but one kind of an ant . . . . Why should not the story be thrown out because of the ant idea entirely? In the next place, his criticism informs us that the fight in which McEwen, as a warrior ant, spitted his enemies with his spear-like tail, poisoned them with formic acid and crushed them with his mandibles is ridiculous. Why? Because it does not appeal to his kind of imagination? . . .
>
> Furthermore, I contend that no man called upon to judge a thing from its scientific side should be allowed to establish the merit of a story as a piece of fiction. What, pray, does the Elkhart, Indiana, reader care whether McEwen was a male or a female so long as he fulfilled the dramatic requirements of the situation and held his interest? What has the fact that one professional reader objects to his being called McEwen after he has been transformed into an ant, got to do with the interest and cleverness of the tale from the standpoint of the general public? He admits that the story is clever; that if the points he objected to were cleared away, the story would be charming. Thereupon, I am told that the Editors of the *Century*, do not find it of sufficient power, etc.

See Dreiser's letter of 9 January 1900 to Robert Underwood Johnson, associate editor of *The Century*, in *Letters*, 1: 45–46.

18. Johnson was later appointed ambassador to Italy, and it is interesting to note in this connection that earlier in his free-lance period Dreiser interviewed such an ambassador and wrote about him. Criticizing the ambassador, Joseph H. Choate, for being untrue to truth itself, Dreiser called Choate a representative who has a moral defect because he fails to represent the people he serves. Dreiser further accused Choate of a lack of sympathy in his work: "It seems to be a frame of mind in which one goes about to make a display of the narrowness and meanness of another, to put forth plainly a detail of the sufferings and misfortunes and sad, hard necessities of the erring of this world, without experiencing any sensations one way or the other. A rather machine-like quality, to say the least, or, an attitude of mind allied to that of the surgeon who uses the scalpel upon a cadaver." See "The Real Choate," *Ainslee's* 3 (April 1899): 324–33.

19. Dreiser, "When the Old Century Was New," *Pearson's* 11 (January 1901): 132. Dreiser seems to be confused here with dates. The story takes place in the spring of 1801 as he says in the beginning. Since John Adams was the president from 1797 to 1801, he means Thomas Jefferson, who was then the newly elected president.

20. Matthiessen, *Theodore Dreiser*, p. 52.

21. Robert E. Spiller, "Theodore Dreiser," *Literary History of the United States*, ed. Robert E. Spiller et al. rev. ed. in one vol. (New York, 1959), p. 1198.

22. Eliseo Vivas, "Dreiser, an Inconsistent Mechanist," *The Stature of Theodore Dreiser*, ed. Kazin and Shapiro, p. 245.

CHAPTER 8: *Sister Carrie*

1. Quoted in Dorothy Dudley, *Dreiser and the Land of the Free*, p. 152.

2. Dreiser, *Dawn*, p. 109.

3. Dreiser's letter of 13 May 1916, to H. L. Mencken, in *Letters*, 1: 213.

4. Dudley, p. 160.

5. Richard Duffy, "When They Were Twenty-One," *The Bookman* 38 (January 1914): 524.

6. *Letters*, 1: 213.

7. Ibid., 213. Dudley gives a similar account by quoting Dreiser as saying, "I had reached the place where Hurstwood robs the safe. I didn't know where I was going; I had lost the thread . . . ." See Dudley, p. 162.

8. Dudley, p. 162; cf. Dreiser's letter of 13 May 1916 to Mencken in *Letters*, 1: 210-14. Henry, leaving his wife and child, then married Anna Mallon. Dreiser's "Rona Murtha," in which Henry appears as Winnie Vlasto, is a nonfictional portrait based on Anna Mallon. See *A Gallery of Women* (New York, 1929), 2: 567–624.

9. Dudley, p. 162.

10. New York *Herald*, 7 July 1907.

11. Dreiser, *Sister Carrie*, p. 557. All textual references are made to the Doubleday, Page and Company edition and will be incorporated into the text. This edition was reprinted in facsimile by Charles E. Merrill, Columbus, Ohio, 1970.

12. *Letters*, 1: 213.

13. What was cut and why these portions were cut are not known. We can only surmise that Dreiser was following a better judgment. Cf. *Letters*, 1: 213–14.

14. See the account by Jack Salzman, "The Publication of *Sister Carrie*: Fact and Fiction," *Library Chronicle* of the University of Pennsylvania 33 (Spring 1967): 119–33.

15. Philip Rahv, "On the Decline of Naturalism," *Partisan Review* 9 (November-December 1942): 487.

16. Lars Åhnebrink, *The Beginnings of Naturalism in American Fiction* (Upsala, 1950), p. v.

17. "The Barbaric Naturalism of Mr. Dreiser," *The Stature of Theodore Dreiser*, p. 80.

18. Donald Pizer, "Nineteenth-Century American Naturalism: An Essay in Definition," *Bucknell Review* 13 (December 1965): 3.

19. The Dreiser-Gates relationship was first revealed by Dreiser's undated letter to Arthur Woodard, which mentions Dreiser's intention to visit Gates' laboratory (*Letters*, 1: 49). Also see Gates' letter of 11 December 1901 to Dreiser in the University of Pennsylvania Library Dreiser Collection. Recently Ellen Moers made a thorough investigation of this relationship in her book (*Two Dreisers*, pp. 159–61).

20. Dreiser, *Dawn*, pp. 198–99.

21. Subtitle of *Hey Rub-A-Dub-Dub* (New York, 1920) is "A Book of the Mystery and Wonder and Terror of Life."

22. Most of the critics have noticed this quality in Dreiser's fiction, but the most illuminating and detailed study on this subject in *Sister Carrie* is William J. Handy's "A Re-examination of *Sister Carrie*," *Texas Studies in Literature and Language* 1 (1959): 380–93.

23. Ibid., 389.

24. Dreiser, *A Book About Myself*, pp. 1–2.

25. Robert Elias' account of this incident comes largely from Dreiser's manuscript of *Dawn* and his conversation with Elias, but in this account there were certain inaccuracies in the details and in the motives of the sister's flight. Examining the newspaper articles in Chicago, George Steinbrecher, Jr., has reported that the man to whom Dreiser's sister went from the architect was an employee of Chapin and Gore named L. A. Hopkins (not George Hopkins, manager of Hannah and Hogg). He stole $3,500 (not $15,000) and returned all except $800 (not $1,000). She did not allow herself to be deceived into leaving but rather went of her own free will, and they went to Montreal rather than Toronto. The newspapers identified her as "Mamie Tracey Treigh," a "dashing blonde." See George Steinbrecher, Jr., "Inaccurate Accounts of *Sister Carrie*," *American Literature* 23 (January 1952): 490–93. Cf. Elias, *Theodore Dreiser: Apostle of Nature* (New York,

1949), p. 18; F. O. Matthiessen, *Theodore Dreiser*, pp. 65–66. Matthiessen repeats Elias' account almost *verbatim*.

26. Hazard was one of the influential newspaper reporters Dreiser met in 1893 in St. Louis, where he himself was a fledgling reporter. See Chapter 4, Section 3. Cf. Harry R. Burke, *From the Day's Journey*, pp. 165–71.

27. Paul Dresser, "Making Songs for the Million," *Metropolitan* 12 (November 1900): 701.

28. See Dreiser, "Curious Shifts of the Poor," *Demorest's* 36 (November 1899): 27.

29. For instance, in the first chapter: "The entire metropolitan centre possessed a high and mighty air calculated to overawe and abash the common applicant, and to make the gulf between poverty and success seem both wide and deep" (p. 17). In the final chapter:

> A study of these men in broad light proved them to be nearly all of a type. They belonged to the class that sit on the park benches during the endurable days and sleep upon them during the summer nights . . . . Miserable food, ill-timed and greedily eaten, had played havoc with bone and muscle. They were all pale, flabby, sunken-eyed, hollow-chested . . . their ears anæmic in hue, and their shoes broken in leather and run down at heel and toe. They were of the class which simply floats and drifts, every wave of people washing up one, as breakers do driftwood upon a stormy shore.
>
> . . . .
>
> . . . Crowds were hastening to dine. Through bright windows, at every corner, might be seen gay companies in luxuriant restaurants. There were coaches and crowded cable cars.
>
> In his weary and hungry state, he should never have come here. The contrast was too sharp . . . .
>
> . . . .
>
> Once he paused in an aimless, incoherent sort of way and looked through the windows of an imposing restaurant, before which blazed a fire sign, and through the large, plate windows of which could be seen the red and gold decorations, the palms, the white napery, and shining glassware, and, above all, the comfortable crowd. (pp. 540–46)

30. Cf. Dreiser, *A Book About Myself*, pp. 492–98; idem, *Sister Carrie*, pp. 513–14.

31. Harrison Rhodes, "Mr. Dreiser's *Sister Carrie*," *The Bookman* 25 (May 1907): 298.

32. Joseph Katz, ed., *The Portable Stephen Crane*, p. 66.

33. See Dreiser's letter to H. L. Mencken in 1916 in *Letters*, 1: 215.

34. Kazin and Shapiro, ed., *The Stature of Theodore Dreiser*, p. 241.

35. An interview, New York *Times*, 15 January 1901, in *The Stature of Theodore Dreiser*, p. 60.

36. Ford Madox Ford, *Portraits from Life* (Boston, 1937), p. 178.

Bibliography

This bibliography contains only those items cited in the text. The date of original publication for the later editions used in the text appears in brackets following the title.

Works by Dreiser

"After the Rain Storm." Pittsburgh *Dispatch*, 19 May 1894, p. 2.

An American Tragedy [1925]. Cleveland, 1948.

"America's Greatest Portrait Painters." *Success* 2 (11 February 1899): 183–84.

"The Art of MacMonnies and Morgan." *Metropolitan* 7 (February 1898): 143–51.

"Art Work of Irving R. Wiles." *Metropolitan* 7 (April 1898): 357–61.

"Atkinson on National Food Reform." *Success* 3 (January 1900): 4.

"Benjamin Eggleston, Painter." *Ainslee's* 1 (April 1898): 41–47.

"Birth and Growth of a Popular Song." *Metropolitan* 8 (November 1898): 497–502.

"The Black Diva's Concert." St. Louis *Globe-Democrat*, 1 April 1893, p. 8.

A Book About Myself. New York, 1922.

A Book About Myself ms. University of Pennsylvania Library, Philadelphia.

The Bulwark. Garden City, N.Y., 1946.

"Burned to Death." St. Louis *Globe-Democrat*, 22 January 1893, pp. 1–2.

"Butcher Rogaum's Door." *Reedy's Mirror* 11 (12 December 1901): 15–17.

"C.C. Curran." *Truth* 18 (September 1899): 227–31.

"The Camera Club of New York." *Ainslee's* 4 (October 1899): 424–35.

"The Career of a Modern Portia." *Success* 2 (18 February 1899): 205–6.

"Carrier Pigeons in War Time." *Demorest's* 34 (July 1898): 222–23.

"The Chicago Drainage Canal." *Ainslee's* 3 (February 1899): 53–61.

"Christmas in the Tenements." *Harper's Weekly* 46 (6 December 1902): 52–53.

The Color of a Great City. New York, 1923.

"The Color of To-Day." *Harper's Weekly* 45 (14 December 1901): 1272–73.

"Concerning the Author of These Songs." *The Songs of Paul Dresser*. New York, 1927. Pp.v–x.

"Concerning Bruce Crane." *Truth* 18 (June 1899): 143–47.

"A Cripple Whose Energy Gives Inspiration." *Success* 5 (February 1902): 72–73.

"Curious Shifts of the Poor. Strange Ways of Relieving Desperate Poverty.— Last Resources of New York's Most Pitiful Mendicants." *Demorest's* 36 (November 1899): 22–26.

Dawn. New York, 1931.

Dawn ms. The Lilly Library, Indiana University, Bloomington, Ind.

"The Descent of the Horse." *Everybody's* 2 (June 1900): 543–47.

"E. Percy Moran and His Work." *Truth* 18 (February 1899): 31–35.

"Edmund Clarence Stedman at Home." *Munsey's* 20 (March 1899): 931–38.

"Electricity in the Household." *Demorest's* 35 (January 1899): 38–39.

The Financier [1927]. Cleveland, 1946.

Free and Other Stories. New York, 1918.

"From New York to Boston by Trolley." *Ainslee's* 4 (August 1899): 74–84.

The "Genius" [1915]. Cleveland, 1946.

"A Great American Caricaturist." *Ainslee's* 1 (May 1898): 336–41.

"The Harlem River Speedway." *Ainslee's* 2 (August 1898): 49–56.

"The Haunts of Bayard Taylor." *Munsey's* 18 (January 1898): 594–601.

"Haunts of Nathaniel Hawthorne." *Truth* 17 (21 September 1898): 7–9; (28 September 1898): 11–13.

Hey Rub-A-Dub-Dub. New York, 1920.

"A High Priestess of Art." *Success* 1 (January 1898): 55.

"His Own Story." St. Louis *Republic*, 4 June 1893, pp. 1–2.

"Historic Tarrytown." *Ainslee's* 1 (March 1898): 25–31.

"The Home of William Cullen Bryant." *Munsey's* 21 (May 1899): 240–46.

A Hoosier Holiday. New York, 1916.

"The Horseless Age." *Demorest's* 35 (May 1899): 153–55.

"Hospital Violet Days." Pittsburgh *Dispatch*, 12 May 1894, p. 2.

Jennie Gerhardt [1911]. Cleveland, 1946.

"Lawrence E. Earle." *Truth* 20 (February 1901): 27–30.

"A Leader of Young Mankind, Frank W. Gunsaulus." *Success* 2 (15 December 1898): 23–24.

"Lessons I Learned from an Old Man." *Your Life* 2 (January 1938): 6–10.

Letters of Theodore Dreiser. Ed. Robert H. Elias. Philadelphia, 1959.

"Life Stories of Successful Men—No. 10, Philip D. Armour." *Success* 1 (October 1898): 3–4.

"Life Stories of Successful Men—No. 11, Chauncey Mitchell Depew." *Success* 1 (November 1898): 3–4.

"Life Stories of Successful Men—No. 12, Marshall Field." *Success* 2 (8 December 1898): 7–8.

"The Literary Shower." *Ev'ry Month* 2, No. 6 (1 September 1896): 22–23.

"Little Clubmen of the Tenements." *Puritan* 7 (February 1900): 665–72.

"The Log of an Ocean Pilot." *Ainslee's* 3 (July 1899): 683–92.

"The Loneliness of the City." *Tom Watson's Magazine* 2 (October 1905): 474–75.

"The Making of Small Arms." *Ainslee's* 1 (July 1898): 540–49.

"A Master of Photography." *Success* 2 (10 June 1899): 471.

"Mathewson." *Esquire* 1 (May 1934): 20–21, 125; 2 (June 1934): 24–25, 114.

"A Monarch of Metal Workers." *Success* 2 (3 June 1899): 453–54.

"A Negro Lynched." St. Louis *Republic*, 17 September 1893, p. 2.

"The New Knowledge of Weeds." *Ainslee's* 8 (January 1902): 533–38.

"New York's Underground Railroad." *Pearson's* 9 (April 1900): 375–84.

"Nigger Jeff." *Ainslee's* 8 (November 1901): 366–75.

"A Notable Colony: Artistic and Literary People on the Picturesque Bronx." *Demorest's* 35 (August 1899): 240–41.

Notes on Life by Theodore Dreiser. Ed. Marguerite Tjader and John J. McAleer. University, Alabama, 1974.

"Old Scraps of Melody." Pittsburgh *Dispatch*, 7 July 1894, p. 3.

"A Photographic Talk with Edison." *Success* 1 (February 1898): 8–9.

"Plant Life Underground." *Pearson's* 11 (June 1901): 860–64.

"The Problem of the Soil." *Era* 12 (September 1903): 239–49.

"The Railroad and the People: A New Educational Policy Now Operating in the West." *Harper's Monthly* 100 (February 1900): 479–84.

"The Real Choate." *Ainslee's* 3 (April 1899): 324–33.

"The Real Howells." *Ainslee's* 5 (March 1900): 137–42.

"The Real Zangwill." *Ainslee's* 2 (November 1898): 351–57.

"Reapers in the Fields." Pittsburgh *Dispatch*, 6 July 1894, p. 2.

"Reflections." *Ev'ry Month* 2, No. 6 (September 1896): 2–7.

"Reflections." *Ev'ry Month* 3, No. 1 (October 1896): 2–7.

"Reflections." *Ev'ry Month* 3, No. 2 (November 1896): 2–7.

"Reflections." *Ev'ry Month* 3, No. 3 (December 1896): 2–7.

"Reflections." *Ev'ry Month* 3, No. 4 (January 1897): 2–7.

"Reflections." *Ev'ry Month* 3, No. 5 (February 1897): 2–7.

"Reflections." *Ev'ry Month* 3, No. 6 (March 1897): 2–6.

"Reflections." *Ev'ry Month* 4, No. 1 (April 1897): 20–21.

"Reflections." *Ev'ry Month* 4, No. 2 (May 1897): 20–21.

"Reflections." *Ev'ry Month* 4, No. 3 (June 1897): 20–21.

"Reflections." *Ev'ry Month* 4, No. 4 (July 1897): 20.

"Resignation." *Demorest's* 34 (April 1898): 137.

"The Rivers of the Nameless Dead." *Tom Watson's Magazine* 1 (March 1905): 112–13.

"Scenes in a Cartridge Factory." *Cosmopolitan* 25 (July 1898): 321–24.

"The Sculpture of Fernando Miranda." *Ainslee's* 2 (August 1898): 113–18.

"The Shining Slave Makers." *Ainslee's* 7 (June 1901): 445–50.

Sister Carrie. New York, 1900.

"The Smallest and Busiest River in the World." *Metropolitan* 8 (October 1898): 355–63.

"The Story of a Human Nine-Pin." New York *Daily News*, 3 April 1904, p. 3.

"A Tale About Two Cats." Pittsburgh *Dispatch*, 20 May 1894, p. 2.

"A Talk with America's Leading Lawyer." *Success* 1 (January 1898): 40–41.

"The Tenement Toilers." *Success* 5 (April 1902): 213–14, 232.

Theodore Dreiser: A Selection of Uncollected Prose. Ed. Donald Pizer. Detroit, 1977.

"Theosophy and Spiritualism." St. Louis *Globe-Democrat*, 20 January 1893, p. 12.

"Thomas Brackett Reed: The Story of a Great Career." *Success* 3 (June 1900): 215–16.

"Through All Adversity." *Demorest's* 34 (November 1898): 334.

"A Touch of Human Brotherhood." *Success* 5 (March 1902): 140–41, 176.

"The Town of Pullman." *Ainslee's* 3 (March 1899): 189–200.

"The Track Walker." *Tom Watson's Magazine* 1 (June 1905): 502–3.

"The Trade of the Mississippi." *Ainslee's* 4 (January 1900): 735–43.

"The Transmigration of the Sweat Shop." *Puritan* 7 (July 1900): 498–502.

A Traveler at Forty [1913]. New York, 1930.

"The Treasure House of Natural History." *Metropolitan* 8 (December 1898): 595–601.

"True Art Speaks Plainly." *Booklover's Magazine* 1 (February 1903): 129.

Twelve Men. New York, 1919.

"A Vision of Fairy Lamps." *Success* 1 (March 1898): 23.

"When the Old Century Was New." *Pearson's* 11 (January 1901): 131–40.

"Whence the Song." *Harper's Weekly* 44 (8 December 1900): 1165–66a.

"Where Battleships Are Built." *Ainslee's* 1 (June 1898): 433–39.

"With the Nameless Dead." Pittsburgh *Dispatch*, 23 July 1894, p. 3.

"With Whom Is Shadow of Turning." *Demorest's* 34 (June 1898): 189.

"Woes of Dog Catchers." Pittsburgh *Dispatch*, 2 August 1894, p. 3.

Works by Others

Adams, Henry. *The Education of Henry Adams*. New York, 1931.

Åhnebrink, Lars. *The Beginnings of Naturalism in American Fiction*. Upsala, 1950.

———. "Dreiser's *Sister Carrie* and Balzac." *Symposium* 7 (November 1953): 306–22.

Balzac, Honoré de. *Père Goriot* and *Eugénie Grandet*. Trans. E. K. Brown. New York, 1946.

———. *The Wild Ass's Skin*. London, 1895.

Beer, Thomas. *Stephen Crane: A Study in American Letters*. Garden City, N. Y., 1923.

Boynton, Percy H. *America in Contemporary Fiction*. Chicago, 1940.

Burke, Harry R. *From the Day's Journey*. St. Louis, 1924.

Cady, Edwin. *The Light of Common Day: Realism in American Fiction*. Bloomington, Ind., 1971.

Cowley, Malcolm. "Naturalism in American Literature." *Evolutionary Thought in America*. Ed. Stow Persons. New Haven, 1950. Pp. 300–333.

———. "Sister Carrie's Brother." *New Republic* 116 (26 May 1947): 23–25.

———. "The Slow Triumph of Sister Carrie." *New Republic* 116 (23 June 1947): 24–27.

Davis, David Brion. "Dreiser and Naturalism Revisited." *The Stature of Theodore Dreiser*. Ed. Alfred Kazin and Charles Shapiro. Bloomington, Ind., 1955. Pp. 225–36.

Dresser, Paul. "Making Songs for the Million." *Metropolitan* 12 (November 1900): 701–3.

Dudley, Dorothy. *Dreiser and the Land of the Free*. New York, 1946.

Duffus, Robert L. "Dreiser." *American Mercury* 7 (January 1926): 71–76.

Duffy, Richard. "When They Were Twenty-One." *The Bookman* 38 (January 1914): 521–31.

Dugdale, Richard. *The Jukes*. New York, 1877.

Elias, Robert H. *Theodore Dreiser: Apostle of Nature*. New York, 1949.

———. *Theodore Dreiser: Emended Edition*. Ithaca, N. Y., 1970.

Farrell, James T. *The League of Frightened Philistines*. New York, 1945.

Flaubert, Gustave. "On Realism." *Documents of Modern Literary Realism*. Ed. George J. Becker. Princeton, N. J., 1963. Pp. 89–96.

Ford, Ford Madox. *Portraits from Life*. Boston, 1937.

Ford, James L. *The Literary Shop*. New York, 1894.

Garland, Hamlin. *Crumbling Idols*. Ed. Jane Johnson. Cambridge, Mass., 1960.

Hakutani, Yoshinobu. "Sister Carrie and the Problem of Literary Naturalism." *Twentieth Century Literature* 13 (April 1967): 3–17.

———. "Theodore Dreiser's Editorial and Free-Lance Writing." *Library Chronicle* of the University of Pennsylvania 37 (Winter 1971): 70–85.

Handy, William J. "A Re-examination of *Sister Carrie*." *Texas Studies in Literature and Language* 1 (1959): 380–93.

Hartley, J. Scott. "Letters to Dreiser." University of Pennsylvania Library, Philadelphia.

Hemmings, F. W. J. "The Origin of the Terms *Naturalisme, Naturaliste*." *French Studies* 8 (April 1954): 109–21.

Henry, Arthur. *Lodgings in Town*. New York, 1905.

Hodgins, Francis, Jr. "The Dreiser Letters." *Journal of English and Germanic Philology* 59 (1960): 714–20.

Hofstadter, Richard. *Social Darwinism in American Thought*. Philadelphia, 1944.

Holmes, Oliver Wendell. *Elsie Venner—A Romance of Destiny*. New York, 1886.

———. *Pages from an Old Volume of Life*. New York, 1883.

Horton, Rod W., and Herbert W. Edwards. *Backgrounds of American Literary Thought*. New York, 1952.

Huth, John F., Jr. "Theodore Dreiser: 'The Prophet.'" *American Literature* 9 (May 1937): 208–17.

Katz, Joseph. "Theodore Dreiser at Indiana University." *Notes and Queries*, n. s. 13 (March 1966): 100–101.

———. "Theodore Dreiser's *Ev'ry Month*." *Library Chronicle* of the University of Pennsylvania 38 (Winter 1972): 46–66.

———, ed. *The Portable Stephen Crane*. New York, 1969.

Kazin, Alfred. *On Native Grounds: An Interpretation of Modern American Literature*. New York, 1942.

Krause, Sydney J., ed. *Essays on Determinism in American Literature*. Kent, Ohio, 1964.

Lengel, William C. "The 'Genius' Himself." *Esquire* 10 (September 1938): 55, 120, 124, 126.

Marcosson, Isaac F. *Adventures in Interviewing*. New York, 1923.

Marden, Orison Swett, ed. *How They Succeeded: Life Stories of Successful Men Told by Themselves*. Boston, 1901.

——, ed. *Little Visits with Great Americans*. New York, 1903.

——, ed. *Talks with Great Workers*. New York, 1901.

Matthiessen, F. O. *Theodore Dreiser*. New York, 1951.

McDonald, Edward D. "Dreiser Before 'Sister Carrie.'" *The Bookman* (U. S.) 67 (June 1928): 369–74.

Mencken, H. L. *A Book of Prefaces*. New York, 1917.

Miller, Clarence E. "William Marion Reedy: A Patchwork Portrait." *Missouri Historical Society Bulletin* 17 (October 1960): 45–56.

Moers, Ellen. *Two Dreisers*. New York, 1969.

Mott, Frank Luther. *American Journalism: A History of Newspapers*. New York, 1941.

——. *A History of American Magazines, 1885–1905*. Cambridge, Mass., 1957.

Norris, Frank. *The Octopus* [1901]. Garden City, N. Y., 1956.

——. *The Responsibilities of the Novelist* [1903]. Garden City, N. Y., 1928.

Pizer, Donald. "Nineteenth-Century American Naturalism: An Essay in Definition." *Bucknell Review* 13 (December 1965): 1–18.

——. *Realism and Naturalism in Nineteenth-Century American Literature*. Carbondale, Ill., 1966.

——. "Theodore Dreiser's 'Nigger Jeff': The Development of an Aesthetic." *American Literature* 41 (November 1969): 331–41.

Putzel, Max. "Dreiser, Reedy, and 'De Maupassant, Junior.'" *American Literature* 33 (January 1962): 466–84.

——. *The Man in the Mirror: William Marion Reedy and His Magazine*. Cambridge, Mass., 1963.

Rahv, Philip. "On the Decline of Naturalism." *Partisan Review* 9 (November-December 1942): 483–93.

Rhodes, Harrison. "Mr. Dreiser's 'Sister Carrie.'" *The Bookman* 25 (May 1907): 298–99.

Riis, Jacob. *How the Other Half Lives: Studies among the Tenements in New York*. New York, 1890.

Salzman, Jack. "The Publication of *Sister Carrie*: Fact and Fiction." *Library Chronicle* of the University of Pennsylvania 33, (Spring 1967): 119–33.

Shapiro, Charles. *Theodore Dreiser: Our Bitter Patriot*. Carbondale, Ill., 1962.

Sherman, Stuart P. "The Barbaric Naturalism of Mr. Dreiser." *The Stature of*

Theodore Dreiser. Ed. Alfred Kazin and Charles Shapiro. Bloomington, Ind., 1955. Pp. 71–80.

Spiller, Robert E. "Theodore Dreiser." *Literary History of the United States*. Ed. Robert E. Spiller et al. rev. edition in one volume. New York, 1959. Pp. 1197–207.

Steinbrecher, George, Jr. "Inaccurate Accounts of *Sister Carrie*." *American Literature* 23 (January 1952): 490–93.

Swanberg, W. A. *Dreiser*. New York, 1965.

Trilling, Lionel. "Reality in America." *The Stature of Theodore Dreiser*. Ed. Alfred Kazin and Charles Shapiro. Bloomington, Ind., 1955. Pp. 132–45.

Vivas, Eliseo. "Dreiser, an Inconsistent Mechanist." *The Stature of Theodore Dreiser*. Ed. Alfred Kazin and Charles Shapiro. Bloomington, Ind., 1955. Pp. 237–45.

Walcutt, Charles C. *American Literary Naturalism, A Divided Stream*. Minneapolis, 1956.

———. "*Sister Carrie*: Naturalism or Novel of Manners?" *Genre* 1 (January 1968): 76–85.

Wolfe, Don M. *The Image of Man in America*. Dallas, 1957.

Wycherley, H. Alan. "Mechanism and Vitalism in Dreiser's Nonfiction." *Texas Studies in Literature and Language* 11 (1969): 1039–49.

Zola, Émile. *The Experimental Novel*. Trans. Belle M. Sherman. New York, 1893.

Index